SanJuan COUNTRY

For
BARBARA
and
The Boys,
Art and Tom

Thomas M. Griffiths

SAN JUAN COUNTRY

Foreword by David Lavender

PRUETT PUBLISHING COMPANY
Boulder, Colorado

First Edition
1 2 3 4 5 6 7 8 9

Unless otherwise indicated, all photographs
are by the Author

Printed in the United States of America

Library of Congress Cataloging in Publication Data

Griffiths, Thomas Melvin, 1910–
    San Juan country.

    Bibliography: p.
    Includes index.
    1. San Juan Mountains Region (Colo. and N.M.) —
Description and travel. 2. Natural history — San Juan
Mountains Region (Colo. and N.M.). 3. San Juan
Mountains Region (Colo. and N.M.) — History. I. Title.
F782.S19G74   1983   978.8′38   82-16544
ISBN 0-87108-505-4

Acknowledgments

A book is not made by a single person; like Odysseus, "I am a part of all that I have met."

I acknowledge gratefully the "parts" provided by the numerous and unnamed ranchers, cowboys, farmers, merchants, miners, school teachers, professors, journalists, geologists, engineers, publicans, and peers who, through the years, have guided me toward an understanding of San Juan country.

Special thanks must go:

To Elwyn and Louisa Arps, Carl Blaurock, and Dr. Hugo Rodeck, Professor Emeritus, University of Colorado, for their generous help with Colorado History and natural history.

To Chester and Nina Price, Chester for bringing me up to date on livestock ranching and for introducing me to Dwight Lavender many years ago, and Nina for her remembrances of Telluride and the Uncompahgre Valley during my temporary absence.

To Arnold Withers, of Santa Fe, and the late Al Olson, University of Denver, who were especially helpful with San Juan archeology.

Posthumously to Dr. Ross McCafferty, of Montrose, who first directed my footsteps into the high hills, and Louis and Bethel Kuchs, who generously shared their remembrances of San Juan yesteryears.

To the late Sara Williams, pioneer teacher *extraordinaire*, Barbara McCullough Spencer, Verena Rucker Jacobson, Mary Kuchs Griffiths, and the late Ruth Rathmell Wing, who supplied what understanding I have of San Juan country's schools.

Posthumously to Roy Stryker, who, by precept and example, instilled in me an appreciation of the photograph as an historical and socio-economic document, explaining and illuminating the land-man relationship.

To the small cadre of San Juan Mountaineers, living and dead, companions in arms on many adventures: Dwight Lavender, David Lavender, Carleton Long, Gordon Williams, Charles Kane, Bob Ormes, Lloyd Griffiths, Lewis Giesecke, and the McClintock family: Lacy, Charlotte, Mary, Frank, and Ruth; and with very special thanks to David Lavender who did me the honor of supplying a foreword for this book.

To the staffs of the Western History Department of the Denver Public Library and the Colorado Historical Society, who never failed to deliver the most demanding requests, expertly and cheerfully.

To Pruett Publishing's Jerry Keenan, whose editing pruned what had become a formless *opus maximus* to manageable size and who gently led me through the *terra incognito* of publication. And to Nancy Emerson for a skillful job of copyediting.

Finally to my patient and long-suffering wife, Barbara, who has never once reproached me for undertaking this task. We met in San Juan country; this is as much her book as it is mine.

Mel Griffiths
Ouray and Denver,
Colorado

Table of Contents

Mel Griffiths has staked out a unique literary claim to the San Juan Mountains of southwestern Colorado. He grew up near their northern flanks and learned, by sitting still and watching, how the pale shining greenness of new leaves moves up the steep hillsides in the spring and how the duskier reds, oranges, and yellows flow back down in the autumn. Before he was well out of his teens he shivered through a night on the top of Uncompahgre Peak just so he could watch the whole great range take shape under the golden wash of dawn. As a hardrock miner he delved deep into the Camp Bird Mine, where he learned firsthand the tragedies that avalanches can cause. He confronted transportation problems with reluctant donkeys and, later, with four-wheel-drive vehicles that sometimes rebelled, like the donkeys, at going where he pointed them. He built his own house among the aspens near Ouray and has felt with his own skin the cyclical dramas of the mountain seasons and the mountain climate.

By trade he is — or, until his retirement, was — a professor of geography at the University of Denver. This circumstance added, and continues to add, new perceptions to his instinctive understanding of the language of the earth. He can, and in *San Juan Country* does, speak with offhand familiarity about fault lines, unconformities, and rock flows, about pikas, bears, and coyotes. He leads us easily into current theories about how the mountains were formed, deformed, eroded, uplifted again, smothered in volcanic ejecta (he drops in words like that, too), and then reshaped over and over again by the ebb and flow of ice sheets responding to cosmic forces most of the rest of us seldom wonder about.

A universalist, he illuminates his descriptions of phenomena in the relatively small San Juan region with examples drawn from around the world. For example, he uses the formation of a volcanic island in the sea off Iceland to launch into an explanation of how life

forms might have colonized Corbett Ridge above Ouray after it, too, had been blanketed and isolated by lava and volcanic ash. He can absorb us in a graphic description of the tormented topography between Ridgeway and Silverton and then add a sudden new perspective by reminding us that to the astronauts that rugged surface looked as smooth as the skin of an orange.

When words don't suffice, he uses his own pictures, many of them taken from an airplane he was flying himself, to emphasize and clarify his points.

Having employed all these devices so that we can understand the mountains, Griffiths introduces us to the San Juan region's heterogeneous cast of characters. They march through in chronological order, with their private idiosyncrasies — Paleo-Indians, Spaniards, trappers, government explorers, and so on down to the latest land developers. Here again his approach is directed by geography: we see the adjustments that mountain weather, mountain materials, and mountain structures have forced on miners, stockmen, the builders of narrow-gauge railroads, water hustlers, environmentalists, and the rest.

Added to this knowledge of the mountains and their inhabitants are rich helpings of regional lore. He knows the kinds of pasties Cornishmen, the ubiquitous Cousin Jacks of the mining camps, wanted in their lunch boxes. He understands such diverse matters as labor strife in the mines, and schoolteaching under cornices where snowslides hang precariously. And characters! — muleskinners, oddball prospectors, cowboys, glamorous mine superintendents, cantankerous journalists, pioneer skiers, legendary climbers.

Like a good pasty, the whole transcends the parts. You can analyze the ingredients, but that seldom explains the satisfaction. To know what that statement means, start turning the pages that follow this one. Long before you reach the end, I think you'll agree.

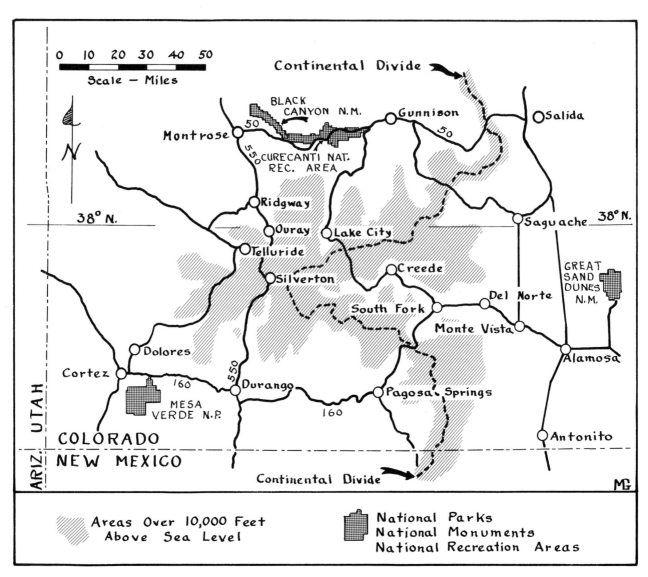

SAN JUAN COUNTRY

San Juan Country

In the West a region is often called a country: Navajo country, Big Bend country, Mormon country, Four Corners country, Powder River country, Hopi country. Perhaps a surfeit of space led the westering pioneers to be profligate with the names they bestowed on the land; a modest region of the West was often larger than a whole European country so it deserved the name. A "country" in this western American sense usually took its name from its distinguishing feature—physical, historical, social, institutional.

In this way the San Juan country of southwestern Colorado came by its name.

San Juan country covers about 20,000 square miles. At its heart lies the mountain mass which gives the region its name. The mountains themselves embrace about 12,000 square miles, with an additional 8,000 square miles of plateau and river valleys adjacent to the mountains. All except the small southeastern tip of San Juan country lies in southwestern Colorado.

The naming of the San Juan Mountains took place between the passage of the Escalante-Dominguez expedition of 1776 and the penetration of the region by Anglo fur trappers during the decades from 1820 through 1840. The name was given by the early Spanish colonists who pushed north of Santa Fe and Taos into the lower San Juan River and San Luis valleys.

In 1778, Don Bernardo de Miera y Pachecoa, who had accompanied the Escalante expedition of 1776, prepared a map of the region which was to be called, in our time, northern New Mexico and Arizona, western Colorado and eastern Utah for the king of Spain. This map is remarkably accurate for its date. Many of its rivers still bear the names given them in the late 1700s: Rio de las Animas, Rio Florida, Rio de los Pinos, Rio de Nuestra Senora de las Dolores, Rio Grande del Norte, Rio Colorado. Mountain ranges whose names have survived include Sierra de la Sal, Sierra de la Plata, Sierra de Abajo. Anglo impatience with foreign language has since stripped most of these of their musical Spanish gracefulness, but the root remains.

One who knows the country depicted by Miera's map can learn a great deal about the state of Spanish knowledge in the 1770s. For example, near the point where the Rio de las Animas empties in the San Juan (Rio de Nabajoo on Miera's map) is the notation, "Here are found the ruins of great towns once occupied by ancient Indians." Did the Spanish colonists of Miera's time know of the Anasazi ruins of the Mesa Verde? Did they know of silver ore in the mountains which they named Sierra de la Plata near present Silverton at the headwaters of the Rio de las Animas? We will probably never know for sure, but so many of the features are in the right locations, and so many of the names have survived for more than 200 years that we want to believe.

Between the headwaters of the Rio Grande del Norte and the tributaries of the San Juan (Miera calls the San Juan the Rio de Nabajoo, "Navajo River") at the place of the east central heart of the present day San Juan Mountains, Miera's map shows a range called Sierra de las Grullas (Mountains of the Cranes). How that range lost the name given it on Miera's map and took up the name of the river which drains its southern flank we do not know, but it seems altogether fitting that during the years this magnificent mountain mass lost the name of "the Mountains of the Cranes" and acquired the name of John, the "beloved disciple."

The San Juan Mountains are a part of the Rocky Mountain system—the great mountain barrier which dominates the western third of the North American continent, separating the waters which flow to the Atlantic from those which drain to the Pacific.

Marching southward from their anchor at the Chukchi Sea on Alaska's northwest coast, the Rocky Mountains cross from Wyoming into Colorado in a phalanx of parallel ranges separated by open parks and river valleys. The eastern edge of the phalanx is guarded from the high plains by the Front Range, the Wet Mountains, and the Sangre de Cristo Mountains. To the west lie North Park, Middle Park, South Park, and the San Luis Valley. West of these high parks and river valleys a jumble of ranges—which include the Elkhead Mountains, the Rabbit Ears Range, the Williams Fork and Gore ranges—eventually coalesce in the vicinity of Tennessee Pass, at the head of the Arkansas Valley. To the west of the valley, the high rampart of the Sawatch Range runs due south for eighty miles to Marshall Pass, serving as a Colorado backbone—besides carrying the Continental Divide, it contains fifteen summits more than 14,000 feet above sea level, including the highest peak in Colorado, Mt. Elbert, 14,433 feet above sea level.

At Marshall Pass the great westward sweep of the San Juan Mountains begins. They are connected to the south end of the Sawatch Range by the low, rolling Cochetopa Hills. Except for this hilly connection, the San Juans lie in splendid isolation from the remainder of the Rocky Mountains.

The San Juans are drained by two major river systems—the Rio Grande and the Colorado. The Continental Divide wriggles southwestward along the umbilical cord of the Cochetopa Hills, sweeps in a great westward arc to the knot of high country between Silverton and the Needle Mountains, then curves back to the southeast, where it enters New Mexico along the narrow, southward prong of the San Juans. A 220-mile section of the "divide" in Colorado is carried along the crest of the San Juans. To the east of this line the numerous tributaries of the Rio Grande flow down to the San Luis Valley and eventually to the Gulf of Mexico. To the north, west, and south of the divide major tributaries of the Colorado River system drain to the Pacific: the Gunnison, Uncompahgre, Dolores, San Miguel, and the San Juan.

Opposite: Miera Map of the region through which the Dominguez-Escalante party traveled in 1776. Herbert E. Bolton, "Pageant in the Wilderness," Utah Historical Quarterly, 1950.

GRADOS DE LONGITUD

Detail near center of Miera Map. Sierra de las Grullas lies at the center of this detail. Herbert E. Bolton, "Pageant in the Wilderness," Utah Historical Quarterly, 1950.

The headwaters of each major river system sends its long tentacles up into the high country, drawing away the moisture produced by groundwater and the melting of the snowpack which accumulates during the cruel winters. Each tributary rootlet has some association with the human population—past or present—Spanish, Anglo, or Indian. Often it takes its name from that association. The procession of names is a catalogue of descriptions, adventures, joys, or past sorrows: Cow Creek, Lou Creek, Cascade Creek, Canyon Creek, Lost Creek, Lime Creek, Mineral Creek, the Hermosa, the Piedra, Los Pinos, Embargo Creek, Cedar Creek, Bear Creek, Half-moon Creek, Noname

Creek, Tabeguache Creek (pronounce this one Tab-a-watch—the Ute tongue grates wryly in Spanish and Anglo mouths). The litany is as long as it is colorful.

Mountains, tablelands, and mesas have names oriented as locally as are streams: Horsefly Peak, Deep Creek Mesa, Sunlight Peak, Trident Mesa, Sheep Mountain, Tongue Mesa, the Lone Cone, Groundhog Mountain, Coal Bank Hill, Potato Hill, American Flat. One could linger for hours over the U.S. Geological Survey (U.S.G.S.) topographic maps and U.S. Forest Service maps of the San Juan country, dreaming up plausible stories to account for the names which man has put upon features. Nor would the stories dreamed up by the uninitiated be any more fanciful than the incidents which prompted the names actually placed there by the pioneers.

The San Juan Mountains contain thirteen summits more than 14,000 feet above sea level. This is the second largest group of peaks of this height in the state. (The Sawatch Range contains fifteen peaks over 14,000 feet above sea level.)

Contained within San Juan country are smaller mountain groups, separated from each other by the deep valleys of drainage tributaries. These include the Needle Mountains, divided into the Grenadier Range, the Main Needles, and the West Needles; the central San Juan, divided into the Uncompahgre Group, the Sneffels Group, the Silverton Group, and the Telluride Group; the San Miguel Mountains; and the La Plata Mountains.

The San Juans are unique, having been carved from one of the thickest masses of young, volcanic ash and volcanic breccia in North America. Brilliantly colored rock and extensive mineralization are found throughout the range. Heavy winter snowfall and attendant avalanches make it a difficult area in which to maintain a transportation system. Mountain basins exposed to the southwest where they can catch the full sweep of winter storms have received snowfalls in excess of 400 inches in some years. Yet the very snows which create "hard" winters and cause difficult transportation, feed meltwater to the numerous tributaries which nourish the Rio Grande and the upper Colorado River. These waters feed thriving irrigation projects in the San Luis Valley, the Uncompahgre and Grand valleys, and the mesas east and west of Durango, before releasing their life-giving surplus downstream to New Mexico, Texas, Arizona, California, and Mexico.

The removal of the Utes from their San Juan homeland, by the Brunot Treaty of 1873, set in motion the great gold and silver rush of the 1870s and 1880s. The San Juan mining stampede, overnight, caught the fancy of the whole United States, as well as investors in Europe. It took up slack just as the Mother Lode country was declining in California and as costs were skyrocketing on the Comstock of Nevada. The San Juans burst on the mining scene contemporaneously with the Black Hills rush. In quick succession Silverton, Ouray, Rico, Telluride, Lake City, and a dozen or more other mining camps sprang into being. The silver panic of 1893 slowed mining all over the world, but it did not bring the San Juan boom to a halt. Many mines had as great or greater values in gold as in silver, so they managed to ride out the panic.

The San Juan still has working mines, although most of the high grade silver and gold values have been worked out now. Uranium and vanadium on the mesas of the San Juan's western flanks, low grade copper and other base metal deposits in the heart of the ranges, and coal and oil shale to the north are now attracting energy-conscious investors.

While the initial mining boom ran its fever, ancillary enterprises came to the valleys and mesas of the San Juans: irrigated agriculture, cattle and sheep ranching, timber and lumber production.

Today the hard-rock mining past of the legendary San Juans has slowly evolved into another type of entrepreneurship. Whereas gold was once extracted from rocks by drilling, blasting, and milling, gold is now extracted from the summer and winter tourist, who comes to hike, climb, ski, fish, hunt, or is satisfied to pay for the privilege of being hauled to the high basins in a stretched jeep over a cliff-hanging trail which once bore freight-wagons and pack mules.

Of Colorado's top ten tourist attractions during 1975, five are in or on the edge of San Juan country: Curecanti National Recreation Area, Mesa Verde National Park, Black Canyon National Monument, Colorado National Monument, and Great Sand Dunes National Monument. The region seems on the threshold of a rush which will eventually eclipse the mineral rush of the last decades of the nineteenth century and the beginning of the twentieth century. Texans, Arizonans, Oklahomans, Nebraskans, Colorado eastern-slopers, as well as a sprinkling of easterners, from farther afield, knowing a good thing when they find it, have bought up second home and summer home property in the San Juans until the influx now approaches the saturation point.

Contemplation of this rebirth in the making will give lovers of the San Juan country pause. The potential for turning it into a true renaissance or a disaster lies with the local communities, the cities, the counties, the state and federal authorities. Enlightened land use practices, more than any other factor can provide a balance between the competing and cooperating uses to which the region has been put in the past and potentially can be put in the future. Somehow the many-faceted environment of the San Juans must be equitably apportioned between its exploitation for watershed, grazing, farming, hydroelectric power, mining, timber, scenic values, recreational use, historic values, wilderness values, and living space. We have the skill; do we have the will?

PART I
THE LAND

CHAPTER 1

The Landscape

San Juan country is mountain country. Mountains are one of nature's most complex creations; they have their roots in a troubled geologic past. The highland surface is chaotic. Individual peaks and ridges soar high above neighboring mountainsides, slopes are steep, valleys and canyons are deep, sunlight and shadow are sharply separated. In the eye of the beholder, mountains give the intuitive impression that all nature is gargantuan in scale. Up and down are the dominant directions.

Standing at the foot of a great mountain, one is overwhelmed by the size and nearness of nature. Standing on the summit of that same peak, one is humbled by the global distance to the horizon. With the psalmist, after such an experience, one is prompted to ask, "What is man, that thou art mindful of him?"

Mountains wear coats of many colors: pristine snow, except on vertical rock, in winter; a hundred hues of green on forest, meadow, and tundra in spring; the riot of wildflower blossoms in summer; the frosty flames of aspen, oak, and oriental-carpeted tundra in fall.

There is a stubbornness about mountains; they are not easily changed or moved by the wounds inflicted by puny man or the disfigurement dealt by geology and time.

We must understand mountains if we are to know the San Juan landscape.

We can best sample this landscape by making a traverse across it. For our transect we will choose the route of U.S. Highway 550, the popular "Million Dollar Highway," which crosses the heart of the mountains from north to south. We will traverse three mountain passes, one above and two just under 11,000

Opposite: Looking southeast from near the junction of Dallas Creek, which flows from the right foreground, with the Uncompahgre River, which flows from the right middle distance. Ridgway lies behind moraine hummock in left middle distance.

feet above sea level. We will course along parts of four upper drainage tributaries and pass through or over three of the major geologic provinces of the San Juans. We will make the inspection trip from north to south.

Our first stop will be at the site of old Dallas, two miles north of Ridgway. Here Dallas Creek enters the Uncompahgre from the west. In the foreground is the sagebrush-covered, hummocky mass of debris carried to this place by the great trunk glacier which flowed down the Uncompahgre Valley. On either side of the valley which comes from the south, a great mountain front rises like the wings at the front of a massive stage set. To the right 14,160-foot Mt. Sneffels dominates the mountain wall; to the left, around the corner, out of sight, 14,309-foot Uncompahgre Peak. This massive north front of the San Juans has been carved from the thick blanket of gray volcanic rock which smothers the center of the San Juan uplift.

Three or four miles ahead, beyond Ridgway, we are able to see the structure more clearly. The valley bottom rises imperceptibly ahead to where it issues from a magnificent bowl in which lies the little mining town of Ouray. Choking the valley beyond and forming the far rim of the bowl is the conical bulk of Mt. Abram. Rimming the valley walls to either side of us, red beds of sedimentary sandstone rise gently and blend into the near rim of the Ouray bowl. They pinch out there beside the town.

Beyond Ouray the road climbs steeply in switchbacks into the canyon of the Uncompahgre River. The river, tumbling from the mountain wall ahead has carved a narrow cleft through unyielding rock — tough, primordial material case-hardened and formed in the deep bowels of the earth.

At the top of the two switchbacks, overlooking Ouray, one can park and become familiar with the three basic elements of the San Juan's geologic past. At this lookout point and for several miles ahead, to the south, up the canyon, one is standing on or driving

3

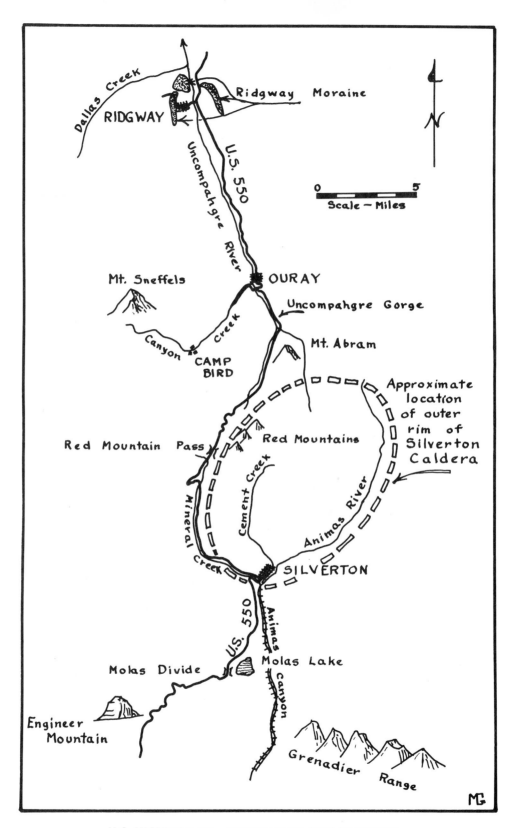

U.S. HIGHWAY 550—RIDGWAY TO MOLAS DIVIDE

through the top of the ancient basement rock of the San Juans. If one is permitted a homely comparison, this basement material is like a scoop of ice cream in the bottom of a sundae dish. On top of this foundation are the red sedimentary beds, which here descend gently to the northward, like a layer of thick chocolate sauce poured on top of and flowing down the sides of the scoop of ice cream. If we look up to the skyline, we see a blanket of gray, horizontally bedded rock, resting on top of the beveled sandstone and basement rock, like a blanket of whipped cream, resting on top of our imaginary sundae. The east and southeast rim of the bowl surrounding Ouray, locally known as the "Amphitheatre," has been carved from a several-thousand-foot thickness of this gray volcanic rock.

For the next five or six miles the route lies in the old, hard, basement rocks—the scoop of ice cream. The canyon is narrow, the walls are steep, spectacular. At Bear Creek, an east-side tributary, Otto Mears, the old "Pathfinder of the San Juan," who built this route as a toll road, placed his tollgate at a precarious bridge over the waterfall, where it was impossible to sneak a man, animal, or vehicle past the toll collector. When you stop to admire the 250-foot waterfall which issues from under the tollgate bridge, look past the rainbow-spanned spray in the plunge-pool to a ribbon of waterfall which tumbles down the opposite side of the main Uncompahgre Canyon—a ninety degree turn to the right. Near the canyon bottom its spray wets the stair tread of gigantic ripple marks, made by wave oscillation in the bottom sands of a shallow sea over a billion years ago—even before the inner fires of earth fused it into the basement material of the mountains.

Still in the basement complex, the road slices across the face of Mt. Abram, turns sharply around the west side of the peak, tiptoes past the grim avalanche tracks of the East and West Riverside avalanches—winter killers, these—climbs three tight switchbacks, and runs out onto the floor of Ironton Park. By now the route has climbed into the gray volcanic rock which blankets the higher parts of the San Juan.

Ahead, on the left side of the valley, as we look south, are three high mountains of fiery red rock. Their splashes of color accent the gray, volcanic talus slopes and the green of aspen, spruce, and tundra. These colorful red mountains (their names are Red Mountain No. 1, No. 2, and No. 3) are also of volcanic rock. They lie on the outer rim of the Silverton Caldera, the westernmost of some sixteen great blisters in the earth's crust from which issued the massive volcanic ash flows which produced the deep gray blanket of rock which covers most of the San Juan uplands.

Through the midst of the Red Mountain Mining District, whose rich veins of gold and silver were injected into the weakened roof and sides of the volcanic superstructures, the highway slips across 11,018-foot Red Mountain Pass to the headwaters of Mineral Creek, which curves southward and eastward, still hugging the outer rim of the Silverton Caldera. From here it is difficult to grasp the immense size of this ruined volcanic feature which is eight to twelve miles in diameter.

Silverton lies on the extreme southern rim of the caldera. There, the Animas River, whose headwaters have traced southward the east rim of the caldera, meets Mineral Creek. Their combined flow bursts through the caldera rim to the outside and enters a narrow canyon carved once more through the overburden to the basement rock.

From Silverton the highway climbs the west side of the canyon, abandoning its river bottom to the narrow gauge railroad. Quickly, the highway reaches the red sedimentary layers again, which here dip gently southward—opposite to the direction of their dip at Ouray.

At Molas Lake, which nestles in a shallow basin scoured by glacial ice, we can look across the water to the southeast into the heart of the Needle Mountains, the highest exposed part of the dome of basement rock over which the covering of sedimentary and volcanic rocks was laid. Here the agents of erosion have stripped away every vestige of the sedimentary and volcanic overburden and have etched deep valleys and left spectacular high peaks of the hard basement rock. The jagged Grenadier Range, visible across the lake, is carved from the same sort of brittle quartzite as the narrow slit of the Uncompahgre Canyon above Ouray, which we passed forty miles earlier—there lying in the bottom of a sunless canyon, here flinging its spires into a 13,900-foot sky.

The summit of Molas Pass, 10,910 feet, is a half-mile ahead. Here for the last time on this route, we see the whole of San Juan geology close at hand: the gray and red-streaked caldera rim to the north and northeast, the exposed ancient rocks of the San Juan basement in the Needles to the east, and to the west, at our feet, the gently southward-dipping red sandstones. Straight ahead to the southwest, sitting on top of the sedimentary rocks in splendid isolation, rests the gray, layered bulk of Engineer Mountain, a truncated cone of the San Juan's gray volcanic overcoat, spared by selective erosion. Beyond, at the blue rim of the earth, beyond the La Platas, rest the buff and green mesas of the Colorado Plateau.

There is no more ennobling view of the San Juan heartland to be had than from this highway and from this vantage point.

CHAPTER 2

Skin Game

Rudyard Kipling, in his *Just So Stories*, explains "How the Rhinoceros Got His Skin"—with a "great fold over his shoulders, and another fold underneath."

It is a fanciful tale of an ancient time when "one Rhinoceros, with a horn on his nose, two piggy eyes, and few manners, came down to the beach from the Altogether Uninhabited Interior and ate a cake which was two feet across and three feet thick" just baked by a hungry and potentially vengeful Parsee, who had retreated to safety in a palm tree. "In those days the Rhinoceros's skin fitted him quite tight. . . . There were no wrinkles in it anywhere. . . . All the same he had no manners then, and he has no manners now, and he never will have any manners.

"Five weeks later, there was a great heat wave on the Red Sea, and everyone took off all the clothes they had. . . . The Rhinoceros took off his skin and carried it over his shoulder as he came down to the beach to bathe. He waddled straight into the water and blew bubbles through his nose, leaving his skin on the beach."

Whereupon the vengeful Parsee, who never ate anything but cake, climbed down from his safe perch in the palm tree, "filled his hat with cake-crumbs . . . and rubbed the Rhinoceros skin . . . just as full of old, dry, stale, tickly cake-crumbs and some burned currants as ever it could *possibly* hold."

When the Rhinoceros came out of the water and put on his skin, he "buttoned it up with the three buttons, and it tickled like cake-crumbs in bed. . . . He rubbed so much and so hard that he rubbed his skin into a great fold over his shoulders, and another fold under-

neath, where the buttons used to be (but he rubbed the buttons off). . . . And it spoiled his temper, but it didn't make the least difference to the cake-crumbs. They were inside his skin and they tickled. So he went home, very angry indeed, and horribly scratchy; and from that day to this every rhinoceros has great folds in his skin and a very bad temper, all on account of the cake-crumbs inside."

Kipling's children's tale has a strange likeness to the modern geologist's descriptions of the earth: a plastic core and mantle inside a wrinkled crust (skin) which has been "rubbed" into folds and wrinkles by the "irritation" created by geothermal energy slowly escaping toward the cooling surface.

The theory of *plate tectonics*, today, defines an outer brittle earth's crust (*lithosphere*) some sixty to seventy miles in thickness which floats on a mantle of soft, viscous, plastic rock called the *Asthenosphere*.

The global crust is broken into seven major segments (plates) and perhaps as many as twelve minor fragments, all moving horizontally with respect to each other, riding on the Asthenosphere like cakes of ice jostling each other as they float on a restless sea. Six of the major plates have continents of lighter rock imbedded in them—North American Plate, South American Plate, Eurasian Plate, African Plate, Australian Plate, and Antarctic Plate. The seventh major plate contains the Pacific Ocean Basin.

The boundaries between plates are zones of crustal deformation. If plates move apart, creating tension, molten lava rises toward the surface in the weak zone and welds itself to the trailing edges of the separating plates. If plates move toward each other, compression forces one plate to dive beneath the other into the plastic mantle. This process (*subduction*) creates a trench in the crust on the side of the plunging plate, while the upper plate is forced into folds and fractures and is uplifted by the subducting plate. In such fashion mountain ranges are thrust upward near converging

Opposite: Grenadier Range and Needle Mountains from the north.

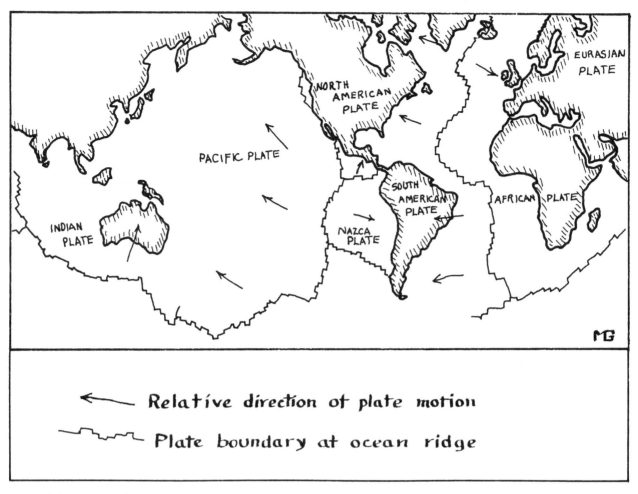

← — Relative direction of plate motion

⌐‾⌐‾⌐ — Plate boundary at ocean ridge

General distribution of crustal plates on a world Mercator projection. Jagged lines show plate boundaries along ocean ridges. Short arrows show relative direction of plate movement. Compiled and modified from various maps and sketches in J. Tuzo Wilson, Continents Adrift, Readings from Scientific American, 1971.

plates — the Alps, the Himalayas, the Andes, and the Rockies. The volcanic island arcs which rim the western margin of the Pacific Ocean Basin also had such an origin. At some boundary locations plates move neither directly toward (compression) nor away (tension) from each other, but grind past each other in shearing (transcurrent — strike-slip) faults. The great San Andreas fault system which borders the western edge of the North American continent is of this sort. These are earthquake-prone regions.

Our fictitious rhinoceros's skin has now been stretched to global proportions; its wrinkles are measured by the same scale. The highest mountains on the earth's surface rise about 5½ miles above sea level; the average diameter of the earth is 7,913 miles. The ratio of diameter to height is 1,440 to 1 — small wonder that the earth looked to the first lunar astronauts, halfway from earth to moon, like a perfectly smooth ball wreathed in cloud garlands. To give significance to mountain wrinkles we must view them at human scale. A field of view which takes in about a quarter part of a Rocky Mountain state will do.

The North American Plate is colliding against the Pacific Plate along the western edge of the North American continent. At most places the Pacific Plate is actively subducting beneath the North American Plate. At others the two plates are grinding past each other in opposite directions, as along the California coast. This collision and grinding between plates is translated into massive wrinkles which have spread eastward from the Pacific coast to the near edge of the continent's great interior plains. Close to the coast, subduction has weakened the crust and created channels along which molten rock from the mantle works its way to the surface, where it erupts in a line of volcanoes from the Aleutian Islands to Mexico and Central America. Farther inland, the great compression created by the colliding plates tilted and wrinkled the crust along the zone now occupied by the Sierra Nevada, the Great Basin, and Rocky Mountains, producing massive highlands, domes, and ridges from which the present ranges have been carved.

Two specific structural elements occupy the site of the San Juan Mountains. Both have their origins in disturbances in the past near the western margin of the North American Plate. One is ancient, one is relatively young in geologic time. Both are linear, and they cross each other at the site of the San Juan Mountains.

The oldest of these structural elements is a great elongated arch, like the top half of a submerged dirigible, thrust upward along an axis running northwest to southeast from the present Colorado-Utah border, west of Grand Junction, to north central New Mexico, west of the Rio Grande Valley. The present trace of this ancient arch is called the Uncompahgre Plateau. The core of the structure consists of ancient igneous and metamorphic rocks uparched during the period when the vast blankets of sedimentary rock were being deposited at the San Juan site. The core of the arch is almost completely hidden by these sediments except at the southeastern end, where it is exposed in the Needle Mountains, and nearer to the flanks of the arch, in the canyons of the Gunnison, the Animas, and the Uncompahgre, where erosion has cut down through the overlay of sedimentary rock.

The second structural element which serves as a foundation for the San Juans is a great transverse belt of fractured crust which extends from the Front Range near Boulder, Colorado, toward the southwest, terminating at the San Juan uplift, where it crosses the southeastern end of the Uncompahgre Plateau.

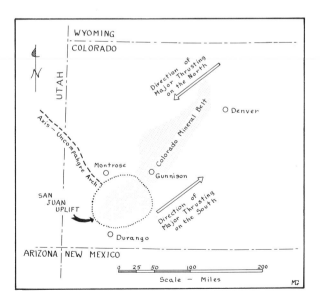

STRUCTURAL ELEMENTS OF THE SAN JUAN UPLIFT. Modified from Atwood and Mather, "Physiography and Quaternary Geology of the San Juan Mountains, Colorado," U.S.G.S. Professional Paper 166, 1932, and Phillip King, "The Evolution of North America," 1959.

This fracture belt came into existence 80 to 70 million years ago—when the Rocky Mountain system was being folded and uplifted. Compression created between the subducting Pacific Plate and the overlying North American Plate created a shearing couple in which the crust on the northwest side of the fracture zone was pushed from west to east while the southeast side was pushed from east to west.

This massive fracturing of the crust produced a zone of weakness through which molten material and hot solutions from the underlying mantle were injected into the overlying crust.

When prospectors, miners, and geologists in the 1870s got around to taking note of the location of Colorado's mining districts, they perceived a pattern which, with a few exceptions, was confined to this northeast-southwest trending zone, which they named the Colorado Mineral Belt. Beginning in the Front Range, west of Denver, the camps were strung out to the southwestward—Boulder, Clear Creek, Central City, Idaho Springs, Silver Plume, Breckenridge, Alma, Leadville, Aspen, Tincup, Bonanza, the San Juans, the La Platas. The only major mining camp to lie outside the fracture zone is Cripple Creek, west of Pikes Peak.

◦ ◦ ◦ ◦

If one could split the San Juans into two halves by cleaving the mountain mass from top to bottom and from edge to edge with a continent-sized knife, as one would cut a huge layer cake, removing one half so that the remaining cut surface could be examined, he would have produced a full-scale cross section of the mountain system. Not having a knife of sufficient size or the power to wield it, the geologist must reconstruct what such a cross section would be like by deducing the probable location and attitude of buried formations. He does this by projecting their probable trend from their surface attitude. He measures their attitude on mountainsides and in canyon walls. He maps formations in mines and deep wells. He probes with diamond drills, seismometers, and gravity measuring instruments.

A scientist "reads" the geologic history of a region, continent, ocean basin, or mountain range by interpreting clues in the rocks, making use of a logic concept called "uniformitarianism." Expressed in another way: "The present is the key to the past." This concept makes the assumption that the natural processes which are going on all around us today have been going on in the past. Swift-flowing streams, today, deposit gravel in their beds. A gravel deposit in an ancient sedimentary bed is a clue to its stream or beach origin. Windblown desert sand is heaped into dunes; a cross-bedded sandstone points to a sand dune origin. A coal seam points to an ancient swamp. A fossil bears

9

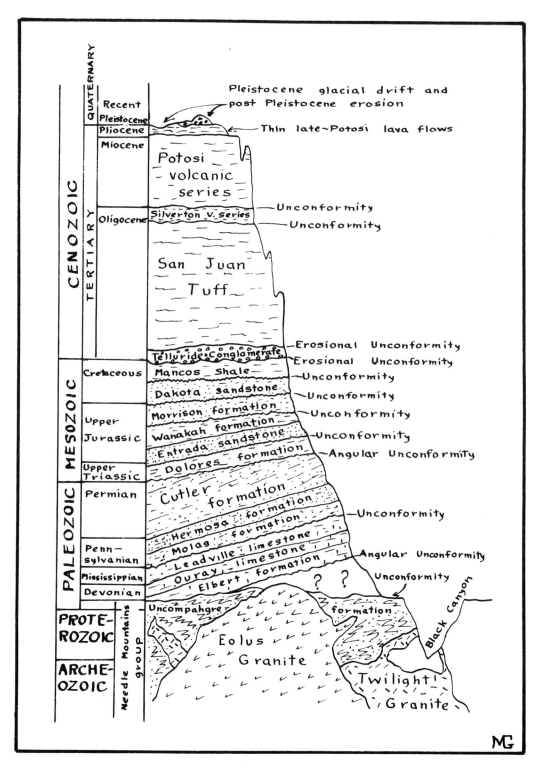

SAN JUAN—GENERALIZED STRATIGRAPHIC COLUMN. *Compiled from Atwood and Mather,* "*Physiography and Quaternary Geology of the San Juan Mountains, Colorado,*" U.S.G.S. *Professional Paper 166, 1932, and Larsen and Cross,* "*Geology and Petrology of the San Juan Region, Southwestern Colorado,*" U.S.G.S. *Professional Paper 258, 1956.*

evidence of the animal which it once was. The catalogue of clues and indicators has multiplied immensely during the past four or five centuries, and new diagnostic tools are added to the geologist's arsenal every day.

Three basic processes are forever at work in and on the surface of the earth's crust, subjecting it to constant change. First is the differential release of energy within and from below the earth's crust. This is usually in the form of heat; its uneven distribution creates forces which jostle the crustal plates, causes upwarping, downwarping, faulting, and tilting. When conditions are favorable it can thrust molten rock from the mantle below the crust into the crust or even through the crust where it erupts as a lava flow or a volcano. Another process is *degradation*, by which the agents of erosion—water, wind, ice, gravity, and chemical action—tear down surface rock and transport it downslope. The third process is *aggradation*, by means of which fragmental, suspended, and material in solutions, as a product of weathering and erosion, is transported to a new resting place, where it may again be consolidated into new rock.

The geologic history of any part of the earth's crust is usually complicated. All three of the basic processes have left their mark, one after the other or even simultaneously during the 4 to 4½ billion years of crustal formation. We will see this as we relate the highlights of San Juan country's geologic odyssey from dawn to present.

The oldest rocks in the San Juan region are gravel conglomerates and volcanic lavas formed 1½ to 2 billion years ago. They survive today around the flanks of the Needle Mountains uplift. Nothing is known of the still older rocks which must have preceded them. A short time later, geologically speaking, floods of molten rock were injected from below into these old materials, accompanied by a general uplift which formed a dome-shaped highland region. This injected molten material survives today as granite mountain summits at the heart of the Needle Mountains, in the walls of the Animas River canyon, and as the brilliant bands of pink granite in the walls of the Black Canyon, east of Montrose.

This upheaval was followed by a prolonged period of quiescence, during which the entire domed upwarp was worn down by erosion to an essentially level plain, which the geologist terms a *peneplain* (almost plain).

The peneplain was then downwarped into a vast shallow bowl which received the sand, gravel, and clay eroded from the surrounding high ground.

Next the region was again upwarped into a broad dome-shaped structure. Accompanying the upwarping, great masses of acidic magma were thrust into the core of the dome. This only melted its way partly to the surface, where it cooled slowly in great igneous masses, called *batholiths*, centered in the Needle Mountains, south of Silverton. This pinkish rock is named the Eolus Granite, for a 14,000-foot peak near the heart of the Needle Mountains.

The igneous activity which produced the Eolus Granite provided the heat, pressure, and hot solutions needed to convert the sandstones and shales deposited earlier in the postpeneplain period into quartzite and slate. These altered (metamorphic) rocks, called the Uncompahgre Formation, lie on the east and north sides of the central Needle Mountains, underlying the magnificent summits of the Grenadier Range (once called the Quartzite Mountains). Farther north, it is found in the bottom thousand feet or so of the Uncompahgre Canyon, just south of Ouray (the "scoop of ice cream" mentioned in the previous chapter).

This ancient phase of San Juan geologic history, marked by upheavals and profound igneous activity, was brought to a close by a prolonged period of erosion which produced another peneplain. By this time, about 550 million years ago, four fifths of the earth's 4½ billion years since the "beginning," had passed.

From 550 million years ago until a scant 60 million years ago, the San Juans were flooded intermittently by shallow seaways into which sand, gravel, and clay were carried from the nearby shores. The resulting layers of sandstone, conglomerate, and shale, which at one time blanketed the entire mountain mass, dip gently away from the center of the uplift, exposed as red and buff sandstone in the canyons of the Animas, Uncompahgre, San Miguel, and Dolores.

This period of sedimentary deposition was brought to a close by a profound upheaval which affected the entire western margins of North America. This period of crustal activity is known as the *Laramide Revolution*. Set in motion by activity along the western edge of the North American Plate, the parallel and overlapping ranges of the Rocky Mountain system, from the Arctic Ocean to Central America were folded, uplifted, and intruded by isolated small masses of magma. This was followed by a long period of erosion which carried great sheets of gravel out of the center of the uplift to be deposited as massive alluvial fans around the flanks of the San Juans.

The stage was now set for the final fiery renaissance of the San Juan mountain complex: a succession of massive volcanic explosions which racked the range from about 35 million years ago to about 28 million years ago. In a zone bounded by the Gunnison River on the north, by the San Luis Valley on the east, the Needle Mountains on the southwest, and the San Miguel Range on the west, twenty or more huge volcanic peaks began to spew out great columns of ash, smoke, and magma. Many of these immense, explo-

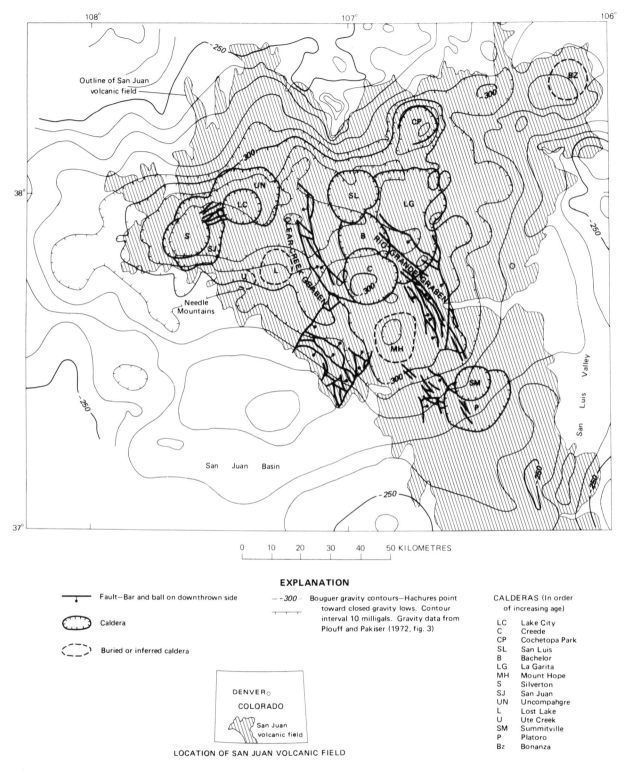

EXPLANATION

Fault—Bar and ball on downthrown side

- -300 - Bouguer gravity contours—Hachures point toward closed gravity lows. Contour interval 10 milligals. Gravity data from Plouff and Pakiser (1972, fig. 3)

Caldera

Buried or inferred caldera

CALDERAS (In order of increasing age)

LC	Lake City
C	Creede
CP	Cochetopa Park
SL	San Luis
B	Bachelor
LG	La Garita
MH	Mount Hope
S	Silverton
SJ	San Juan
UN	Uncompahgre
L	Lost Lake
U	Ute Creek
SM	Summitville
P	Platoro
Bz	Bonanza

0 10 20 30 40 50 KILOMETRES

DENVER○

COLORADO

San Juan volcanic field

LOCATION OF SAN JUAN VOLCANIC FIELD

COLLAPSE CALDERAS OF THE SAN JUAN VOLCANIC FIELD. *From Steven and Lipman, "Calderas of the San Juan Volcanic Field, Southwestern Colorado," U.S.G.S. Professional Paper 958, 1976.*

sive eruptions were so violent that they emptied the magma chambers below the bases of the cones. This usually caused the superstructure of the cone to collapse into the evacuated magma chamber, creating what the volcanologist calls a caldera.

You can best visualize what such a feature looks like today by recalling pictures of Crater Lake, Oregon, where only the base of the original cone remains as a rim around the lake, which occupies the collapsed center of the former cone.

In the San Juans, at least fifteen calderas have now been recognized, and two or three more may exist.

The smallest of the known San Juan calderas is about 4¾ miles in diameter (7 kilometers), the largest is over 25 miles in diameter (40 kilometers).

By about 30 million years ago the first phase of the volcanic activity, which saw the creation of the huge volcanic cones and vents, was completed. The final phase of volcanism, between 30 million years ago and 26 million years ago, witnessed the evacuation of magma chambers and the collapse of the volcanic superstructures.

It is difficult to imagine the volume of ash-flow material ejected onto the surface of the San Juans by the massive eruptions which took place during the short 4 million years of the final period. The eighteen known separate ash-flow sheets produced in that short time have been estimated to contain about 2,760 cubic miles (11,500 cubic kilometers) of material—enough tuff, breccia, and lava to cover the 9,650 square miles (25,000 square kilometers) of the San Juan volcanic field to an average depth of about 1,500 feet (460 meters). This average is distributed between very thin sheets and depths of more than 4,000 feet (1,220 meters).

The San Juan volcanic rocks make up the upper slopes and summits of the high ranges to the north and east of the Needle Mountains. The Needles show no evidence of ever having received any of the lava and ash from the volcanic disturbances which were taking place further to the north and east. Undoubtedly, ejected material spilled over onto the surface of the Needle Mountains, but erosion soon carried it away.

In that part of the range which is buried in volcanics the rock has a neutral gray, elephant-hide color which contrasts sharply with the brilliant green of sedges and grass above timberline. In a number of places, such as the summits of Red Mountain, south of Ouray, on the northwest rim of the Silverton Caldera, invading hot mineral solutions have added great swatches of red and ochre oxidation to the volcanic rocks. Numerous other local patches and streaks of mineralized coloration relieve the monotony of the gray volcanic rock.

The hues of the high country are augmented by the red and buff of the sedimentary beds on the flanks of the range, which are often clothed in the green of needle leaf trees and aspen. The resulting ensemble presents one of the most colorful ranges on the continent.

At the end of the volcanic episode, the calderas from which the ash flows had emanated were fractured and faulted zones of weakness in the roofs of the major magma chambers.

Meanwhile recharge material from below was forming into a large shallow batholith beneath the entire area. The complex network of fractures provided numerous avenues along which igneous intrusive material and hot mineralized solutions could make their way toward the surface. This mineralization took place for the most part from 2 to 10 million years after the final collapse of the calderas—say from 22 million years to 16 million years ago.

The mineral veins of the San Juan Mountains region, which have produced about $725 million in gold, silver, copper, lead, and zinc, lie mostly in the fractured rims or floors of earlier calderas. The ancient rocks of the Needle Mountain section and the flanking sedimentaries have, so far, shown little mineralization.

The topmost surface material on the stratigraphic column of the San Juans is composed of a few late lava flows in the eastern part of the range and the products of weathering and erosion left after the ceaseless work of wind, water, ice, and gravity.

CHAPTER 3

The Mills of God

Two processes are at work in the carving of a landscape. One is *weathering*, the other is *erosion*. They have been going on since the beginning of geologic time.

Weathering breaks down solid rock into smaller and smaller fragments; erosion is the process whereby these fragments are transported away from their point of origin by water, wind, or ice.

Weathering is both a chemical and physical process by which solid rock is slowly broken down into smaller and weaker components. For example, rust is a visible result of chemical weathering. In the presence of water, iron is converted to a hydrated form of ferric oxide which is immeasurably softer than the metallic iron from which it was produced. A similar process works on rock.

Recent news releases have pointed out that Cleopatra's Needle, a granite obelisk which was transplanted from the dry climate of lower Egypt to Central Park in New York City, less than 100 years ago, has suffered greater deterioration during its short sojourn in the New World from noxious urban fumes than it suffered in its whole 3,400 years of exposure to the dry climate of the north African desert. Weathering weakens the initial mineral bonds which hold earth materials together.

Chemical reactions are not the only processes which weaken rocks. Freezing and thawing of water in the small interstitial spaces between rock components wedges them apart. Water expands in volume when changing its physical state from liquid to solid, exerting a powerful force which prys rocks apart. Rootlets in tiny cracks expand as they grow, adding to the burden of dissolution inherent in all earth materials. Weather-

Opposite: Upper Sneffels Creek from the summit of Potosi Peak. Looking west. A rock glacier, in sunlight, flows down from the north side of Gilpin Peak.

ing is the initial stage in the process of soil formation. Darwin once pointed out the extreme importance of the lowly earthworm in the breaking down of parent material to a stage which permits the cultivation of plants.

Weathering prepares rock for the process of erosion. The smaller fragments resulting from all of these processes can more easily be moved from one part of the landscape to another.

Longfellow put it more poetically when he observed: "Though the mills of God grind slowly, yet they grind exceedingly small."

Erosion, the second sculpturing process, has to do with transportation. Weathered material is carried by one of the agents of erosion, which include gravity, water, wind, and ice, from one part of the earth's surface to another. The transported material may travel only a short distance during each transport episode, but it will be picked up and moved again and again. Its ultimate resting place is the bottom of some coastal sea which may lie half a continent away.

In a sense, a mountain range can be characterized as a magnificent ruin standing in the debris of its own dissolution, like one of the ancient cities of the Middle East which is marked by a mound of debris, or "tell," on the desert plain. Old cities, like old ranges, have lost many of the recognizable features of their once proud structures. The Appalachians and Ozarks, much as Nineveh and Ur, rise like gentle ghosts above the plains which surround their sites.

Young ranges and young cities are otherwise. The San Juan is a young range. Its towers and summits stand proudly above a limited apron of debris—much as the Parthenon soars above its hill at Athens, or the eleventh-century abbey pierces the sky above the summit of Mont-Saint-Michel, off the Normandie coast of France.

The basic transporting agents of erosion are four in number—gravity, water, ice, and wind. In a way,

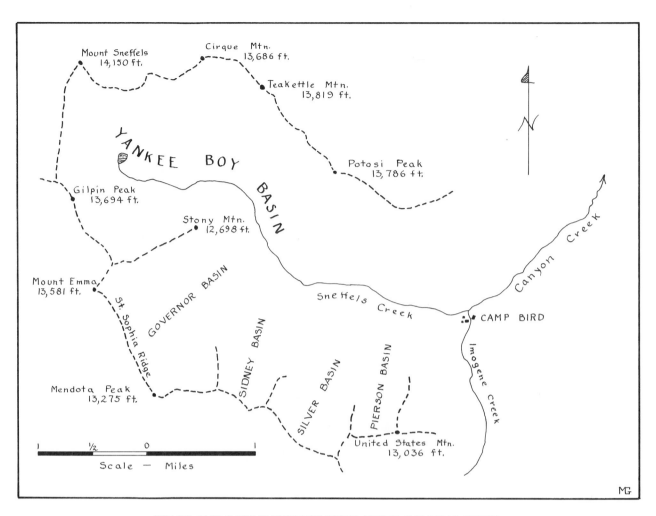

PEAKS AND BASINS SURROUNDING UPPER CANYON CREEK

gravity is the chief of all the rest. It is the prime mover. The force of gravity is elemental—ubiquitous. If we push a rock off the summit of a mountain, it will go careening down the slope in response to the force of the attraction between its mass and the mass of the earth.

I'm not suggesting that you push a rock off the summit of a mountain! It would be one of the most dangerous and thoughtless acts you could ever perform. One never knows what or who might be below—don't!

Our hypothetical rock would prefer to be attracted directly toward the center of the earth, but if mountain slopes get in the way it will roll or slide down them in the general direction of the earth's center until it reaches a point where the attraction between its mass and that of the earth is not great enough to overcome the resistance of friction, where it comes to rest.

Gravity attracts unattached objects toward the center of the earth. It is also the prime mover which pulls the three transporting agents downhill. Water runs downhill like a falling rock. Glacial ice, formed

from fallen snow, responds to the same urging although at a much slower pace. Even air has mass and responds to differences in pressure (weight).

Each of the agents of erosion (gravity, water, ice, and wind) does work as it responds to the tug of gravity. Each agent, being of a different nature and responding in a different way, leaves its individualized signature on the land.

Canyon Creek heads in a glacial basin high on the south slopes of Mt. Sneffels. As it makes its way to lower country, it has scoured a deep, spectacular canyon through the gray volcanic rock which caps the northern part of the San Juans. At about 9,000 feet above sea level, it is joined from the south by the stream which tumbles from Imogene Basin, which cradles the famous Camp Bird Mine. The dark red Camp Bird mill, long since destroyed by a spectacular fire, once stood in the timber-girt bowl where the two tributaries join.

At the junction, the canyon turns northeast and plunges more or less as straight as an arrow toward

16

the mountain-rimmed amphitheatre which cradles Ouray. Just below the Camp Bird mill, the canyon tilts downward over the lip of a resistant formation and knifes deeply into the red and buff sandstones and shales which underlie the gray volcanics. By the time the creek has cut down to the level of the Uncompahgre River, which it joins at the edge of Ouray, it has eroded its canyon through the whole column of geologic formations in this part of the San Juan. In the process it has cut backward in time from the glacial and gravity-eroded rocks on the top of the range, which are only a few brief decades in age, to the Precambrian Uncompahgre Formation, where it joins the Uncompahgre River at the bottom of the valley. This represents somewhat more than one billion years of geologic time. Even the walls of the Grand Canyon scarcely expose a longer record.

From a spectacular vantage point on the broad summit of Potosi Peak (pronounced Pō-tō-see, with the accent on the final "see" — named for San Luis Potosi, a Mexican silver mining center), one can look down on a type of erosion unique to high mountain country.

On the nearby sides of the chasm in which Canyon Creek curls around the foot of Potosi, the lower, gentler, softly rounded slopes are clothed in green. Only occasionally is the tundra broken by the scars of bare rock slides which have been carried downslope along overflowing small watercourses. Higher, the canyon sides spring up sharply toward the ridge crests which encircle the canyon-head basin.

Across the valley several tributary glacial cirques open into the canyon from the valley side. They have relatively flat bottoms at about timberline and sheer headwalls which have been cut into the general upland like the handiwork of a giant biscuit cutter. The wash of emerald forest and lighter green tundra rises into the bottoms of the cirque basins but stops at the foot of the encircling cliffs, like the upper limits of high tide on a beach. On flat land higher up, tundra again clothes the meager soil, but the oversteepened slopes everywhere are the domain of gravity erosion.

The agents of weathering, chemical and physical, disintegrate the extrusive volcanics of the San Juan into masses of platy fragments which gravity urges downward as soon as each fragment is prized from the bedrock. Usually the talus slopes are steep enough for individual fragments to only barely overcome friction; they creep valleyward with glacial slowness. But sometimes a single boulder which is larger and heavier than its neighbors will careen from the top of a mountain clear to its base, sending down showers of fragments where it caroms off the mountainside sending up puffs of sulphurous smoke.

The south slope of Cirque Peak, just to our right, feeds a smooth blanket of talus down to the lower lip of the basin. There, where the angle pitches downward steeply, there is a break in the talus. It has exceeded the angle of repose. Individual fragments now begin to break away from the tightly packed mass and tumble over the brink of the steepened slope like a stream over a waterfall. Usually, movement of weathered debris by gravity is of doddering slowness — measured in inches per century; here the occasional clink of individual rockfalls reaches ones ears.

Debris prized from the vertical cirque headwalls across the valley falls in disordered heaps at their feet and spreads down the less precipitous slopes in aprons.

At the foot of Gilpin Peak, across the amphitheatre, the apron of debris has spread out in a startling, different form. Its surface has concentric sweeping curves, successive waves which parallel the outer edge of its tongue-shaped mass, like a nest of overlapping saucers with exposed rims, while their bodies were still buried in the hillside. Viewed from above, this feature resembles nothing so much as a huge mound of thick, ropy molasses which was poured out on the slope from a gargantuan narrow-necked jug on a cold day. The surface has every appearance of having flowed to its present position in waves and then been frozen.

Across and farther down the main valley, the floor of Silver Basin contains another of these lobate tongues of debris. If the mass of talus appears familiar it is because its picture has been reproduced in more geology and geomorphology textbooks than almost any other mass-wasting feature in the world.

The geologists of the fledgling U.S. Geological Survey, who examined the area during the last quarter of the nineteenth century, reported these unique features, photographed them, and recorded their field observations in scientific journals. As is often the case with a newly observed phenomena or process, a controversy arose in the literature as to the proper interpretation of the mode of origin of these features. It continues to this day.

These features are known as "rock glaciers," or as sometimes appears in the literature, "rock streams." Because of the uniform blocky nature of the products of weathering in the San Juans, the abundance of such material, and the great extent of slopes, there seems to be a greater number of these features in the San Juans than anywhere else in the world. The intense glaciation of the San Juan also seems to have played a part in the formation of rock glaciers.

Although the San Juans have become a sort of type area for these features, they are not unique there. They have been reported in Canada, Alaska, the Sierra Nevadas, Switzerland, Spitsbergen, and even the Falkland Islands off the Argentine coast.

About 140 years ago, in *The Voyage of the Beagle*, Charles Darwin described "streams of stone" which he observed in the Falkland Islands during his visit in

South-southeast from the summit of Mt. Sneffels. All of these peaks have been eroded from thick, flat-lying beds of volcanic tuff and breccia. The hardest beds have formed vertical cliffs, while more easily eroded strata form moderate slopes covered with talus.

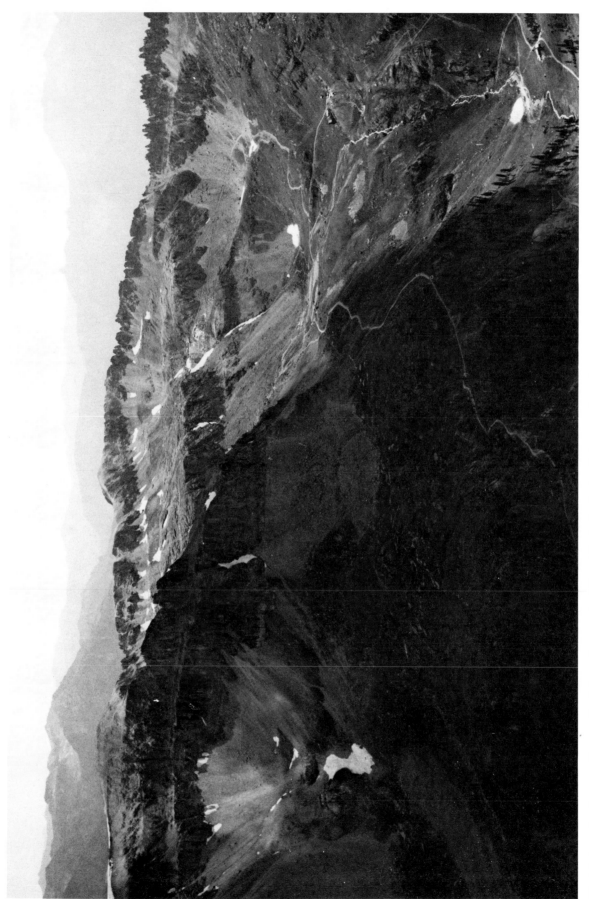

Glacial cirque heads across Canyon Creek from the summit of Potosi Peak. St. Sophia Ridge is at the right end of the middle distant ridge. Governor Basin, with numerous mine buildings and roads lies at the foot of St. Sophia Ridge. The stair-step bottoms of the cirques has resulted from alternate hard and soft rock layers on which the ice has scoured. Telluride lies in the valley beyond the sunlit ridge in the middle distance. On the skyline to the right is the San Miguel Range, west of Telluride. To its left is the narrow spire of Lizard Head.

Silver Basin, above the Revenue Mine, west of Ouray, cradles this lobate mass of rock — the Silver Basin rock glacier. These features are sometimes called rock glaciers and sometimes rock streams; the terms are interchangeable. The lobate rock mass

probably came to its present location on the back (surface) of the dying mass of glacier ice which occupied the cirque floor at the end of the ice age.

Gilpin Peak on the right, Mount Emma to the left of it, from the summit of Mt. Sneffels. The talus at the foot of Gilpin Peak's summit cliff has moved slowly down into a rock stream (rock glacier) in the lower left corner of the picture.

1834. Although, from his description, they do not appear to exactly match the San Juan rock glaciers, they are near enough to be classified among this type of mass-wasting phenomenon.

A recent study based its conclusions on a count of at least 756 rock glaciers within those portions of the San Juan Mountains lying inside Colorado. There are rocks glaciers in other Colorado ranges just as they are found in other parts of the world, but nowhere else are they found in such profusion.

A visit to the Silver Basin rock glacier provides a face-to-face view of this type of feature. From the ruins of the old Revenue Mine beside Canyon Creek, eight miles from Ouray, the route climbs on an unused wagon road into the upper bowl of the cirque, beyond the last timber. Near the lower lip of this upper basin a magnificent turquoise tarn nestles at the foot of the Silver Basin rock glacier.

The cirque walls leap up almost vertically in a semi-circle, like the upper bleachers in the end of a football stadium or the seats in an ancient Greek theatre. At the outer ends of the semicircular walls a thin blade of ridge ravels out into thin air where the side of the Silver Basin cirque meets the side of the next cirque down valley — rather like slightly overlapping biscuit cuts in thick dough. The upper rim of the cirque is topped by the upland surface which caps this part of the range, the remnant of an ancient peneplain left by an earlier erosion cycle.

The gentler slopes at the side and floor of the cirque which are not filled with either talus or the rock glacier are clothed in a carpet of bright tundra. Festoons of rock debris drape down the lower parts of the encircling cliffs which have been swept bare of loose talus as soon as it has been prized from the cirque headwall. The massive curtain of talus at the foot of the upper headwall feeds down in ropy ridges onto the upper surface of the rock glacier, fanning out into encircling ridges which outline the tongue-shaped mass of debris. At its outer limit, the mass of the rock glacier termi-nates in a steep front down which loose talus tumbles at the angle of repose into the blue-green waters of the tarn.

At one time geologists felt that rock glaciers were the result of massive landslides. But when their form was compared to massive landslides which had oc-curred in more recent times, like the Turtle Mountain Slide at Frank, Alberta; the Hope, a British Columbia slide; the Gros Ventre Slide in Wyoming; the Elm Slide in Switzerland — it was found that there were salient differences in structure and form. It was noted that rock glaciers were always associated in some way with glaciation or past glaciation.

In Hurricane Basin, near Henson Creek, between Ouray and Lake City, a mine tunnel driven through the base of a rock glacier to get to bedrock traversed over 300 feet of debris-choked ice. Other evidence has come from such clues as movement, interstitial ice, orientation, meltwater amounts, overall distribution. Many workers now feel that rock glaciers hide the dying remnants of once much larger glaciers which occupied mountain cirques during the final deglacia-tion of the ice age. Debris moving down the cirque headwall fed out onto the ice and was moved slowly forward by the shrinking mass of ice. Eventually, when the ice had melted to such a small remnant that it was no longer able to move the massive load carried on its back, it became stagnant and the cargo of rock de-bris, which still showed the lines of glacial movement, settled onto the floor of the cirque.

The world of mass wasting is evident throughout the San Juans; it is the natural realm closest to bedrock yet at the same time at the surface, the theater where mountains are reduced to heaps of rubble — ruins buried in the debris of their own dissolution.

CHAPTER 4

Water, Snow, and Ice

The great prime mover of weathered rock debris is water; water is the great sculptor of the mountain landscape. The movement of weathered material on very steep slopes may initially be gravity, but as slope angles decrease water must take over more and more of the burden.

Water is carried to mountain slopes and summits by the hydrologic cycle: evaporated from the ocean basins, it is carried as water vapor by prevailing winds over the land, where it falls as rain or snow and then begins its journey back to the nearest ocean. In its course downslope it transports weathered rock debris, *eroding* and shaping the surface.

The sediment carried by moving water is graded and classified by its size and the water velocity. Material which is dissolved chemically in the water is known as *dissolved load.* Salts and alkalies, which are washed out of the soil are carried invisibly in this way. Fine particles of weathered rock, such as clay, silt, and extremely fine particles of sand, may be stirred up in turbulent water and transported as a *suspended load.* A muddy stream is carrying a suspended load. Larger fragments, such as gravel, cobbles, and boulders are too bulky to be suspended, even at the greatest velocity; however, they can be nudged or dragged along the course of the stream as a *bed load* or *traction load.* It is startling to discover the size and weight of boulders which can be moved by a large quantity of swift-flowing water. It is not uncommon to find some as big as a small automobile.

As water flows downslope, it seeks the steepest gradient, concentrating its flow in such a way as to shorten its trip toward its ultimate goal, the sea. By joining forces with other streams hurrying in the same general direction it magnifies its volume, which at the same time increases its ability to do work. The concentration of flow in a channel, by increasing the mass of water and debris in a narrow space, intensifies the amount of scouring which is accomplished, a sort of self-perpetuating process. The more water, the bigger the channel; the wider and deeper the channel, the more water it can carry.

As water is concentrated into ever-larger channels downstream, the tiny trickle from a snowbank combines with others to form a brook which flows into a creek which becomes a rivulet, then swells to a river, which eventually grows to the master stream for a whole region. Each branch of the system does its part to add to the magnitude of the whole. The little upstream tributaries gnaw away at the very summits and upper slopes of the highlands. The intermediate streams round off the middle slopes while the great rivers coil sluggishly away from the ruins of the ranges, having collected the sediment and water from half a country and pushed it on toward the ocean.

If there is a single term which can be applied to the work of streams in a mountain setting, it is "canyon." A canyon can be described as a narrow deep watercourse which carries its burden of mountain sediment like charges of shot down an unrifled gunbarrel.

In the high country of the San Juans, every stream, from the tiniest snowbank-fed streamlet to full-blown river, has some part of its course crowded between the confining walls of a canyon. The walls are steepest and deepest and the course straightest at those places where the stream traverses the exposures of hardest rock. At such places the channel, once it has started to saw its way downward into the hard rock, must hew to the course which it began.

Dr. Wallace W. Atwood, senior author of a U.S. Geological Survey monograph on the physiography

Opposite: Inside Box Canyon, within the city limits of Ouray, Colorado. (Starns-Orendorf)

and glacial geology of the San Juan Mountains was carried away from his usual scientific reserve in the following passage:

> The glory of the lofty peaks that contributes so generously to the scenic beauty of the San Juan Mountains is rivaled only by the grandeur of the gigantic canyons that intervene between the peaks and radiate from the heart of the range. The mountaineer enjoying the vista from some vantage point high on an eerie crag is entranced by the glimpse of a mighty river so far beneath him that it appears merely as a silver thread winding in and out among the grassy lowland meadows, or is thrilled by the abysses that open at his feet, where this selfsame stream has carved a chasm deep into the heart of the mountain massif. Again, as he pursues his circuitous route along the bank of a swift rivulet, he is constantly awed by the towering cliffs and precipitous walls which rise almost vertically to dizzy heights from either bank of the foam-lashed stream and which with their pinnacles and palisades sculptured by wind and rain lend endless variety to the always glorious views. It is the canyons that contribute to the picturesqueness of the mountain scenery and make life in the mountains most joyous.

As happened so many times among the midwestern and eastern-trained scientists who were commissioned to do the early geologic exploration of the West, Atwood was caught up in wonder at the splendid vistas which he was commissioned to map and investigate. He was not alone. Some of the most lyrical descriptions of the unspoiled West are to be found in the scientific writings of such investigators as Gilbert, Powell, Hayden, Holmes, Dutton, and King. Perhaps their training led them to see more clearly the framework of the landscape; perhaps they were poets at heart.

The city of Ouray has a "pet" canyon in its backyard. In fact, it has several, but one caught the fancy of the locals before the others. In the days of the mining boom, when the warm water springs and aspirations toward late Victorian tourism caused locals to bill the region as the "Switzerland of America," the cliff above the canyon sported a large electric sign proclaiming "Box Canyon" to the world.

Box Canyon is the lower end of Canyon Creek, which we met in the previous chapter. At this point, the stream and its load of transported rock debris, collected further up the valley, is funneled through a narrow slit which has been scoured deep into the Uncompahgre quartzite. At the lower end of the slit, the stream falls sheer more than a hundred feet into a dark chasm constantly wet with spray. The inner reaches of the chasm never receive sunlight—only dark twilight and the blackness of night reign there.

The visitor approaches the fall on a wooden trestle and hanging bridge bolted to the smooth rock. The most lasting impression from the inner reaches of the gorge is the deafening roar of the fall as it beats great gobbets of water, sand, and occasional cobbles against the walls and bottom of the slit. At the very back of the gorge the pounding water has cut a vertical hole through the rock so that part of the waterfall is hidden behind a curtain of rock. It is as though one looked through a window in the side of a well in which a furious maelstrom plunges ever down into a bowl-shaped pit.

Box Canyon is an impressive monument to the abrasive power of water. All along the sides of the gorge can be seen the smooth waterworn channels cut at earlier stages of the canyon's formation. These smooth sanded hollows high above the present stream level serve as high-water marks, measuring earlier and higher levels of the canyon bottom.

All of the smaller streams flowing out of the San Juans have canyoned sections along their courses. These are the places where adamant formations have preserved the narrow course of the stream. Some of these gorges are small, as befits a brook or creek, others are of gigantic proportions which seem to belie the size of the water courses which occupy their bottoms. The larger streams have also carved befitting gorges.

The San Miguel, which drains the glacial basins above Telluride, plunges into an impressive series of canyons as it flows through the red sedimentary rocks which flank the San Juans on the northwest. The Uncompahgre and its tributaries thread their way through the miniature canyons we have just described. The Rio Grande, even after it has traversed the gates of the mountains at Wagon Wheel Gap and escaped into the broad San Luis Valley, must run a further gauntlet through vertical walls of volcanic rock from the lower lip of the San Luis Valley, south of Alamosa, to the open valley above Bernilillo and Albuquerque.

The San Juan's most awesome canyon has enjoyed national status since its establishment in 1933 as the Black Canyon National Monument. Visitors to its rim often express disbelief that this 2,000-foot-deep granite gorge was carved by the tiny sliver of river which brawls between the jumbled, house-sized boulders which choke the canyon bottom. Seeking an easier explanation, they invoke some cataclysm such as an earthquake, flood, or volcanic upheaval to explain what seems incomprehensible. But all of the geologic evidence points inescapably to water erosion.

The doubters reckon without the span of time involved. If the ancestral Gunnison River began to entrench itself at the beginning of the Laramide Revolution, 60 million years ago, cutting a 2,000-foot-deep canyon since that time, it took 30,000 years, on the average, to lower the river course 1 foot, or 2,500 years per inch. Expressed another way, this average rate of erosion amounts to 0.0004 inch per year—about 105½ years to lower the canyon bottom as much as the thick-

Bottom of the Black Canyon of the Gunnison, at one of its deepest points. The figure gives scale to the size of the boulders. Water-scoured surfaces can be seen thirty and forty feet above the present stream level, which is hidden here under the mass of boulders which have fallen from the canyon walls.

Blanca Peak, across the San Luis valley from the southern San Juans. The three prominent valleys which course down this west side of the Blanca massif display the characteristic U-shaped cross profile of glaciation.

ness of one sheet of 20 # bond paper. Somehow, this figure is slightly easier to live with than 2,000 feet or 60 million years.

Little drops of water, given enough of them, charged with enough abrasive load, and given time enough, can indeed transport the mightiest of mountain ranges to the distant sea, carving an awesome canyon along the way.

. . . .

Whereas the hallmark of mountain stream erosion is the canyon, glacial erosion leaves a much different signature on the land: valley cross sections are U-shaped, with smooth rounded bottoms and sides, scoured by the passage of ice; valley heads are fretted at summit levels in scooped-out cirques; high mountains are defined by knife-edged ridges which converge at arrow-head summits; great jumbled masses of ice-borne debris choke valley bottoms and sides at the farthest extent of the ice, in the ridges of lateral and terminal moraines.

For one trained to see such tokens, the evidences of past glaciation meets the eye everywhere in the mountain world of the San Juan: the dramatic U-shaped valleys which cradle Telluride, Ouray, and Silverton; the same U-shaped profile of the Animas Valley above Durango; grooves planed in the surface of Uncompahgre quartzite at Bear Creek Falls; the Matterhorn-shaped summit of Wetterhorn Peak, Pigeon Peak, Jagged Mountain, Arrow, and Vestal; the bow-shaped terminal moraine above Durango; lateral moraines hung high on the sides of most valleys. How did all of this come about?

Two million or so years ago, world climatic conditions began a slow change. The geologist calls this epoch the Pleistocene. It was followed by geologic time's final epoch, the Recent, in which we now live.

According to one of the more persuasive theories of the ice age, at the start of the Pleistocene, the Arctic Ocean was probably an ice-free ocean, surrounded by ice-free land. Today, it is covered by frozen sea ice (pack ice), which drifts in a clockwise direction around the pole. At the beginning of the Pleistocene, it would have been possible for an ocean-going ship to sail from the mouth of the Mackenzie River in Canada's Northwest Territory, across the North Pole to Murmansk, Russia's ice-free port on the Kola Peninsula, without encountering pack ice. Warm north Atlantic and north Pacific water circulated freely over the thresholds at the Bering Strait and between Greenland and Norway, into the Arctic Basin, keeping it ice free.

Cores from sea bottom sediments, deposited at those long ago times, tell us the temperature of the sea water in which they settled.

A changed wind system began then to carry moist air from the open Arctic sea toward the lands which surround it. The average annual temperatures were low; most of the precipitation was in the form of snow. During the long sunless winters, in high latitudes, more snow was accumulated than could be melted during the ensuing short summers. The surplus snow which was left at the end of each year was slowly compressed into more dense material, called "firn." After centuries of such accumulation and compression, the firn was metamorphosed into crystalline, milky, bubbly, glacial ice; its weight eventually caused it to squeeze outward from the initial accumulation zone.

The outward-moving ice overwhelmed everything in its path. In North America, the principal accumulation areas were on the Labrador Peninsula, in the shallow depression now occupied by Hudson Bay, and the Keewatin barren lands to the west of Hudson Bay. Here the ice accumulated to great depth; estimates have placed its greatest thickness at somewhere between 10,000 and 15,000 feet. The pressure of increasing weight squeezed the ice outward at its fringes, like thin batter on a warm griddle.

The outer border of the expanding ice sheet soon invaded milder climes. Here the outer fringe of the ice sheet underwent greater melting than the central accumulation zone. Eventually the outer limit of the ice sheet was melting at the same rate that snow was accumulating in northern Canada and being forced outward from the nourishment zones. At this time the ice sheet had reached a state of equilibrium.

A glacier or ice sheet operates on a budget, which might be likened to a household budget or a bank balance. Snowfall in the accumulation areas is reckoned as a deposit to the account. Melting at the snout or edge of the ice sheet or glacier, plus melting from the surface, wherever it occurs, is reckoned as a withdrawal from the account. When the deposits are just equal to the withdrawals the glacier is said to be in a state of equilibrium. If deposits are greater than withdrawals the glacier is said to have a positive budget, and it advances or grows in size; if withdrawals are greater than deposits it is said to have a negative budget and the glacier or ice sheet shrinks or retreats. Four times during the approximately 2 million years of the Pleistocene, the accumulation zones overflowed and ice swept southward, the outer fringe reaching its maximum extent at mid-continent—in Nebraska, Kansas, Illinois, and Wisconsin. Four times the warm, dry climate of the south brought the advance to a halt and then melted the ice edge back to its starting place. The inland icecap of Greenland and the smaller icecaps of Baffin Island and Ellesmere Island in the Canadian Arctic, are the only remaining remnants of this last advance. In North America the glaciologist calls these four separate ice advances the Nebraskan, Kansan, Illinoian, and Wisconsin, from oldest to youngest; named for the states where the best preserved evidence of the outer boundaries of the ice for each advance is found.

As the ice moved south during each period of advance, it rearranged the landscape. Like a vast bulldozer it scoured loose material, soil, and plants from the surface over which it moved. Sometimes the material scooped from a northerly landscape was carried great distances to the south, where it was eventually released from the grip of the ice as it melted. Sand and gravel held in the bottom of the ice sheet acted like a rasp, or sandpaper, smoothing the land over which it moved. Almost a million square miles of Canada, north of the Great Lakes, was smoothed in this fashion.

At the south end of this debris transportation system, the material which had been picked up in the north was slowly lowered to the surface of the land as the ice melted under the southern sun. The scraping and scouring are evident everywhere in the north; a disordered veneer of glacial debris marks the landscapes south of the Great Lakes. As the ice edge melted back it usually left a great ridge of material marking its outer position, called a terminal moraine. In other places, sheets of jumbled rock, sand, and silt blanketed the ground, causing a rearrangement of the drainage pattern, leaving hummocks in places and basins in others. The myriads of lakes in Minnesota and Wisconsin occupy many of these depressions. Such a veneer of randomly assorted material left by glacial action is called a *till sheet* or *ground moraine.*

During the massive deglaciation great floods of meltwater from the retreating ice front rushed southward to form the rivers which skirted the dying ice sheet.

During each of the ice advances and subsequent retreats the changes were so gradual that natural vegetation could adapt quickly. As ice advanced over a particular location the vegetation was wiped out; as the ice later retreated, exposing the glacial debris, vegetation quickly regained a foothold and advanced northward following the retreating ice. Lichens and mosses recolonized the bare rock. Grasses, sedges, ground cover, and eventually trees crept north from one pocket of soil to another.

Along with the grass and sedges, the herbivores which grazed upon them, and the predators which preyed upon the herbivores advanced and retreated south of the moving ice front. Man joined the movement as a predator, particularly during the last period of deglaciation. Remains of the mastodon and woolly mammoth have been found as far north as Alaska

and Siberia; they have also been found as far south as Arizona and central Europe, where they had been driven during periods of ice advance. The camel, the wild ox, and the ancestor of the modern horse followed the same pioneering migrations, taking advantage of the changes of climate and environment.

The great climatic oscillations which brought about the onset and demise of each ice advance and retreat were global in extent and effect. What was happening on the North American continent was happening at the same time in Eurasia. What happened in the Northern Hemisphere was likewise happening in the Southern Hemisphere. What was happening to the northern and eastern part of North America was happening in the mountains of the West. Because of their height above sea level, the deep freeze extended much further southward in the mountains than in the lowlands of the mid-continent. Altitude above sea level has an effect upon climate which is directly comparable to the effect produced by latitude.

The San Juans lie on the main stem of the southward-pointing highlands of the Rocky Mountains. Simultaneously with each of the major ice advances out of North America's northern accumulation zones, the high plateaus and summits of the San Juans became a secondary, isolated accumulation zone. Here, because of altitude, more snow accumulated each winter than could be melted the following summer. Season after season the surplus snow compacted into firn and then glacial ice. By the mere weight of surplus mass it eventually began to move away from the high accumulation zone toward the edge of the highlands. The readiest avenue of escape to the lowlands was along the numerous valleys and canyons already carved by the streams flowing outward like the spokes of a wheel from the heart of the ranges.

During these times the upper portion of the San Juan was occupied by a great central icecap which buried even the very highest summits. The San Juan icecap must have looked like the Columbia Icefield, of the Canadian Rockies, or the Greenland inland ice do today. At the edges of the icecap the outward-moving ice collected into the headward channels of the major streams and flowed down them as discharge glaciers. Each discharge glacier eventually reached a lower elevation where melting at the snout just balanced the rate at which ice was being fed down the channel from the inland ice above. As in the case of continental glaciation, at the outer end of each discharge glacier huge disordered masses of boulders, gravel, sand, and silt collected where it was released from the grip of the ice which had carried it from the mountains. Such a mass of ice-borne material, deposited at the snout of a glacier, is called a terminal moraine. Beyond the

Glacial outwash terrace along the Uncompahgre valley a few miles north of Ridgway, Colorado. The terrace is veneered with outwash gravel carried down the river course when it was carrying vast quantities of melt water from retreating glaciers. This is just downstream from the Ridgway terminal moraine.

Sunlight Peak in the Needle Mountains. Sunlight is a frost-shattered remnant of the much larger Needle Mountain uplift. The two dark peaks in the right middle distance are Arrow Peak and Vestal Peak in the Grenadier Range. (H. L. Standley)

terminal moraine, stream-side terraces extend for miles along both sides of the stream which carried meltwater away from the melting glacier.

Even more impressive than the great masses of till and the outwash terraces which mark the deposition sites of the ice-borne material around the skirts of the range is the fretwork of ice sculpture among the highest summits themselves. Almost every tributary stream in the heart of the range heads in a glacial cirque. These great semicircular headwalls eat into the mountain summit level like the scalloping of a gigantic biscuit cutter. Below the head of each stream most valleys have been polished out to a U-shaped profile. Many San Juan tributary valleys have the cross profile of the inside of a hollowed-log canoe. At the zenith of the Pleistocene, it was not uncommon for a thousand-foot-deep river of ice to crawl down a valley. The rock imbedded in the bottom of the ice was dragged along the bed of the valley scouring and smoothing everything over which it moved, like a rasp or coarse sandpaper. One thousand feet of ice presses down with the weight of two and one half tons per square foot of surface. A more efficient, large-scouring tool could hardly be devised.

At the apex of the range, the handiwork of glacial erosion shows at its finest. Here the biscuit-cutter imprint of two or more coalescing cirques has frequently eaten away the upland to a residual remnant, standing like a concave-profiled, vertical-sided pyramid. Many of the San Juan's highest summits bear the imprint of the past work of ice: Uncompahgre Peak, Wetterhorn Peak, and Wildhorse at the northeast end of the range; Arrow, Vestal, Pigeon, Turret, Jagged Mountain, Windom, Sunlight, and Eolus in the Needles and Grenadiers; every summit along the northwest front of the range from Whitehouse on the east to Hayden Peak on the west, including Cirque, Teakettle, Sneffels, Kismet, Gilpin, Dallas, Wolcott, Mears, and Last Dollar; every summit in the San Miguel Range; and the summits in the La Platas; a hundred more, unnamed. After the Matterhorn-type peaks come the knife-blade-thin ridges sharpened between opposite and advancing cirque headwalls—St. Sophia Ridge, Needle Ridge, Ramshorn Ridge, Cimarron Ridge, each a replica of the classic European *Arête*, and much admired as safe routes to difficult summits over rotten rock.

CHAPTER 5

A Self-made Climate

There is a sumptuous variety about the New England weather that compels the stranger's admiration – and regret. The weather is always doing something there; always attending strictly to business; always getting up new designs and trying them on people to see how they will go. But it gets through more business in Spring than in any other season. In the Spring I have counted one hundred and thirty-six different kinds of weather inside of twenty-four hours.

The above quotation is from a speech delivered by Mark Twain, in New York on December 22, 1876, before the New England Society. Although Twain was in fine humorous fettle, his observations about the fickleness of the New England weather could apply with only slight modification to the San Juans, or any other of the world's mountain regions. Changeability is the watchword.

About this same time Mark Twain is reputed to have made another witticism about weather which is no longer true of at least the San Juan region: "Everyone talks about the weather but no one ever does anything about it."

During the past few years, at several locations in the San Juans, the Bureau of Reclamation of the U.S. Interior Department, has been engaged in a weather modification program which looks toward the increase of winter snowfall. It is too early to assess the results of the program. However, the importance of the San Juan watershed to the run-off volume of the upper Colorado River and Rio Grande drainages is critical.

It gives pause to consider that weather and climate in the mountains of Colorado controls to a large extent

Opposite: The north face of Mt. Sneffels in a February snowstorm, taken from the summit of Blaine Peak.

the economic well-being of a vegetable farmer in Brawley or Mexicali or a citrus grower in Harlingen or Matamoros.

The British climatologist, W. G. Kendrew, is reported to have said "Mountains make their own climates." Note that "climates" was expressed in the plural. He was stating in another way that every mountain region is different from every other mountain region, and that each mountain region does not have a single climate but many climates. Weather forecasters hate to practice their skills in a mountain region – their forecasts are wrong more often than the law of averages would allow.

Let us make a distinction between weather and climate. Weather is the day-to-day occurrences of atmospheric phenomena. Climate is the average of these individual phenomena over a period of time. Weather is a storm which dumps an inch of rainfall at one location in forty-eight hours; climate is the average annual precipitation computed over fifty years of record at that same place. Climate is the result of statistical manipulation; weather is the measured impact of a single meterological event, or of each of a group of such events. Weather phenomena are measured by rain gauges, barometers, anemometers, sling psychrometers, recording hygrometers, thermistors, and such sophisticated tools as radar and radio sondes. We must describe a region's climate in terms of the statistical handling of data from measured weather phenomena.

The normal annual precipitation (a climatic element) at Montrose, at the north edge of the San Juans, measured during the period 1881 to 1956, was 9.65 inches. But no single year during that period recorded that precise amount of rainfall. Some years showed as high as 18 inches, some went as low as 6 inches. The yearly averages were composed of monthly averages and the monthly averages were composed of daily averages. If we wished to carry this manipulation to an absurdity

West from 13,000-foot elevation on Mt. Sneffels in mid-winter. Black pinnacles on near right are on the southwest ridge of Sneffels; twin-summited peak in center is Dallas Peak. Block-top summit of Gilpin Peak on extreme left. Small section of San Miguel Range, west of Telluride, shows through saddle to left of Dallas Peak.

Winter, changing recording drum of hygrothermograph at weather station above timberline.

Right: The SNOTEL remote snowpack station at Red Mountain Pass near Highway 550, between Ouray and Silverton, Colorado. Since the 1930s agencies of state and federal government have been forecasting runoff from snowmelt in the West. In recent years this duty has been taken up by the Soil Conservation Service of the Department of Agriculture. Seventy-five percent of the annual flow in western rivers such as the Colorado, the Rio Grande, the Arkansas, and the Platte, comes from the spring and summer melt of winter snow. In order to forecast the next year's runoff, the Soil Conservation Service, during the years, has established in the Rockies and the Sierra Nevada mountains a network of 1,700 snow courses, where field crews take snow samples once a month in the winter and weigh the samples to determine the water content. During the past five years or so, 480 new SNOTEL stations have been placed at strategic snow course sites, with the object of eventually replacing the older sampling method. SNOTEL is an acronym derived from SNOw TELemetry. These unattended stations automatically measure snow water content, precipitation totals, and air temperatures on a continuous basis. These data are transmitted daily to two monitoring stations at Boise, Idaho, and Ogden, Utah.

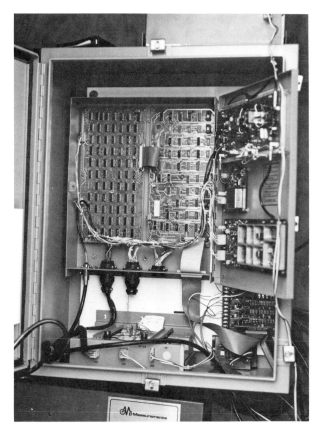

Left: Monitoring, computer, and short-wave transmission equipment at the Red Mountain SNOTEL site. Analog data from the precipitation gauge, the air temperature thermistors, and the snow pressure pillows at the site are converted in the computer to digital information, which is then stored in a buffer ready for transmission when called for. Equipment for the monitoring, storage, and VHF transmission is operated by storage batteries which are charged by solar cells. (See the cell panels halfway up the radio mast in photo on page 39, bottom.) Transmission beyond the horizon is made possible by bouncing signals off ionized meteor burst trails seventy-five miles or so above the Earth's surface. By reflecting signals in this way, data is transmitted between stations up to 1,200 miles apart. Consequently, the two monitoring stations at Boise and Ogden are able to communicate with remote stations in all of the Western states.

we would need to weigh every raindrop and every snowflake, adding its mass to the sum.

Nor is this the end of the measuring and manipulation. Weather and climate consist of many more components than just precipitation. The temperature regime at a given station is also an important part of its climatic dossier as are: wind directions and intensities; the distinction between precipitation which arrives in the form of rain and that which arrives in the form of snow; amounts of incoming solar radiation; length of the frost-free period (this is sometimes called the "growing season"); daily and annual duration of cloud cover; sensible temperature (the comfort index); barometric pressure differences; the tracks and speeds of cyclonic storms; evaporation rates; soil temperatures. Nor does this end the list of climate elements at the average lowland station. Elements which are peculiar to a mountain region add a still greater dimension of complexity.

For example, barometric pressure measurements which are collected at the vast network of weather-reporting stations all over the world are raised to sea level equivalents. This provides a uniform base for the determination of horizontal pressure differences. These horizontal differences are plotted on weather maps as high and low pressure areas and provide a basis for predicting wind and storm directions at the earth's surface. But the weather which occurs at a mountain station doesn't take place in a pressure system altered to sea level equivalents. Instead it takes place in an atmospheric pressure which is naturally lowered because of the elevation of the station. Weather phenomena take place in a real atmosphere not a hypothetical one, the pressure of which has been altered statistically to satisfy the need for a uniform base of computation.

There are other real mountain-world controls which make the weather elements of a region such as the San Juans "different." These include slope orientation: In a typical mountain valley the morning summer sun doesn't reach the west-facing slope until after nine in the morning, but sunset lingers over the far valley ridge until nine in the evening on the longest days. The other side of the valley is awakened by the sun at six in the morning and must endure the shadows after five in the afternoon. In mountainous regions the orientation of ridges and ridge crests to prevailing wind directions produces wet, windward slopes and dry, lee slopes, known as "rain shadows." Because air is compressible, more water vapor, condensation nuclei, and microscopic dust particles are packed into its lower layers than into the thin air which bathes the mountain tops. For this reason, at high elevations there is a slower, less efficient, transfer of energy from the sun, and a less active transfer of moisture from the vapor state to the liquid state than in the higher pressure air which

occupies the lowlands. The distance of a mountain region from the nearest source of moisture (the ocean), can have a profound effect on the precipitation regime of the range. Moisture-laden air must cross 650 miles of desert and semidesert before it reaches the San Juans. It may have been milked of some of its burden of moisture before it reaches the mountains. When air is forced to rise over the ranges, cooling it to the condensation level, it tends to lavish its remaining moisture content on the west and southwest sides of the mountains. The heaviest recorded snowfalls for the San Juans have been found in the west and southwest-facing basins above Telluride on the west side of the range. The least recorded precipitation is found at lower elevations on the east, northeast, and north sides of the range — the rain shadow side.

An old-time mountain dweller is reported to have once remarked, "If you don't like today's weather, wait 'till tomorrow; it'll change."

One of the first basic research tasks undertaken by the Bureau of Reclamation in connection with the San Juan weather modification program, begun in 1970, was an effort to reconstruct the past 100 years of weather and climate in the test area. This was done from surviving weather records, often fragmental or from stations at the edge of the mountain area or located in low elevation valleys, the recollections of old-timers, and the dendrochronological and dendroecological records left by the growth rings of trees sampled in or near the test area. In spite of this fragmental and sometimes circumstantial evidence, the record provides a recognizable trend for the past 100 years. The abstract of the "Historical Climatology" section of the project's final report states, "Temperature fluctuations during the period indicate regional cooling from the late 1860s until about 1930, when a reversal of the trend occurred. These temperature trends are the opposite of those noted for many areas in the Northern Hemisphere. Precipitation variations tend to be inversely related to temperature trends in the San Juan region." Stated in another way, the San Juans seem to have been getting gradually cooler and wetter from the 1850s to the 1930s and have been getting warmer and drier from the 1930s to the present. The San Juans seem to be unique in that the trends before and after 1930 are exactly opposite to the trends found in most other Northern Hemisphere regions.

A characteristic of the San Juan climate, which is generally applicable to most mountain and dry climate

Opposite: Reconnoitre Peak, now named Mount Ridgway, through an opening in winter storm clouds. Northwest ridge of Cirque Peak in middle distance. Blaine Basin in foreground.

Three pinnacles, the Hand, the Penguin, and the Thumb on the northwest flank of Mt. Sneffels during a winter snowstorm.

locations, is the extreme fluctuation in mean annual temperatures and mean annual precipitation from year to year. Often a year of drought will be followed by a wet year, or several years running of drought or overabundance will be followed by a single year of change. Unpredictability is the only stable characteristic of the climate.

Seasonally, the greatest mean precipitation occurs in the winter, followed usually by the summer, fall, and spring—in that order.

In the mountain West, precipitation amounts increase as elevation increases. In the San Juans the relief (difference in elevation between the lowest and highest places), amounts to about 9,000 feet—from 5,000 feet to 14,000 feet. On average, the mean annual precipitation increases just over 3 inches per 1,000 feet of elevation change. The mountains are surrounded by a lowland region of relatively low annual precipitation, in the range of 15 inches to 20 inches. The highest summits should receive by this reckoning an annual mean precipitation near 43 to 45 inches in amount. Since there are no recording stations on the summits of the highest peaks this amount is deduced by extrapolation. It is known, however, that some locations, because of special orientations or conditions, exceed these projected figures, while others fall short. For example, the Wolf Creek Pass station, at 9,425 feet, during the period 1951–1960 recorded a mean annual precipitation of 42.55 inches, clearly much

higher than a regression figure of 3.15 inches per thousand feet would have indicated.

There is usually enough snow cover in a San Juan winter to make the entire region subject to severe avalanche danger. When the hand of drought is on the land there is not enough water to satisfy the overallocated needs of downstream users on the Colorado and Rio Grande.

The narrow gauge railroads which probed their way into the high country were sometimes blocked by drifts and avalanches for whole months at a time. Highway 550, "the Million Dollar Highway," which traverses the region from north to south, is closed sometimes for several days by avalanches and dangerous conditions. One winter Red Mountain Pass got away from the road crews and had to be closed for several weeks while they dug away at thirty-foot drifts.

By the time gale-blown snow banners stream out from the high ridges and peaks, every hibernating species has long since gone to den, and the deer, elk, and mountain sheep have sought the lowland benches.

But the San Juan climate is not all storm and strife. To sit on a gentle tundra slope among a riot of columbine and paintbrush and watch fleecy cumulous clouds drift across an incredibly blue sky past high crags, or walk in the fall through a gentle aspen forest, each golden leaf dancing on the vagrant breeze, is to enjoy one of the greatest privileges God can bestow on mortal man.

On the last day of 1951 a storm lashed into the Colorado Rockies from the southwest. Three days later it had earned a dubious distinction: the "worst" storm in the history of the region. For those with long memories, elements of this same storm were to howl on across the country and out into the Atlantic, where they crippled a freighter, *The Flying Enterprise,* and helped eventually to make a hero of her skipper, Captain Kurt Carlsen.

In the Colorado Rockies, the death toll in the wake of the storm was higher than it was on the Atlantic. When the mountain country finally dug out on January 7, 1952, fatalities totaled seven: one storm-induced heart failure, one aircraft fatality, attributed to lethal flying weather, two frozen to death after abandoning their stalled automobile, and three deaths resulting from avalanches.

As the storm began to pick up intensity, the afternoon of December 31, Reynolds Bradshaw, Earl Croft, and Melvin Herron jockeyed a big tractor and semi-trailer truck eastward from Durango, in southwestern Colorado. Northeast of Pagosa Springs, at the west foot of Wolf Creek Pass, the road became icy. They put on chains. The thought of turning back from the pass never occurred to them. Storms, even on 11,000-foot mountain passes, are no deterrent to through freight, particularly perishables. The highway maintenance crews were out on the road. In another hour or so the truck would be over the summit and rolling down toward Alamosa and the evening meal.

The snow was now falling in a heavy curtain. The driver switched on the running lights and ground down into low and then into compound as the truck hit the

first real grade above the Newton Ranch. Herron climbed into the bunk at the back of the cab to get some sleep. This decision probably saved his life.

Half an hour later, as the truck labored upward through deepening drifts, a huge avalanche hurled itself across the road, sweeping the tractor and trailer into the canyon below. Somehow, Herron was thrown from his place in the bunk and clear of the cab—he doesn't to this day know how or why. Bradshaw and Croft rode the tractor into the canyon.

A week later, on January 6, the tractor was found 350 feet below the road, buried under eight feet of snow. The cab was packed solidly with rocks, tree limbs, and snow which it picked up during its plunge. Bradshaw and Croft's bodies had to be gotten out through a hole chopped in the roof. Herron, meantime, had fought his way back to the road and eventually staggered half-frozen to a highway maintenance shelter.

It is easy to say, in retrospect, "They shouldn't have tried to cross the pass in a storm." Yet how were they or the highway crews or the fourteen other people, including several children, who were trapped on the pass, to know that this storm portended any more danger from avalanches than numerous previous storms, during which the highway had been kept open and freight had gone through? It was their sad misfortune to be in the path of one of the most destructive and unpredictable of the great forces of nature.

During this same storm, a few miles to the north, the caretaker at the Highland Mary Mine, in Cunningham Gulch, near Silverton, Colorado, was killed by an avalanche.

The first three days of the storm saw all high passes in the state closed by avalanches. It was more than a week before traffic was back to wintertime normal. The road equipment had relatively little trouble handling the storm's normal accumulation of snow. What

Opposite: Small avalanche falling from cliffs on south side of Canyon Creek several miles below Camp Bird lower mill.

kept the passes closed and the maintenance crews straining their hearts out, were the hundreds of avalanches which choked the rights-of-way with marble-hard snow, boulders, trees, and debris carried down from the slopes above.

Bad as it was, why did this storm go down in the records as the worst in the history of the region? The characterization certainly did not imply that more snow fell, or more avalanches were set in motion, or the temperatures dropped to lower figures, or that wind velocities were higher than during any previous storm. The weather records show otherwise. The term "worst" pointed up a new fact: More people were on the mountain highways, where they could be stalled, maimed, or killed by nature's ruthless power. Where fifty years ago tens were venturing into or living in the high country during the winter months, today hundreds venture as skiers, motorists, truck drivers, road maintenance crews, power line crews, or live the year round at mines, logging camps, power stations, and vacation homes. The number and value of "sitting-duck" targets provided for this capricious killer, the snow avalanche, has been multiplied prodigiously by man's rising tempo of utilization in the mountain West.

The picture-postcard image of the winter time San Juans is good for the tourist trade, but no old-timer who has lived through several San Juan winters is easily taken in by the sham. It is too easy to dredge up figures, such as those for the winter of 1906, when in San Juan County alone, between January 26 and March 24, twenty-four lives were lost in thirty separate avalanche incidents. Betsy R. Armstrong, in a compilation of avalanche damage in San Juan County, entitled *Century of Struggle Against Snow: A History of Avalanche Hazard in San Juan County, Colorado,* has tabulated for the period from 1875 to 1938, ninety-eight deaths from avalanches; twenty-one persons buried, dug out alive, injured; and ninety buried, dug out alive, uninjured. This was during the period of the major mining activity in the San Juans. Mines large and small were found on most slopes and in most valleys of the northern half of the San Juans. The narrow gauge railroad entered this region from the south and penetrated up the Animas as far as Eureka and over Red Mountain Pass and down the north side as far as Ironton Park. Otto Mears' toll road threaded the upper Uncompahgre Canyon between the end of the railroad and Ouray. There were mine access routes up Cunningham Gulch, Cement Creek, Canyon Creek, Poughkeepsie Gulch, Henson Creek, the upper Lake Fork of the Gunnison, the upper San Miguel, over Lizard Head Pass, and to the high basins above Telluride. Everywhere there was a mine there was either a wagon road or at least a mule trail to get equipment

and fuel in and ore out. The commerce of the San Juans moved along these tenuous arteries, every one of which were threatened by avalanches during the winter season.

In the San Juans, what is, on more formal occasions, called an avalanche, is known as a snowslide. Outwardly, a snowslide seems to be one of the most easily understood of natural phenomena. Its only necessary elements are a steep slope covered with snow and the ever-present force of gravity.

Avalanche research has been going on for a number of years at numerous mountain centers throughout the world, including the Institute of Arctic and Alpine Research (INSTAAR), University of Colorado, in the San Juans. Although much work remains to be done, the research of all of these institutions has established a basic understanding of this natural phenomenon.

Snow lying on a slope has weight. The force of gravity which acts vertically is resolved into two components, one acting parallel to the slope, the other acting at right angles to the slope. The component of gravity which is resolved at right angles to the slope tends to hold the snow in place; the component which is resolved parallel to the slope causes the snow to slide or glide downslope.

One type of dry snow avalanche occurs when fresh snow has not yet consolidated. It lacks cohesion. In its unconsolidated state it responds uncontrolled to the force of gravity. Such avalanches are extremely unpredictable and are likely to be set in motion during a storm, just as are the more destructive slab avalanches which occur after snow has consolidated more fully.

When snow first falls in the autumn it lies on an uneven surface which is likely to supply enough friction to hold it in place, overcoming the gravity component which is trying to pull it downward parallel to the slope. The next and succeeding snowstorms fall on a slope which is already covered with snow. The strength with which the second and subsequent layers adhere to the layers which have already been deposited determines the overall internal strength of the snow cover. The total snow cover at any point in time might be compared to a deck of cards; each card in the deck represents the accumulation of an individual snowstorm, except that snowstorms do not deposit layers of uniform thickness like individual playing cards. To continue the analogy, if the individual cards in a deck are sticky (perhaps the youngsters played with them while they were eating honey) they will not slide past each other easily. If you laid such a deck on an inclined plane it would be likely to stay together as a single unit. On the other hand, if the deck was newly shuffled, freshly out of its wrapper, the individual cards would be likely to slide over each other in "slabs" (individual cards) if placed on an inclined plane. It is a lack of cohesion between individual layers which serves as the basic characteristic of the common slab avalanche.

The most destructive avalanches in the San Juan country are slab avalanches of the type just described. The most destructive of all are those in which the failure occurs between two of the lowest slabs in the pile, allowing the major part of the snow load to be projected down the slope.

Studies by INSTAAR clearly indicate that snow cover in the San Juans has, on the average, lower mechanical strength and less cohesion between layers than snow cover in many regions where avalanches have previously been studied. The center of the San Juans lies at about 37° 37′ north latitude, 750 miles further south than the Alps; they have a mean altitude of about 10,000 feet; they have a dry, continental, interior location. This combination of high average altitude, low latitude, and interior location leads to a unique solar radiation regime. The Institute's consultants have called the San Juan winter climate a *radiation snow climate*. The rapid and profound changes the snow cover undergoes after it falls creates a complex internal structure which weakens cohesion between layers. Rapid radiation creates unstable voids and depth hoar within the layers. Rapid surface melting on south-facing slopes introduces large amounts of meltwater into surface layers, which sets up stresses when refrozen, during repeated freeze-thaw cycles.

As a result of these complex and unique conditions, the San Juan is a region of impressive depths of weak, unstable, winter snow on appallingly steep slopes, on which are located—at least were located during the heyday of the mining boom—a great many works of man such as mines, mills, dwellings, and transportation routes. The whole ensemble is a catastrophe ripe for happening.

The ultimate trigger of an avalanche can be as complex and unknown as the characteristics and dimensions of separate avalanches: a falling rock, sudden freezing or thawing, a snowstorm, high wind, spring rain, an ice fall, some animal (man included), a loud noise—any or all can trigger the snow blanket into action. Many an old-timer would like to add "just plain cussedness" to the list. I have seen slides hang up and weather out several wet, sloppy storms, which should have sent them thundering down, only to see them run later on a calm, clear day, when they should have stayed put.

No one who has seen an avalanche in action, or helped recover its victims, or survived burial in one is ever complacent about it afterward. Familiarity with this powerful natural force breeds anything but

contempt. Take the case of R. F. Dunn. "Rough," as he was known with respect to the miners and management of the King Lease of the historic Camp Bird Mine, was the mine superintendent.

At 9:43 A.M., February 25, 1936, Dunn walked into the snowshed leading from the Camp Bird mill to the mine adit, bound on an underground tour of inspection. He had just left the shop, where Ralph Klinger, the blacksmith, was sharpening drill steel. Midmorning, winter peace lay over Imogene Basin. From the 11,500-foot elevation of the mine to the rim of the basin, 2,000 feet higher, a layer of fresh snow buried every rock and ridge under a 10–20-foot blanket. It had stormed spasmodically for the past forty-eight hours, and the fitful flurries were to go on for more hours. But for the time being, a pale sun struggled to pierce through to the white earth.

The flotation mill rumbled and ground away at its 100-ton quota of gold-bearing rock. The compressor popped off periodically with an echo-awakening "choof!" The jaw crusher's metallic crunching shook the mantle of white on the buildings.

Upstairs in the corrugated iron boarding house, a few hundred feet downhill from the mill and stable, the night shift slept off their labors. Downstairs, Mrs. Rose Israel, the cook, started her baking for the noon and evening meals. The dishwasher finished the last of the breakfast dishes. A mule skinner, Evan Roberts, warmed himself by the big range and exchanged pleasantries with the kitchen crew; the early morning struggle with the pack string up the three miles of snowblotted trail from the end of the road at the old mill had left him chilled to the bone.

Chapp Woods, the mill "super," was in the little pump house below the mill. Punctually, day in and day out, fair weather or foul, he went to the small house about ten o'clock to check the lubrication of the centrifugal pump and look over the edge of the big tank to note the water level.

A mile underground, the day shift drilled and blasted at the earth's vitals. The mine's whole intricate organization functioned perfectly, like the movement of a fine watch.

At 9:44 A.M., just one minute later, the finely meshed organization was shattered. Not a wheel turned. The mill and the blacksmith shop lay in desolation. The lower story of the boarding house was crushed like an eggshell. The mine adit lay under forty feet of snow, the pump house under ten.

In the interim, some disturbance (a falling rock, a temperature-induced contraction or expansion of the snow, gravity alone—man will never know) had occurred at the headwall of the basin. The blanket of snow slid downward, slowly at first and then with terrifying acceleration. What had started as a small

Left: The clock in the Camp Bird boarding house was stopped by the avalanche at 9:44 a.m., 25 February, 1936.

Wreckage of upper Camp Bird mill after avalanche of 25 February 1936. (Mel Griffiths from W. O. Winters)

Damage to the upper Camp Bird mill. (Mel Griffiths from W. O. Winters)

thing grew, through the short span of seconds, into a tons-heavy avalanche of snow, sweeping everything before it. Like the white cloud of powder snow which geysered upward from the snow-swept mountainside, it whirled away the value of $100,000 worth of physical plant, which a moment before had been earning its way. But more tragic: three lives were lost.

Mrs. Israel, the cook, heard the slide as it first gathered momentum. She rushed to the door to see it. Walt Rogers, one of the mill men, shouted, "Rose! Get back!" When she did not turn, he ran and caught her hand to pull her from the door. At that instant the snow struck the building. Mrs. Israel was torn from Rogers' grasp, carried outside, and crushed under fourteen feet of heavy snow. Walt is alive today; Mrs. Israel is not. Yet only an arm's length separated them when the avalanche struck.

Ralph Klinger, the blacksmith, died at his work. Ten hours later they dug his body from beneath the workbench in the shop. It was frozen stiff in such a grotesquely broken shape that the rescue crew had trouble lashing it to a toboggan for the trip to the lower mill.

Through twenty-eight feverish hours the rescue crew probed through the debris-littered mass of snow with long steel rods, searching for the pump house. The destruction had so altered things that even men who had worked at the mine for years could not tell where the little building should be. It was early afternoon of the next day when one of the rods finally struck the roof of the building. Swift shovels sliced through ten feet of snow. A hole was chopped in the roof.

There was air space inside! But the slight hope this discovery held forth was immediately dashed. Chapp Wood's body was found hanging head down in the water tank—drowned. The authorities concluded that the mill "super" had been struck on the head by the collapsing roof and knocked into the tank. Ironically, Chapp never had a chance to use the air space the pump house afforded.

Meanwhile, what of Dunn? He was in the snowshed when the slide struck. One moment he had been walking down the tunnellike shed which led to the mine adit; the next he was pinned under fifteen feet of snow, with an eight-by-eight timber crushing his chest. The depth of snow above him might as well have been a thousand feet, for all he could do to save himself. In his pain-dimmed mind was room for only one thought: "I'm trapped!" He could not move—not even a finger. His chest was cracking like a flimsy bird cage. He was spitting blood. He could breathe only with difficulty.

The eight-by-eight which was crushing out his life had formed a sheltering pocket above his head. There was a little air. Though his tortured lungs rebelled at the task, he gritted his teeth, gulped in air, and yelled. The feeble croak was muffled in the heavy snow blanket almost before it passed his lips. He yelled again and again, his injured chest paining fiercely with each effort.

The seconds dragged by—the minutes. His shouts grew more feeble. The darkness and cold pressed in. An hour passed—two hours. If he could have lost consciousness, the waiting for the end would have been easier. He did not shout any more.

A sound reached his ears. He tried to turn his head so he could determine its direction. It came again—a metallic hissing—a shovel slicing through granular ice. He filled his lungs and shouted, "Here! Here!" Gray light invaded the space above his head. With it came a rush of cold air. He heard voices. More of the snow was sliced away and the timber was lifted carefully from his chest.

"Rough" Dunn was lucky. Frank Reed and Slim Erickson had seen him go into the snowshed a few seconds before the havoc. They were safe themselves behind a barricade of baled hay in the stable. When the slide came to rest, they snatched up shovels and began digging for him. Three hours later, after uncovering a length of the snowshed, they stumbled onto the place where he lay. Not one of his shouts had carried beyond the muffling quiet of his crypt.

Watching an early winter, powder snow avalanche is a revelation in the laws of motion—an eddying puff of white rolls up from the top of the steep slope. For a space of perhaps three seconds one sees no further movement. Then the whole slope, from bottom to top, is alive. The snow in the valley is moving almost as soon as that at the headwall. It is as though a long white hall runner has lain on the slope, and an invisible hand has jerked it down from the bottom. It is easy to see why a man can hear an avalanche start and be overwhelmed before he can take more than a dozen steps. Calculations by experts in the Alps have placed the speed of dry snow avalanches as high as 150 to 200 miles per hour. The movement at the top of the slope seems to be transmitted downward like a sound wave, which sets the whole slope in motion. A blast of wind-driven powder shoots ahead of the moving snow on the slope, hurling itself against the opposite slope. White mushrooms of powder snow spew upward all down the mountainside. They form in a dense cloud and blossom. The white column boils against the sparkling blue sky, its top higher than the surrounding peaks. The slight breeze tugs and curls at the plume. The atmosphere shakes over a mile away, before the rumble arrives.

The concussion and noise stops as suddenly as it had started. The white cloud eddies away and settles. There is no further movement on the distant slope. The spectator could hold his breath through the whole time, so swiftly does it come and go.

50

Rescuers searching through debris in a snowstorm, Camp Bird avalanche, 25 February 1936.

Moving R. F. Dunn, the injured mine superintendent, to the lower mill for evacuation to the Ouray hospital.

Preparing bodies of Rose Israel, the cook, and Chapp Woods, the mill superintendent, for transportation to the lower mill for evacuation to Ouray.

First contingent of miners with Rose Israel's body arriving at the lower mill.

Snowslides can do damage as freakish as any done by a tornado. Several years ago a mill worker took me to the downhill side of the tramway and bin floor of the Smuggler Union stamp mill, at Pandora, near Telluride, Colorado. This same building has been used for a number of years to house the flotation mill of the Idarado Mine. All along the studding and planking of the wall were embedded innumerable pieces of glass. Pointing to the queer mosaic, he said, "The Ajax did that a few years back. It dropped off the cliff behind the mill early one morning and ran past the end of the building — didn't even touch it. But the concussion knocked out every window on the uphill side. It blew the ten-by-twelve panes of glass clean across the bin floor and into this wall. Some of the panes were driven in edgewise, stuck so tight you couldn't pull them out without breaking them off. And they were still all in one piece, not broken, just driven in edgewise."

Another miner at the Smuggler says, "See that foundation and floor there, where there's no house now? That used to be the mill 'super's' place. His wife and baby was in there when the slide run. It didn't come closer than a hundred feet from the house, but all the doors and windows was shut. When the slide went past, that house blew up, just like you'd set off a couple of boxes of powder inside it. Wasn't nothing left but the floor and the foundation. We found window frames and part of the roof clear down past the flotation mill. It bruised the missus up some, but the baby wasn't hurt none. The house just went in every direction and left them sittin' there."

That miner wasn't imagining things. It has happened more than once. A fast-moving avalanche leaves an area of low air pressure in its wake. A tightly closed building in that area, though the slide may not touch it, often explodes from the normal air pressure on the inside pushing against the greatly reduced pressure on the outside.

Following the lead of the Swiss, who were the first to experiment with artillery, the Colorado Highway Department now routinely shoots down threatening slides along Highway 550 between Ouray and Silverton, with only "partial success."

Highway 550 sees considerable traffic during the winter months since it is the sole surface link between the northern and central parts of the San Juan. The East and West Riverside slides cross the highway about five miles south of Ouray, where it threads the bottom of the narrow canyon of Red Mountain Creek. At one period in recent years, when families were living at the Idarado Mine on Red Mountain, schoolchildren were bused to and from Ouray every school day during the winter.

The local newspapers have recorded a tragic list of deaths and near-misses at the Riverside Slide since 1888. In December of 1809, Elias Fritz, a miner working at the Treasury Tunnel, was killed at the Riverside. On March 3, 1963, the Reverend Marvin Hudson and his two daughters, Amelia and Pauline, were killed by the Riverside while the Reverend Hudson was on his way to conduct church services in Silverton. On March 2, 1970, Bob Miller, a state highway employee, was killed by the Riverside Slide while clearing earlier slide debris. The latest Riverside victim was Terry Kishbaugh, another state highway employee, who was also clearing away earlier Riverside Slide debris on February 10, 1978.

The last five victims might have been saved if a 1909 proposal to build a highway tunnel or massive snowshed at the Riverside site had been carried out. The latest death has stirred up a storm of pleas and protests to the state and federal highway authorities to build such structures, but it is too early to know what will be the outcome. If one is as cynical about politicians and administrators as their track record warrants, miners, mail carriers, and schoolchildren will still have to sneak fearfully past the Riverside Slide on bad winter days into the foreseeable future.

The San Juans saw the first efforts to deal with avalanche hazard by legislative means. The *Silverton Standard* of Saturday, April 7, 1906, proposed, "to have a state law enacted by which mining counties may appoint inspectors, or a commission, clothed with the power of protecting, so far as possible, lives and property from snowslides." The *Standard* writer proposed that the "commission" be granted the power "to decide whether sites for such buildings (surface mine and mill structures) are safe or unsafe, and their licenses issued accordingly."

It should be noted that this proposal followed the particularly severe losses of life and property which occurred during the winter of 1905–1906, when twenty-four lives were lost in San Juan County alone in the short two months between late January and late March.

Unfortunately, this proposal for an "Avalanche Hazard Commission" was not acted upon at the time, when memories were fresh. As with other similar legislation, the problem sort of "went away" as mining activity declined. Only in response to recent mountain recreational development, particularly skiing, has a move been reinitiated to provide zoning protection from avalanche hazard. Colorado House Bill 1041, passed in 1974, is a start in that direction. As a further indication of concern, the U.S. Weather Service now issues avalanche warnings as a regular part of its forecasting service when conditions are severe.

Skiers, mountaineers, and travelers who have to traverse winter slide country learn to stay away from steep, open slopes, and to use ridges where possible.

The following advice was once voiced: "Stay away from any slope so steep that a cow wouldn't feel comfortable on it." Unfortunately many mountain roads traverse slopes which feel uncomfortable to even a mountain goat.

A tough breed inhabits San Juan country in the winter months. Just how tough, is revealed by Father Gibbons of the Ouray, Colorado, parish in the 1890s. He describes a friend, Billy Maher, who lived with his Italian partner in a rude cabin close to the crest, near the Virginius Mine, in Governor Basin. During a heavy winter snowstorm, Billy was horribly mangled by the explosion of several sticks of frozen dynamite while they were being thawed near the cabin stove. The Italian partner, who was not so severely injured, finally managed to summon a rescue party from the nearby Virginius Mine.

The four rescuers managed to improvise a sled and start Billy down the mountain, requesting, at the Virginius, that a relief party be sent to Porter's (three miles down the hill) to spell the original crew.

When the relief crew didn't arrive at Porter's, the original crew struggled the remaining eight miles to the Ouray hospital, no mean task considering the conditions. Father Gibbons continues the narrative:

When the evacuation crew came back the next afternoon they met one of the men from the Virginius and reproached him for not having sent the promised help, thus compelling them to carry the wounded man the whole way. "We did send four men," he said, "at dusk yesterday evening." They all instinctively turned and looked down the mountain side. There they beheld the track of an awful snowslide and knew the fate of the four miners. Looking closely they saw a hat on the snow, and following the track of the slide soon came to a hand, frozen stiff, protruding from the snow. They digged around it carefully and presently reached the head of a man. The man was standing up as straight as an arrow with his hands thrown out, as if to ward off a crushing blow, or perhaps to keep them free from that horrible snow packing which ensues, when the crunching mass closes around an object. I remember the case of a victim of a snowslide who had worked his way through the mass of snow with his fingers, and when he issued from the living tomb was fingerless, the fingers having been worn out in the effort to free himself.

Meanwhile, poor Billy Maher had died at the Ouray hospital.

CHAPTER 7

Life on an Ash Flow

In November of 1963, on the axis of the Mid-Atlantic Ridge—just off the south coast of Iceland—steam, ash, and lava began to boil up through the floor of the shallow sea. The fiery pillar of smoke and ash was visible off the Icelandic shore for the next three and one half years. During this time material from the volcanic vent built an island one square mile in extent and 560 feet above the level of the sea. The column of steam and ash rose four miles in height at the peak of the eruptions, and it rained debris over hundreds of square miles. In 1965, the government of Iceland named the new island Surtsey, for Sutur, the god of fire in Icelandic mythology.

The scientific world recognized immediately a unique opportunity. Here was an island, cut off from all other contact with the earth except through its vent beneath the sea—a new speck of land fashioned out of primordial material from the earth's mantle. When it had cooled sufficiently to provide a foothold, living organisms would begin to colonize it. When they did, they would provide the scientific world with a measure of the rates of colonization and the priorities chosen by nature for the establishment of fresh new plant and animal life. The Icelandic government, in concert with the United States, has engaged in an ongoing biological watch on Surtsey since its initial formation. They have guarded it from accidental contamination and have kept careful records of the types of plants and animals which have begun the colonization, and the order in which they have taken up residence.

* * * * *

Just north of Ouray, Colorado, on the west side of the Uncompahgre Valley, rises a great, gray, 13,000-foot peak, known as Corbett Ridge. Viewed from the other side of the valley it appears drab and undistinguished because the upper thousand feet or so of the peak consists of gray andesite flows sandwiched between two separate beds of volcanic tuff. The beds from which this upper part of the peak has been carved were deposited perhaps 30 million years ago when the great calderas of the San Juan Volcanic Field were belching out their fiery ejecta. It takes only a slight turn of the imagination to see the mountain flanks as having just cooled from a rain of pumice, ash, and steam as did the flanks of Surtsey during the past few years. Thirty million years ago, the flanks of Corbett Ridge were ready to receive new plant and animal colonists, just as Surtsey has been made ready more recently. The plant succession which finally stabilized during the past 30 million years did so on slopes which were once sterile rock fresh from the mantle which lies just beneath earth's outermost crust.

There are dangers in comparing the faunal and botanical recolonization of a volcanic island just arisen from the sea, and the recolonization of a mountain mass surrounded by dry land. However, the situations are comparable enough to serve as a colorful analogue, so long as no scientific pretensions are claimed.

The plant zones which are recognizable on Corbett Ridge today did not descend in an unbroken line from the plants which gained a tentative foothold just after the rock had cooled sufficiently to receive them. A succession of rhythmic climatic fluctuations occurred during the intervening years. Sometimes dry sectors of the cycle shaped a plant community which pushed drought-tolerant species up the mountainsides to greater and greater height. At other times, cold, wet segments of the cycle laid a frigid hand on the heights, lowering the timberline and forcing the zonation down the mountainsides to escape the rigors of the polar mountaintops. During the past two million years, the highest mountains were completely inundated in ice, and it is likely that all plant habitat was completely obliterated during these ice advances, making it necessary for a new plant succession to get under way following each ice retreat.

The plants which clothe the sides of Corbett Ridge today probably began their colonization only 12 to 15 thousand years ago at the end of Wisconsin glaciation, which is a far cry from 26 to 28 million years and brings the comparison to Surtsey somewhat closer to reality.

The east slope of Corbett Ridge has been deeply scoured by Corbett Creek. Erosional debris from the upper half of the slope has been funneled by a series of tributaries down to the center line, where the creek plunges over a waterfall into a narrow canyon which furrows the lower half of the slope. The upper tributaries are working in the gray volcanic rock, reaching their filamentlike runnels up to the very skyline ridge. The narrow canyon, below, into which all water on this side of the mountain collects, has cleaved its way through the layered red sedimentary beds which rise gently along the main valley side, lapping up onto the core of the range.

The zonal arrangement of the dominant species on the slope serves as a guide to the seasonal and altitudinal changes in vegetation. Like the tiers of a layer cake, the successive life zones are spread across the slopes stacked one above the other. Altitude above sea level is the dominant control. This factor controls the length of the growing season: the number of days of frost, the intensity of incoming solar energy during the warm season, the soil temperature, and the other amenities to which each plant species has become habituated during the millennia.

At the foot of the slope on the benches to either side of the valley bottom, piñon-juniper woodland dominates. Below, along the river itself, ranks of huge cottonwood trees crowd the stream banks.

The piñon-juniper woodland is characterized by occasional patches of cactus, rabbit brush, and sagebrush. Although trees are the dominant vegetation here, this is at the very upper limit of what botanists call the Upper Sonoran life zone. The elevation is just below 8,000 feet above sea level. Above the Upper Sonoran life zone lies the Transition Zone, which is dominated by ponderosa pine. This great western yellow pine is much sought for rustic furniture lumber. Mixed with the ponderosa are great hillsides of scrub oak. Occasionally a grove of aspen joins the festivities. The upper limit of this Transition Zone is reached at about 8,500 feet. Above this zone is the Canadian Zone, dominated by Douglas fir and pine, which reaches from about 10,000 to 10,500 feet. In well-watered locations, aspen shoulders aside the fir, spruce, and pine. Above the Canadian Zone the Hudsonian Zone extends to timberline, which in the San Juans is between 11,500 feet and occasionally as high as 12,000 feet. This zone is dominated by Engelmann spruce and alpine fir. Above the timberline a complex association of sedges, herbs, and grasses reaches to the very tops of snow-covered heights. This is the arctic-alpine zone — arctic if latitude is the chief determinant, alpine if height above sea level is the desideratum.

One can experience this succession of life zones in either of two ways — by staying at the same latitude and climbing the sides of a mountain such as Corbett Ridge, or remaining at approximately the same altitude and traveling northward in latitude. Either route will lead the explorer through the succession of life zones we have just described. The trade-off is roughly 250 miles of latitude for 1,000 feet of altitude. Timberline, which is a significant natural boundary in the plant kingdom, lies at about 14,000 feet above sea level on the great volcanoes on the central plateau of Mexico, 11,750 feet in the San Juans of southwestern Colorado, and 2,500 feet on the slopes of Mt. McKinley in Alaska.

The dominant tree types for each of the life zones are not exclusive. Other varieties are often present: blue spruce, box elder, birch, willow, limber pine, lodgepole pine, plus a host of smaller plants and shrubs.

More intriguing than the catalogue of species, their elevation ranges, or the sort of guide which would permit the uninitiated to recognize the separate species, is the overall ensemble which changes hourly with the shifting sun angles or the slow transformations wrought under the alchemy of the growing season.

The shades of green reflected from the growing things on the slope change perceptibly from early morning flat light to the back light of afternoon. The colors of the rock formations on the slopes are mixed with the colors of the individual trees and plants like the patches on a whirling color wheel. Trees on the brilliant red sandstone slopes do not appear to be precisely the same shade as the same species on the gray volcanic slopes above. Conifers hold steadfast at their posts throughout the seasons like faithful sentinels, as unmoved by summer's rain as by winter's snow; not so their changeable neighbors, the aspens, oak, and cottonwoods.

In their season two distinctive colors are overpowering to the casual observer; the background color seems only to enhance them. One is the pistachio hue of tender new aspen leaflets just as soon as they have burst their buds. After they are unfurled on the slope, the color rapidly intensifies, starting in the groves at the foot of the mountain and passing up the flanks like a wave, each day advancing higher. Ahead of the wave stand gray-green trunks still bare of leaves; behind, the darker mature leaves dilute the exuberant yellow-green of this initial spring dress. It is as though nature were heralding the wave of the future as it soars higher and higher toward the vaulting sky.

The other color which shoulders aside all trifling from the background is the bright-burning flame of those same aspen leaves when fall frost touches the slopes. Then the first turncoats appear near the top of the mountain just below timberline where aspens have sought out sheltered coves. At first only a few errant individuals signal the coming season, but the change gathers strength as the chill winds of autumn flow down from the heights. Usually the warm color is so overpowering that it can hold back for a while the gray advance of inevitable winter. As the color consolidates further down the mountainsides, the yellow is sometimes punctuated by a single tree whose leaves are a deep rusty red — a freak of local soil nutrients or individual plant chemistry.

Sometimes sooner, sometimes later, the seasonal urgings which are bringing about the aspen change spread out to the oak brush and mountain mahogany. Here, splashes of red, brown and rich, residual olive-green give the valley walls the subdued pattern and hues of a rich Persian rug.

Finally, the cottonwoods in the valley bottoms are touched and their golden files trace the watercourses which provide their needed moisture.

The spectator at this coming and going of the seasons watches the tide of change rise from the bottom to top of a mountainside in the late spring, sees it rest on tundra slopes during the all-too-brief summer, and then sees it recede again in the fall like the tide coming into and going out of a narrow embayment. The whole scene is impossible to embrace at a single glance; the memory of it must be reconstructed of bits and pieces borne up and down by the tide of the seasons.

The flotsam and jetsam which marks the passing year can include such minutia as five elk grazing across a steep slope above timberline; wisps of cloud on a wet fall evening growing and dissolving momentarily along the same steep slope; the waterfall at the center of the slope frozen into a fifty-foot icicle; brilliant spokes of sunlight bursting through a late-day cloud rack beyond the ridge, directing the spotlight of a solitary shaft on the rain-glistened crown of an up-valley summit; dead-of-winter snow banners whipped across knife-blade ridges, shaping shadowed cornices; a brittle, white snow-weighted slope etched against a winter's deep blue morning sky; the warm fingers of alpenglow reaching around the edges of the mountain from the already extinguished sun, sunk beyond Utah.

CHAPTER 8

Wildlife

San Juan country is environment for a rich assemblage of continental, North American, medium and high altitude native fauna: terrestrial mammals, birds, insects, reptiles, fish, and amphibians. The constraints of altitude, in the absence of large latitudinal extent, just as in the plant world, tend to distribute fauna groups into habitat zones, one above the other.

The arctic-alpine zone, above timberline, hosts a fauna as unique to it as that found on the piñon-juniper tablelands surrounding the mountain core, and the forested hill lands between.

When the Utes controlled the San Juan, the only large herbivore customarily hunted outside their homeland was the bison. Hunts for these large mammals, so necessary to the Ute way of life, were usually successful by going no farther than South Park or the San Luis Valley on the eastern edge of the southern San Juan Mountains, although for raiding purposes the Utes often sallied forth onto the high plains, east of the mountain zone.

During the last million years, four Pleistocene ice advances drove fauna out of the high country, but the interstadial periods of deglaciation always were accompanied by a recolonization of the highlands. In consequence, although there was vertical, temporary, displacement of species, the effects were slight in horizontal extent; today, the native wildlife of the San Juan highlands is almost identical to that at the same altitude in other parts of the Rocky Mountains and Sierra Nevada, and in the arctic zone, at lower elevations, in Alaska and Labrador.

When the environment permitted, the earliest white settlers tried to extinguish homesickness by introduc-

Opposite: Buck pronghorn antelope. (Colorado Division of Wildlife)

ing flora and fauna with which they were familiar back home. Sometimes these transplanted species offered better sport or were an adjunct to the hunter's larder. Under such sponsorship, the Chinese ring-necked pheasant and the chucker partridge were introduced to the San Juan valleys and mesas in the 1930s. At an earlier period German brown trout and rainbow trout were planted to supplement the native cutthroat. The Division of Wildlife of the Colorado State Department of Natural Resources, is now introducing some exotic, warm-water fish in the numerous hydroelectric and irrigation reservoirs of the Western Slope.

The Utes hunted pronghorn antelope on the sage plains at the southwest flank of the San Juan Mountains a hundred years ago. But soon after the white settlement, the antelope disappeared. Today, antelope are being transplanted from the state's eastern high plains, to their former San Juan habitat.

Other introduced or reintroduced species in the San Juans include the Rocky Mountain goat, the river otter, and the fox squirrel.

During the mining boom many a prospector kept his larder filled with trout, deer, elk, mountain sheep, and bear. In more recent times, the judicious management of the region's wild herds by the Division of Wildlife brings hundreds of out-of-state hunters and fishermen to the high streams, reservoirs, lakes, and timbered slopes during open seasons, much to the delight of local merchants and chambers of commerce.

In March of 1940, *The Western Sportsman*, a short-lived local magazine, reported: "By actual count, the Colorado State Game and Fish Commission fed 8,100 head of deer in the Gunnison-Sapinero area during the winter. With an estimated 10 percent missed in the count, the total number of deer winter fed in this area was in the neighborhood of 9,000 with 2,000 head of elk also on the relief rolls." The *Sportsman's* article goes on to describe a method of branding some deer at each feeding ground with sheep branding paint to prevent their being counted twice if they changed feeding ground when the counting was going on. To brand the animals, a rubber ball-tipped arrow was dipped in paint and shot from a bow.

The feeding of deer and elk was started during the 1930s when several consecutive harsh winters caused both deer and elk losses, as well as widespread damage to ranchers' haystacks. A Game Damage Law has been on the Colorado statute books since that time, but feeding was stopped sometime in the 1940s. It is now felt by Division of Wildlife scientists that winter feeding does more harm than good. It is almost impossible to compound a satisfactory feed for deer; they are browsers who prefer twigs and bark to grass or alfalfa. Elk do well on second or third cutting alfalfa. Crowding large numbers of deer on feeding grounds spreads diseases, including parasites and infections common to sheep and other domestic livestock. Since deer don't do well on artificial feed, the losses of animals on feed are almost as high as if the animals were not fed. Feeding deer tends to lower their resistance to cold and inclement weather, circumventing nature's culling process. It is now felt that natural selection and allowing the law of survival of the fittest to operate is the best policy. Today there is little or no feeding, except in the most dire circumstances, although the Division of Wildlife pays ranchers from the Game Damage Fund when justified.

• • • •

One who has spent most of a lifetime outdoors in the San Juan is bound to have had contact with wildlife on numerous occasions and under many circumstances. Many years ago when plodding up the Columbine Pass Trail from the head of Needle Creek in the southern Needle Mountains, I made the acquaintance of three bachelor elk. The trail climbs in long switchbacks in heavy timber up a steep hillside. When standing and looking out from the downhill side of the trail it was impossible to see more than a few feet because of spruce branches. When about halfway up a long switchback I sat down on the uphill bank of the trail for a breather. With my head lowered I could then see downslope along the ground beneath the canopy of spruce branches.

Not more than thirty feet below the trail stood three young bull elk with their racks and heads turned sideways, close to the ground, so they could look up the slope under the trees. They had obviously been watching my lower legs and feet walking up the trail, thinking all the while that if they remained motionless I would go away without discovering them.

When I sat down, they were caught flat footed. As soon as I saw them, I tried to remain motionless. But the stillness and lack of motion began to make them nervous. Nervousness grew into apprehension, and

after about a minute they could no longer endure the suspense. As though at a prearranged signal, they exploded like Fourth of July fireworks, rattling their horns and hooves in three directions.

• • • •

Years ago mountain sheep used to come down to the narrow-gauge railroad station at Ouray, when snow was deep in the high country, for handouts of baled hay. Four winters ago, a small band of mountain sheep — ewes, lambs, and several rams — as though certifying what had been commonplace in decades past, spent a few weeks on the benches north of Ouray, before local dogs drove them to higher ground.

My own conviction that the bighorn sheep is one of nature's hardiest animals, came from an almost daily observation, in the early 1930s, of a small group of seven ewes and five yearling lambs which wintered on the 13,000-foot shoulder of Cirque Peak, in the Sneffels Range. After the first heavy snowfall in November, the snowfields surrounding the ridge were too deep and soft for escape. The crest of the ridge was swept free of snow by high winds. The brown, frozen grass had to be pawed up, or an occasional blade found in the lee of a random boulder. That they survived seemed a miracle. Similar episodes are undoubtedly responsible for the occasional bighorn skull and horns found on isolated ridges in the high country.

• • • •

Year round residents of Ouray have running battles with deer and elk who make nocturnal raids on town gardens when flower blossoms are tenderest and strawberries are set on the vines.

Tarry with me for a summer afternoon in a high basin above timberline. On the tundra slope below us, a random scattering of earth mounds, beside or below well-anchored boulders, show the presence of some burrowing animal. If we wait quietly, a fat gray-brown marmot will eventually scramble up to blink at the sun or spread out lazily on a nearby rock to soak in some of the warmth. If the day is gray and he isn't disturbed he will graze busily, adding to the layers of fat which he needs to sustain him through a long winter hibernation. If he is alarmed he will send out a sharp whistle to warn others, a shrill call something like the blast made by an exuberant boy by putting his fingers to his mouth and expelling air through a gap in his teeth.

Occasionally we can hear a higher-pitched, piping-like whistle from the jumbled piles of talus higher on the slope. Closer examination discloses mounds of cut plant stems and leaves piled between the rocks where they can receive a maximum of sunlight, like a rancher's mown hay raked into windrows to cure. This is exactly what the mounds are. Our patience and quiet will soon be rewarded by a darting bundle of fur flash-

Left: Sponge rubber ball on tip of arrow being dipped in yellow paint to mark deer to prevent double counting at feeding grounds.

Archer taking aim with sponge rubber ball tipped arrow for marking deer at feeding ground.

Deer at feeding trough on slope of Soap Creek near Sapinero, Colorado, near Gunnison.

Bull and cow elk. (Colorado Division of Wildlife)

Mountain sheep. (Colorado Division of Wildlife)

ing into our line of vision. He carries a leafed plant stem in his mouth to add to the haystack. This is a pika. He is sometimes called a cony by locals, at other times a "rock rabbit." He is indeed a member of the rabbit family, about the size of a guinea pig. His gray fur blends perfectly into the background of elephant-gray talus. Although his body has the compact shape of a cottontail, his ears are tiny and rounded, his face looks forth alertly through two small black eyes, and he seems to have no tail at all. He darts from point to point among the rocks with incredible swiftness.

When the hay, which he gathers during the short summer growing season, has cured sufficiently to forestall any chance of its spoiling, it is carried underground in the galleries inside the talus pile as winter food supply.

Unlike the marmot, the pika does not hibernate during the long cruel winter. His cache of cured hay serves as his winter larder until the snow melts the following summer. One never hears the descriptive phrase, "As snug as a pika in a rock pile," but it might be apt. The deep blanket of winter snow cuts out wind and some cold. The summer-long industry in the above-timber-line meadows has provided an ample store of food.

Two predators are a constant threat to pika colonies. One strikes from the air — a bird of prey such as an eagle, hawk, or falcon — the other invades the very corridors and passageways of the warren — the weasel.

Once high in Yankee Boy Basin I watched a weasel in golden summer coat thread his way into and out of openings on the surface of a gentle talus slope. He would slither into an opening like a snake and pop to the surface again a dozen feet away. Although I had heard the shrill, piping whistle of pikas before the

weasel put in his appearance, the cries suddenly stopped on the instant my eye caught the first flash of his lanky undulating figure. Although I didn't see blood on his face, nor did I see him drag a pika from a passageway, I could only imagine what clashes, alarms, and evasions were racketing through the dark corridors deep in the stone pile.

• • • •

As a boy of sixteen, on a midsummer dusk, I watched, with mounting apprehension, a full grown cougar follow me at fifty yard's distance down the rutted wagon road between the Silver Jack Mine and the Jackson ranger station, on the east fork of the Cimarron River. Each time I stopped for a hasty look over my shoulder, the cat sat down with his thick, furry tail curled around his forefeet and watched me curiously. I fancied his eyes glowing in the dusk, and an overactive imagination could almost anticipate the spring which would launch his raking claws onto my fleeing back.

Each time I nervously resumed my retreat, the mountain lion arose from his haunches and padded along behind me at the same pace. I now became certain that I was being stalked and was about to become cougar supper.

About a quarter mile from the ranger station, the road goes around the end of a promontory which juts out into the valley. Looking back as I started out to the point, I saw the lion leap gracefully from the road onto the cutbank above and disappear into the spruces. In my mind's eye, I could see the animal trotting across the narrow base of the promontory to ambush me at the other end of the detour. In a panic, I broke and ran the last quarter mile to the ranger station.

Yellow-bellied marmot. (National Park Service)

Satellite image of San Juan country. This composite picture was made from a NASA orbiting satellite about 500 miles above the earth. Reflected light from the near infra red portion of the spectrum formed the image. Green vegetation, such as forest, is rendered a brilliant red in this color print.

The La Sal Mountains on the Colorado-Utah border (above).

The Silver Basin rock stream—"its picture has been reproduced in more geology and geomorphology textbooks than almost any other mass-wasting feature in the world" (left).

Looking west from Mt. Sneffels (opposite, above).

West end of Grenadier Range from Molas Lake (opposite, below).

Looking south from Mt. Sneffels (centerfold).

Air view looking north along the east side of the San Luis Valley (above).

A field of Columbine and Scarlet Paintbrush in lower Yankee Boy Basin (left).

Columbines near timberline on west slope of Potosi Peak (opposite, above).

Fairy Slipper (opposite, below left).

Columbine blossoms in Silver Basin, west of Ouray (opposite, below right).

Oak brush and lichen on Dallas Creek, near Ridgway.

Lake Lenore near Ouray.

Mountain lion. (Colorado Division of Wildlife)

Black bear. (Colorado Division of Wildlife)

I didn't see the cat again.

In sober reflection, I realize that the animal was satisfying its curiosity rather than stalking me, but at the time a surge of adrenaline convinced me otherwise.

Even today, I watch a farm cat stalk mice with a trace of apprehension, and I find it difficult at the zoo to look one of the big cats in the eye with complete equanimity. Blake's evocative lines have a special meaning for me:

> Tiger! Tiger! burning bright
> In the forests of the night,
> What immortal hand or eye
> Could frame they fearful symmetry?
>
> . . .
>
> Did He who made the lamb make thee?

. . . . .

Last summer, my wife and I, while walking to a nearby neighbor's home, watched a full-grown black bear leisurely sampling the chokecherries and rose hips in our backyard grove, not more than seventy-five feet away. This is within a mile of Ouray and a shorter distance from several dozen neighbors. This was no half-tame, national park, garbage-dump bear. All the while we watched, he, or she, showed no evidence of being aware of our presence — a result of the bear's preoccupation with berrying rather than a tribute to our stalking ability.

Several years ago a bow hunter in the southern San Juan managed to kill a grizzly bear. At first his tale

Opposite: Coyote. (Colorado Division of Wildlife)

was not believed, but it was authenticated later by game biologists from the State Department of Wildlife, after examining the animal. It had been thought that the last grizzly in Colorado had been killed in the early 1900s. The grizzly is far ranging, and this isolated animal could have drifted into the San Juan from as far away as Canada or Mexico, places where grizzlies are still found in some numbers.

. . . . .

Each year as fall and winter advance, a family of coyotes circles the hillside above our cabin, every few days, stopping occasionally in the wee small hours of the morning to serenade us. When I was a boy my father ran sheep in the San Juans. One of my old and good friends is a sheep rancher, and I know how he and his stock-raising friends regard coyotes. Nevertheless, I can't help but feel a touch of admiration and appreciation for the wily quartet which has escaped traps and poison so far and is able to share a few notes of wild song with us.

. . . . .

The August 24, 1978, issue of the *Ouray County Plaindealer* contains the following item:

James Dustin Johnson of Salem, Oregon, comes to the Ouray area every year, to mine up at Poughkeepsie Gulch. He contacted *The Plaindealer* last week with information that has plainly disturbed him, and will probably be disturbing information to area residents who care about the local wildlife. Johnson said he sighted 150 marmots at the mine area in 1976, only 40 to 50 in 1977, and only saw one this year. Last year, Johnson said he saw dozens of people in jeeps going up with their guns and shooting the marmots, then just letting them lie without disposing of the corpses.

PART II
THE HUMAN INTERFACE

CHAPTER 9

Native Americans

Sometime between 50,000 and 25,000 years ago the first New World humans began a migration which was eventually to spread them into every nook and cranny of both North and South America. The initial immigrants ventured across the narrow ribbon of water which separates Asia from Alaska at the Bering Strait. Because of climatic change, vast quantities of water from the world ocean lay on land, stored in the great continental ice sheets. Sea level stood several hundred feet lower than now. The Bering Strait must have looked like an estuary from which the ocean had drained. The first Americans could pick their way, dry shod, between the tidal pools.

By the time of the last interstadial (interval between ice advances), paleolithic man in Eurasia, having several times followed retreating continental ice northward and moved southward again as it advanced, had eventually pushed into the grasslands of northeastern Asia, poised for continent-hopping. Except for the highest mountaintops, neither northeast Asia nor Alaska was heavily glaciated during the final ice advance. The receding waters from the Bering Strait must have opened an inviting avenue to these ice age hunters. The woolly mammoth, the wild ox, buffalo, camel, and other species were crossing the strait in both directions by this time, providing an invitation for paleolithic man to do the same in search of his primary food source.

Once across the strait it was an easy matter for the pioneers to move slowly southward. Ice-free avenues were open between the ranges of the Rocky Mountain system. Likewise, as the Wisconsin mid-continent ice sheet retreated, great open prairies opened up to the east of the Rockies.

Opposite: Old Eskimo woman cutting dwarf willows for firewood at a Chandler Lake camp, Brooks Range, northern Alaska. The ooloo (woman's knife) can be used as readily for cutting firewood as for skinning a walrus or seal.

By perhaps 20,000 to 15,000 years ago the ancestors of North America's Indian population had overrun the habitable parts of the continent, had crossed the Isthmus of Panama, and were actively colonizing South America.

The mesas and flanks of the San Juans had, by this time, become an ideal habitat for the animals which served as primitive man's most important source of food. The great sheets of volcanic ejecta had by then been carved into rugged mountain forms by water and glaciers during the last 2 million years. As the glaciers retreated, grass, forest, tundra, and eventually the whole complex zonation of natural vegetation returned to the mesa tops and mountainsides.

We have no direct evidence for the earliest humans in the San Juan region. We must make inferences from evidence found at other places around the San Juans, such locations as the Murray Spring Site in the San Pedro Valley, near Tucson, Arizona; the Danger Cave Site, near Wendover, Utah, west of the Great Salt Lake; the Lindenmeier Site, near Fort Collins, Colorado; the Folsom Site in northeastern New Mexico; the Sandia Site, near Albuquerque, New Mexico; the Clovis Site in eastern New Mexico; the Sulphur Springs and Naco-Lahner sites in southeastern Arizona. These sites provide evidence that the early humans there were living in close proximity with or actually preying upon the large mammals such as mammoth, extinct bison, the giant ground sloth, and extinct camel. The anthropologist designates these people, *Paleo Indians.* They have also been called the "Great Hunters"—with good reason. It takes an act of will and faith, to envision skin-clad shaggy men attacking and killing a mammoth with stone-tipped spears. Yet such must have been their hunting prowess.

About 6000 B.C. conditions began to change slowly in the Southwest. The climate gradually became warmer and drier. The vast herds of herbivores began to drift eastward out of the expanding deserts of the South-

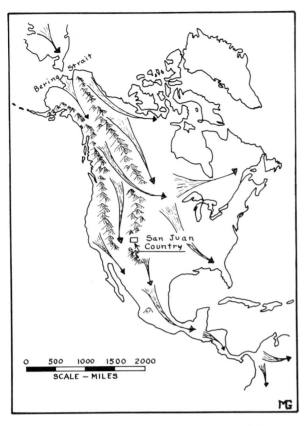

THE PEOPLING OF NORTH AMERICA

intergroup trade routes which had linked New World man since the crossing at the Bering Strait. At first the new agriculture made little headway against the hunting and gathering tradition of the Desert Archaic people, but it was eventually to change them into a sedentary agricultural society, which has survived to the present. By 1000 B.C. beans and squash were added to the diet.

About 300 B.C. the Desert Culture began a subtle change. The manufacture and use of pottery first comes onto the scene. This was followed, about 300 years later, by the erection of simple pit houses which were clustered in tiny communal villages on the mesa tops. Shortly after one A.D. the bow and arrow were introduced, followed by the mano and metate (mortar and pestle stones for grinding seeds and corn), and a variety of implements made of shell, bone, and stone. This inheritor of the Desert Archaic culture was centered in the low country south of the Mogollon Rim in central Arizona and was known as the *Mogollon* tradition.

By about 1100 A.D. it had been absorbed and taken over by a new tradition, the *Anasazi*, which reached the peak of its development in the Four Corners region, embracing the adjacent quarters of Colorado, Utah, Arizona, and New Mexico — principally the San Juan River Basin which drains the south and southwest side of the San Juan Mountains.

The Anasazi flowering took over a thousand years to reach fruition in the great communal apartment complexes in the cliff caves at Mesa Verde, the great surface pueblos near Aztec and at Chaco Canyon, the dwellings at Betatakin and Kiet Siel on the Tsegi. Its rise overlapped with the decline of the Mogollon tradition, further to the south.

The Anasazi tradition was extinguished with bewildering rapidity; almost overnight the great communal pueblos became silent cities. A change of climatic regime, not conquering enemies, caused the extinction. The great silent cities of the Anasazi are monument's to man's propensity to exceed the carrying capacity of his environment. When the deserts and steppes of the Southwest were first settled by the Anasazi, the streams and timber were adequate for the expanding population. Eventually, after many centuries, the balance between population and environment reached a point of equilibrium, at about the time the great apartment complexes reached their maximum size. By that time, from the vast settlement of Pueblo Bonito in Chaco Canyon, it was necessary to travel as far as sixty miles to bring back timber for roof beams. This was an energy consuming trip for a people who did not yet have draft animals — the horse was introduced by the Spanish about 1500 A.D. Water had always been marginal, but adequate. As watershed was denuded the water table began to drop. A diminishing stream

west into the great plains and the piedmont at the east edge of the Rockies. Following their food supply, the hunting culture continued its tradition under a new label: *Clovis* and *Folsom*. The projectile points which they fashioned from flint, obsidian, and quartzite changed in shape and size, although they continued a hunting and gathering tradition.

As the big game hunters withdrew from the Southwest to the plains, a new culture took their place from the desert basins, the California desert rim, and the mountains and basins of northern Mexico. These people, in an old stage of cultural development although on the eve of the transition from hunting and gathering to the beginnings of sedentary, primitive plant husbandry, are known as the *Desert Archaic* or *Desert Culture*. They occupied all the habitable parts of the "Greater Southwest" — a term applied loosely to the southwestern quarter of the United States. The San Juan occupies the northeastern part of this realm. Their tenure extended from about 6000 B.C. to about the time of Christ.

This Desert Culture became the foundation upon which modern Indian populations were eventually built. About 8000–2500 B.C., maize (Indian corn) was carried north out of its cradle in Mexico along the

Eskimo women and children at Chandler Lake, northern Alaska. The dome-shaped tent on the left, stretched over a framework of willows, is modeled after the Mongolian yurt whose users, like the Eskimo's, are descended from a common ancestor.

flow is at the surface for all to see; a dropping water table is not so evident, although those who had to use wells must have been aware of it. A declining ground water supply is not as easy to replenish as a surface supply. The great drought of 1276–1299, which marked the abandonment of the Mesa Verde and Tsegi Canyon areas, strained the carrying capacity of the environment beyond its limits.

The Anasazi were not fools. They apparently abandoned their overpopulated, unsupportable settlements in a relatively few years. In the parlance of the gambler: "They cut their losses, cashed in their chips, and got out of the game."

They divided into smaller social units which placed less strain on the environment. Gradually they transplanted themselves further south to the Hopi villages on First, Second, and Third Mesas, in Arizona, and the pueblos of the middle Rio Grande Valley.

Today the Anasazi way of life, much as it was once lived at Cliff Palace or Pueblo Bonito, can be found at Zuni, Walpi, Oraibi, Cochiti, Santo Domingo, or San Ildefonso.

. . . . .

Two Indian groups came to the San Juans after the

Anasazi had abandoned their apartment complexes on the western flanks of the mountains. These were the Navajo and the Utes.

The Navajo are an Athabascan people who did not cross the Bering Strait until about 3,000 years ago. This may have been as much as 20,000 years after the arrival of the "Great Hunters." The Athabascans are a subfamily of the major group which linguists call the *Nadene*, which include the *Tlingit, Eyak,* and *Haida.* Some of them were fishermen on the Pacific Northwest coasts, others were hunters and gatherers who diffused through the forests and river valleys of Alaska and Canada, eventually working their way southward along the eastern foothills of the Rockies as far as northern Mexico.

These southward-moving Athabascans had reached southeastern Colorado by about 1500 A.D. From there they dispersed into western Kansas, the panhandle of Oklahoma, central west Texas, southwestern Texas, and northern New Mexico. One group, the Navajo, moved farther west into the upper drainage of the San Juan River.

The Anasazi, the former occupants of this region, had an ill-fitted culture to cope with declining water levels. Their successors, the Navajo, had only recently

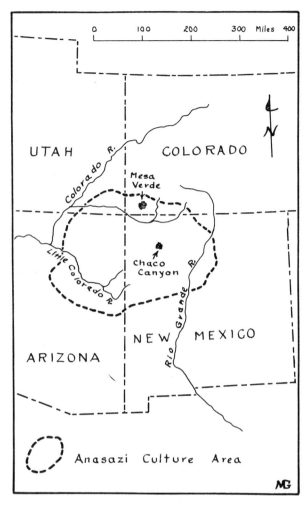

ANASAZI CULTURE AREA. (Redrawn from H. M. Wormington, Ancient Man in North America, *Denver Museum of Natural History, 1957.)*

when the whites first arrived. Their realm extended from the driest desert fringes, in the south and west, to the high mountain slopes above timberline. The Utes were reluctant to relinquish the mountain fastnesses and fertile valleys which had nourished them since time out of mind; the whites looked upon this same realm as an inexhaustible storehouse of mineral wealth and agricultural land. Furthermore, the whites looked upon it as their birthright by virtue of "manifest destiny."

From the first there were incidents — some became full-blown hostilities such as the Meeker Massacre and the Thornburg ambush — others were little more than skirmishes — most stemmed from the Indian's steadfast refusal to accept without question the white man's way of life. The two cultures never came fully to understand each other.

The Utes, along with the Arapahoes and Cheyennes, are among the oldest Indian inhabitants of Colorado. The Arapahoes and Cheyennes, buffalo-hunting plains Indians, kept east of the Front Range for the most part. The Utes roamed the Western Slope, the mountain valleys, and the four large intermountain parks — North, Middle, South, and the San Luis Valley. About the time the first whites appeared in the territory the Utes had begun to make buffalo-hunting forays onto the high plains to the east of the mountains. Occasionally, young Utes took part in raiding war parties against their plains enemies.

The Utes were a Shoshonean-speaking tribe, kin to the Piute, Shoshoni, and certain California tribes. Their origins were to the northwest of their ultimate tribal lands on the Western Slope. The Utes have been described by Rockwell as "short, hardy, and muscular with a tendency toward portliness around middle age. They were so dark skinned that the other tribes referred to them as the "black Indians."

The tribe consisted of a loose confederation of seven bands. Three of these bands composed the Southern Utes, who were located in extreme southwestern Colorado. There they served as a frontier buffer between the remainder of the Ute bands and the Navajo and Apache tribes to the south. The Utes were deadly enemies with the Navajos. With the Jicarilla Apaches, the Utes were on better terms, sometimes marrying their women. The three Southern Ute bands were the Weeminuche, the Mouache, and the Capote. In the center of the state on the west, northwest, north, and northeast of the San Juans was the Tabeguache band. This band was also called the Uncompahgre band. It was the largest single band of the Utes. The Northern Utes, which were confined to northwestern Colorado and adjacent parts of Utah, consisted of the Grand River, Yampa, and Uintah bands. The seven bands, in toto, probably never exceeded 10,000 members. The Tabeguache band, at its largest, probably numbered 3,000.

come from northern climes and still retained a resilient hunting and gathering economy, unfettered by large, fixed dwelling places. The theft of sheep and horses from the Spanish soon widened their horizons; they were then on their way to economic success.

From about 1500 A.D. to the present time the Navajo have followed their pastoral life among the silent cities of the Anasazi. Anasazi is a Navajo word, given by them to the ancient people whose abandoned dwellings they found when they first entered the Four Corners country. In a vague sort of way it meant, "the Ancient Enemies." The Navajos have long feared "Chindees," the ghosts of the ancient ones.

The Navajos have prevailed in a land which their forerunners abandoned. They have even increased their population during their relatively short tenure in the desert and mesa realm.

The Utes controlled the heart of San Juan country

Cliff Palace, one of the largest Anasazi ruins in Mesa Verde National Park, southwestern Colorado.

Right: Alonzo Hartman. (Sidney Jocknick, Early Days on the Western Slope of Colorado, 1870–1883.*)*

Below: FORT MASSACHUSETTS. (U.S. Pacific Railroad Exploration and Surveys, 38th and 39th Parallels [Gunnison Report]. J. M. Stanley from a sketch by R. H. Kern.)

The Utes were horse Indians. They lived in skin tepees, used the bow and arrow, and took up the gun as soon as it was introduced to their culture. They were much feared by most of their Indian neighbors, although their record with the whites was a relatively peaceful one.

Between 1630 and 1640 the Utes came in contact with the Spanish in the upper Rio Grande Valley. The Utes traded meat and hides for agricultural produce. The trade item which the Utes most coveted from the Spaniard was the horse. The price in meat and hides was invariably too high. But the Utes quickly found that they could trade their young children for horses. In return the Spaniards trained these Ute children as cattle and sheep herders. Later the Utes discovered that they could do better by stealing horses than they could by trading their children for them. The Utes never became pastoralists, as did the Navajo. When they stole sheep or cattle from the Spanish they usually shot the animals for immediate consumption rather than keep them as breeding stock to build up a supply of beef or mutton.

Brushes between Utes and other Indian tribes or between Utes and whites were usually hit and run raids or the taking of targets of opportunity.

Old Bill Williams, who accompanied Doc Kern back up the Rio Grande to retrieve some of Kern's maps, notes, and other possessions, after Frémont's ignominious retreat during the 1848 expedition, was killed by Utes. Isolated miners and ranchers were occasionally attacked by young war parties headed on forays against other tribes.

The confrontation which brought on the Meeker Massacre and the Thornburg ambush, in 1879, grew out of attempts to turn the Utes by threats, bribes, and coercion from their hunting-gathering life-style to that of sedentary agriculturalists and pastoralists. Nathan Meeker, the agent at the White River Agency, spitefully plowed up the Indians' horse pasture, where they had been accustomed to conduct race meets. This only fired them to more determined opposition to the agent's attempts to convert them to the plow. For this violation of Ute customs Meeker died of gunshot wounds, and a stake driven through his head.

Alonzo Hartman, in charge of the Tabeguache Agency beef herd, which in the 1870s was run from a camp near present day Gunnison, has told how reluctant the Utes were to take up any of the white man's ways; they had no desire to become farmers or cattle raisers. By treaty, the Tabeguache band was to be supplied, at the Los Pinos Agency, 100 beef animals per month, on the hoof, along with other rations of flour, potatoes, beans, rice, sugar, and coffee. The Utes came in full force to the agency on ration day, as many as 2,000 men, women, and children. After the staple rations had been distributed by the tribal elders, and the

woman had packed the horses with their family share, the beef cattle which had been bunched in a corral, were "booed" out of the gate. At this point the braves who had shed their blankets and were armed to the teeth, raced after the fleeing cattle, shooting them on the run for all the world like plains Indians on a buffalo "run." Occasionally a pony fell in a gopher hole, throwing its rider tail over tin-cup, but the agency doctor usually succeeded in mending the fallen rider sufficiently to take part in the next month's melee. The squaws skinned and butchered the downed cattle on the spot and carried off the meat to be either consumed immediately or the surplus to be "jerked" — cut in thin slices and dried. The Utes preferred to have their cattle raised for them and delivered on the hoof.

As the relationships between the Utes and whites became more strained — primarily because the whites soon realized the tremendous mining, ranching, and farming potential of the San Juan lands — the necessity for cool heads on both sides became urgent. In 1870–1871 gold discoveries were made near the present site of Silverton, which was then called Baker's Park. From that time forward, the Utes' control of their ancestral hunting grounds was doomed.

The first official treaty between the U.S. government and the Utes was negotiated in 1849, a year after the treaty of Guadalupe Hidalgo ended the Mexican War. The southern flanks of the San Juans had been Mexican territory until then. Under this treaty the Utes promised only that they would be friendly and would not depart from their accustomed living and hunting territory. In the middle 1850s the Utes went on the warpath, the San Luis Valley being the principal scene of their depredations. Mexican settlers had been pushing north up the Rio Grande Valley during the preceding decades, coming into abrasive contact with the Utes. Federal troops from Fort Massachusetts at the foot of Blanca Peak, six miles north of present day Fort Garland, put down the uprising.

In 1863, the Tabeguache Utes agreed to be confined to a reservation which included much of the north and northeast sectors of the San Juan. However, neither the U.S. government nor the Utes lived up to any of the treaty provisions. The treaty might have been "writ in water," to paraphrase Keat's epitaph.

In order to get the Utes out of the San Luis Valley, another treaty was negotiated in 1868, which restricted more severely, the size of the Ute Reservation and stabilized agencies for the three groups — Southern Utes, Northern Utes, and Tabeguache Utes.

During the negotiations which preceded the writing of the 1863 Treaty, Ouray, a full member of the Tabeguache band, caught the attention of the negotiators by translating the Ute speeches into Spanish, from which the official government interpreter made the English translation.

Chief Ouray with his friend Otto Mears. "The Pathfinder of the San Juan." (Sidney Jocknick, Early Days on the Western Slope of Colorado, 1870–1883.*)*

The final exodus of the Utes from Colorado. (Crossing Grand River [The Colorado near Grand Junction]. Sidney Jocknick, Early Days on the Western Slope of Colorado, 1870–1883.)

Ouray was probably born near Taos, New Mexico, about 1833, of a Jicarilla Apache father and Tabeguache mother. He spent his youth, to the age of about eighteen, as a sheepherder on the larger Mexican ranches in that part of the Rio Grande Valley. He spoke Ute, several other Indian dialects, good Spanish, and passable English. By the age of eighteen, he had gone back to life as a full-time "wild" Indian, as a member of the Tabeguache band. However, those earlier years had thoroughly habituated him to the white man's ways.

In Washington, D.C. prior to the writing of the 1868 Treaty, the federal government recognized Ouray as the spokesman for all seven bands of Utes. This meant that he owed his position as de-facto spokesman to white interference in the internal affairs of his tribe. He could not have survived the jealousies and connivance of other band leaders had he not prevailed by persuasion, diplomacy, and the sheer forcefulness of his character and personality. There were unsuccessful attempts on his life by other band chiefs and their followers, although he always retained the loyalty of the Tabeguache band throughout his life. He was a good and great Indian chief.

Ouray's place in Ute history is based on his standing among his Indian peers and his ability to see clearly that the whites had superior numbers, superior weapons, and an absolutely irresistible will to prevail. Ouray was, above all else, a realist. Caught between an irresistible force and an immovable object, he chose that course which did him and his people the least violence.

The old homestead of Chief Ouray and his wife Chipeta, which had been their last home just prior to the removal of the Tabeguache and Northern Ute bands to their reservation in eastern Utah in 1880, was located about a mile south of Montrose.

When the remains of Ouray's widow, Chipeta, were returned to her old agency home in March of 1925, for burial in a mausoleum which had been prepared by a committee of Montrose citizens, the whole community turned out to do her honor, something it had hardly thought of doing while she was still living, blind, and in relative poverty on the Uintah Reservation. The local high school band turned out in force, schoolchildren were excused from classes, several hundred spectators showed up, while orators cleared their throats and held forth from prepared texts. McCook,

Left: The mausoleum containing the remains of Chipeta, Chief Ouray's widow, on the Ute Museum grounds near Montrose, Colorado. Chipeta's brother, John McCook, is buried under the white marker to the right of the concrete vault.

Right: Ute Indian cemetery, Ignacio, Colorado. Looking from east to west. White cobblestone pyramid on left marks the grave of Chief Ouray. White fence post stubs, in line from foreground to grave, at center of picture, are remains of fence which once divided Catholic and Protestant halves of cemetery.

Chipeta's brother, was in the funeral procession. He had served a similar function at Ouray's obsequies forty-five years earlier. A few years later he was laid to rest beside the remains of his sister.

Chipeta's husband, Ouray, did not find his final resting place at the old Uncompahgre homestead beside his wife and brother-in-law. Ouray had died over forty years earlier, in 1880, while on a trip to the Southern Ute Agency at Ignacio, on the Los Pinos River in southern Colorado. His mission was to persuade the Southern Ute chiefs to sign the allotment provisions of the Brunot Treaty which confined the Southern Utes to a southern Colorado reservation and the Tabeguache and Northern Ute bands to a reservation in eastern Utah. Before his mission was accomplished he fell ill and died. Three white doctors examined him but were not permitted to prescribe. It was their opinion that he suffered from Bright's disease. The Ute medicine men who were in attendance were unable to help. After his death, his remains were wrapped in a blanket and secreted in a cave under a rocky eminence on a mesa south of the Ignacio Agency. Following Indian custom, three (some say five) of his horses were killed and buried under the rocks along with their owner.

The unmarked resting place was not disturbed until 1925, shortly after Chipeta was buried near Montrose. At that time, a committee of Montrose civic leaders asked McCook to intercede with the Southern Utes at Ignacio, in an attempt to persuade them to permit Ouray's remains to be disinterred and placed with Chipeta's at the Ouray Memorial Park which by then had been developed at the site of Ouray and Chipeta's

old agency home. The site has since been given to the Colorado State Historical Society and is the location of a fine Ute Museum. The request met with a chauvinistic response. It seems that turnabout was fair play. If Montrose had Chipeta's remains, Ignacio would keep Ouray's.

McCook, who had been with Ouray at the time of his death, and had been one of the subchiefs who had taken part in the secret burial of the great chief, induced the other three living witnesses to break their silence. Buckskin Charley, Naneese, Joseph Price, and McCook disclosed the location of the grave and later acted as pallbearers. Ouray's bones were disinterred and—with four days of Indian ceremonies—were reburied in the Indian cemetery at Ignacio. The ceremonies were ended with Christian services, both Catholic and Protestant.

A curious difference of opinion surfaced during the preparations for the reburial services. One Ute faction wished to have Ouray in the Catholic portion of the Indian cemetery, while another faction wished, just as vehemently, to see him interred in the Protestant part of the cemetery.

Although Ouray, because of his youth in the Rio Grande Valley, had probably professed, or had at least been exposed to, Catholicism during his early career, he is said to have embraced the Methodist faith several years before his demise, thus laying some foundation for his dichotomous state of grace at the time of his death. The Gordian knot was cut by taking down a portion of the fence which separated the two parts of the cemetery and the grave was dug on the fence line so that Ouray's bones shared both sides.

CHAPTER 10

The White Man Arrives

The little expedition set off from Santa Fe during that same hot summer that the delegates wrestled with the successive drafts of a Declaration of Independence in Philadelphia. The party enjoyed the sanction of the Church and had implored the patronage of the "Virgin Mary, Our Lady of the Immaculate Conception, and of the most holy patriarch Joseph her most happy spouse." Herbert E. Bolton called it a "Pageant in the Wilderness"; it enjoyed the services of the first chronicler whose narrative has preserved a description of the San Juans and the adjacent Colorado Plateau.

The chronicler's name was Escalante — Fray Silvestre Veléz de Escalante. Although he was actually second in command, because of his chronicle the expedition has come down in history as the Escalante expedition. Escalante's superior, Fray Francisco Atanasio Dominguez, had been sent out from Mexico as superior of the Franciscan missions in New Mexico. Among other duties he had been charged with finding, if possible, a viable route — a *camino* — from the missions of the upper Rio Grande Valley to the new missions which had only recently been established along the California coast — particularly Monterey.

Another missionary, Fray Francisco Garcés, using San Xavier del Bac in southern Arizona as a base of operations, had explored up the Colorado River as far as Havasupai Canyon, on the south rim of the Grand Canyon. From there he had worked his way southeastward to Oraibi, one of the Hopi villages of north central Arizona. On the evening of July 3, 1776, he bribed a young Hopi to carry a message to the missionary at the pueblo of Zuni. The missionary at that pueblo was Escalante. The Oraibi locals were restless

and sullen, hence the circumspection; Garcés was not even permitted to sleep in any of the vacant rooms at the pueblo. The message, which was dispatched when it was already early morning in Philadelphia of the day when the soon-to-be-adopted Declaration of Independence was published to all the land, suggested that the two missionaries open communications between Santa Fe and California. Escalante had already gone from Zuni to Santa Fe at the summons of Dominguez. The message eventually found its way into the archives in Mexico, with no notation as to whether or not it had been received by Escalante.

In the meantime Escalante's expedition had already been set in motion. Knowing of the intransigence of the Hopis on their mesas and the outright belligerence of the Apaches along the Gila River, he reasoned that the most likely successful route from the upper Rio Grande to the California coast would lie somewhere north of the Grand Canyon. Consequently, he chose to follow a route which had been pioneered by traders out of the upper Rio Grande Valley.

At least as early as 1761, Juan Maria de Rivera had, under orders of the governor of New Mexico, explored north from Santa Fe around the south, west, and northwest sides of the San Juan Mountains to the junction of the Uncompahgre and Gunnison rivers near the site of present-day Delta, Colorado. At an even earlier date, Mexican prospectors had found traces of silver in the La Plata (Silver) Mountains west of Durango, Colorado. For some time traders and prospectors had trafficked in hides with the Utes around the southern borders of the San Juan Mountains, giving names to some of the tributaries of the San Juan River — Los Pinos, Florida, and Las Animas. Even earlier the name Sierra de las Grullas had been given to the high peaks from which these rivers flowed.

Consequently, when Escalante and Dominguez set their course north from Santa Fe they were entering a region which had already been trodden and named —

Opposite: Along the Escalante route between Abiquiu and Tierra Amarilla, about sixty-five miles northwest of Santa Fe.

83

but only as far as the north side of the San Juans. The dates and routes of these earlier trips have been reconstructed from tenuous evidence. Not so Escalante's trip; he kept a diary which carefully recorded directions and distances. Furthermore, one of the members of the party was a retired military engineer, named Don Bernardo Miera y Pacheco, who kept detailed navigational notes during the trip. He carried an astrolabe with which he made sixteen observations for latitude. A magnetic compass served as another important item of navigational gear.

Don Bernardo's latitude determinations consistently place him from 50 to 100 miles further north than modern figures. This may have been caused by some instrumental error, or by some systematic error in the observing technique. Measurements were made from both meridian altitudes of the sun and the altitude of the North Star, Polaris.

Although the north and south distance travelled could be checked by latitude determinations, at the time of this expedition there was no reliable method for determining east-west locations—longitude. The chronometer had not yet been invented, and the more sophisticated methods of determining longitudes, such as occultations of certain stars by the disc of the moon, were beyond the capabilities of the instruments taken

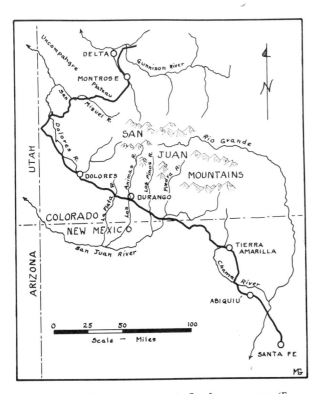

The Escalante-Dominguez route in San Juan country. (From diary and maps in Herbert E. Bolton, Pageant in the Wilderness, the story of the Escalante expedition to the Interior Basin, 1776, including the diary and itinerary of Father Escalante, translated and annotated — 1950 — Utah Historical Society, Salt Lake City, Utah.)

on this rough-and-tumble wilderness trip. Longitude had to be determined by dead reckoning, just as it had been determined since the days of the pharaohs. The navigator made as close an estimate as he could of the amount of "eastering" and "westering" made good each day, worked out from the distances and the compass directions travelled during the day.

Considering the means at their disposal, the padres and Miera y Pacheco produced a remarkably accurate map in both latitude and longitude. Escalante's diary provided an itinerary which made it possible for Dr. Herbert E. Bolton, in 1950, to produce a modern map which shows the site of each night's camp.

The first thirty days of the expedition passed through or near San Juan country. The party left Santa Fe on July 29, 1776. They had planned to depart on July 4 (what a windfall this would have been for those who read significance into dates) but some of the Santa Fe garrison had to go out on a campaign against marauding Comanches, and Escalante was obliged to accompany them as chaplain. Only when they returned was he free to set forth on the great adventure.

The party reached the Uncompahgre River a few miles south of present day Montrose on August 26. From that time on they moved steadily away from the San Juans, going north and northwest. They reached a point near the site of present day Provo, Utah, on the shores of Utah Lake, before they turned back toward Santa Fe, which they reached on January 2, 1777.

(In the following discussion we have made use of the modern names of villages and features.)

At the beginning, they were not pioneering a new route. They moved northwestward from Santa Fe past Abiquiú, Tierra Amarilla, Dulce, Ignacio, to just south of Durango, crossing the San Juan, Piedras, Los Pinos, Florida, and Las Animas rivers. Thence across the La Plata at Hesperus, past Mancos to Dolores. At Dolores, where they halted long enough to take one of their unreliable latitude observations, they plunged into country which is even yet only sparsely settled. They had been on the flanks of the San Juans since they were a few miles north of Abiquiú. They would remain within sight of the high summits until they crossed Grand Mesa and dropped down onto the Colorado River between Grand Valley and DeBeque.

The only incident worth mentioning as far as Dolores, occurred just north of Abiquiú. Besides horses and mules to carry men, supplies, and gear, the expedition drove a small herd of cattle to meet their needs for meat. These animals were undoubtedly of the native, mixed creollo stock, hardy trail animals but not producers of succulent steaks and roasts. I once heard an old cowboy describe such an animal as "All hide, horns and asshole!" Texas longhorns were descended from such stock. What they lacked in beef qualities they made up in native cunning and survival instincts. They were scarcely more tame than wild animals.

The herders lost four of the commissary stock in the heavy brush. Escalante describes it this way: "We turned north, and entered a wooded canyon in which, for the distance of a quarter of a league, there is a grove of small oaks so dense that while passing through it we lost track of four animals and had to stop to hunt for them, but they were soon found." (The old Spanish land league was 2.63 miles in length.)

They were lucky the animals were soon found. Many a stock drover has lost "bunch quitters" under such circumstances. I once came upon such an animal in a dense oak brush thicket. He was literally down on his front knees slithering through openings which would have stopped a greased pig.

From the present town site of Dolores, the route lay down the middle canyon of the Dolores River. Here it was necessary to leave the canyon and travel on the mesa tops on the west side, coming back to the canyon for water on either the main stream or one of its tributaries.

From where Disappointment Creek enters the Dolores the party tried to go further downstream, but the canyon quickly became impassable so they climbed up onto the mesa to the north of Disappointment Creek, then along Gypsum Creek (Cajón del Yeso) and crossed the higher ground to the San Miguel River near present day Naturita. In doing so they had some very hard going while climbing out of Gypsum Valley. Escalante says that the animals left "their tracks on the rocks with the blood of their feet!"

Just before they reached the site of Naturita, the party crossed the east end of Paradox Valley. They would have had a fine view westward down the valley to the imposing, timber-covered slopes of the La Sals, just across the present Utah line.

Escalante remarks: "Near here is the small range which they call Sierra de la Sal because close to it there are salt flats, where according to what we are told the Yutas who live hereabouts get their salt."

On August 25 the party crossed the Uncompahgre Plateau a little north of Horsefly Peak and camped at the head of Loghill Mesa. Summer homes are now be-

The Chama River near Abiquiu, where the Escalante expedition crossed it shortly after leaving Santa Fe.

ginning to dot the landscape where the 1776 party must have been impressed by the stunning facade of the Sneffels sector of the San Juans.

The next day the party reached the banks of the Uncompahgre River at a marshy area just a few miles south of the present site of Montrose. Interestingly, the party reached the river quite close to the point where Chief Ouray and his wife, Chipeta, were provided with a homestead site when the Ute Agency was moved to the Uncompahgre Valley in 1875. Today, the site is administered by the Colorado State Historical Society and is the location of the Ute Museum.

To this point the Escalante party had not seen Utes in any numbers, although they were in the heart of Ute country.

The name given to the Uncompahgre River was Rio de San Francisco, the first camp there, La Cienega de San Francisco. From this place the party trailed across the barren hills between the Uncompahgre and the Gunnison, the latter of which they crossed several miles east of the junction of the two streams. Although they did not visit it, Escalante mentions that Don Maria de Rivera had visited the junction of the Uncompahgre and the Gunnison in 1761 and carved there on a large second-growth cottonwood "a cross, the characters of which spell his name and the year of his expedition."

At this Uncompahgre stop (La Cienega) Escalante appends to his diary and itinerary a "Description of the Sierras Thus Far Seen." Names which are still current and accurately located in the diary include Sierra de la Plata, Sierra de la Sal, and Sierra de Abajo. The Sierra de los Tabehuaches (named for the Tabeguache band of the Utes—what we know as the Uncompahgre Plateau), is especially well described:

> The Sierra de los Tabehuaches, which we have just crossed, runs northwest. It must be about thirty leagues long, and in the place where we crossed it is eight or ten leagues wide. It abounds in good pasturage, is very moist, and has good lands for crops without irrigation. It produces in abundance pinon, spruce (pinabete), royal pine, dwarf oak, several kinds of wild fruits and, in some places, flax. In it there are stags, fallow-deer and other animals, and some fowls of a size and form similar to ordinary domestic hens, from which they differ in not having combs. Their flesh is very savory. [Escalante was probably describing grouse.]

Escalante's description of the Uncompahgre Valley just south of Montrose could have been written by an overeager local chamber of commerce publicist: "This Rio de San Francisco is medium-sized and a little larger

Opposite: The Escalante expedition crossed the Green River from the east (far) side to the west (near) side, a few miles east of Jensen, Utah. Mouth of Split Mountain Gorge in the middle background.

Pikes Peak from the high plains.

rescued through diplomatic channels and were repatriated at Natchitoches, Louisiana, in 1807. Some of the notes and maps were recovered from the Mexico City archives a hundred years later.

Pike's tenuous association with the San Juans consisted of an inspiring view of the range from Poncha Pass, across the San Luis Valley, skirting along the edge of the La Garita Hills as the party moved south down the west side of the San Luis Valley, and ascending the Conejos Valley far enough to reach the site of the winter quarters "fort" where the party was apprehended.

As a result of Pike's exploration the knowledge of a magnificent range of mountains tucked away behind the easternmost Front Range had now made its way into official U.S. archives, waiting to be useful at some future needful time, although San Juan country was still Mexican territory.

. . . .

The pattern of North American climatology dictates that the west sides of the overlapping mountain ranges, which fill the western quarter of the continent, are wetter and greener than the eastern sides. Streams are more numerous and carry greater heads of water down the western flanks of the ranges.

The beaver, an aquatic animal, favored these better-watered sides of the western ranges, although he was indigenous to the whole region.

The fur brigades of mountain men who invaded the Rockies in pursuit of beaver after the return of the Lewis and Clark expedition, were not content to confine their trapping to the tributaries of the Missouri and Mississippi. In defiance of hostile tribesmen, mountain men trapped their way up these tributaries and crossed over one pass after another to the network of streams which drained the better-watered western side of the individual ranges. In doing so they found, one after another, the intermontane pockets, parks, and valleys which soon served as winter quarters and rendezvous sites in the rich beaver country west of the divides—Jackson's Hole, Pierre's Hole, Cache Valley, the Portneuf, Green River, Ham's Fork, Black Fork, Bear Lake, the Hoback, the Uintah, and Brown's Hole.

By 1840, the bubble had burst. The demand for beaver hats had fallen disastrously in the span of a brief thirty-five years. A turbulent era had run its course. But the edges of San Juan country were brushed by the goings and comings of the traders and trappers. Escalante's old trail was a natural route between the Spanish settlements on the Rio Grande and the fur trading posts on Green River west of South Pass, such as Fort Bridger and the rendezvous site in Pierre's Hole.

than the Dolores. It is composed of several small streams which flow down the western slope of the Sierra de las Grullas and runs to the northwest. In the place where we saw it there is a meadow about three leagues long, of good land for crops and with facilities for irrigation and everything else needed for the establishment of good settlement."

. . . .

Aside from frequent Spanish incursions up the Rio Grande Valley, the next recorded white entry into the San Juan is little more than a footnote of history. Following the Louisiana Purchase in 1803, Jefferson launched several expeditions to explore and map the newly acquired territory. Lewis and Clark's two-year journey to the Pacific, and return, got most of the contemporary attention. However, another exploration by the less publicized Lt. Zebulon Montgomery Pike pushed closer to the San Juans.

In 1806, the Pike party, probing the northern boundary of Mexican territory, explored almost to the head of the Arkansas River, attempted to climb, without success, the peak which now bears Pike's name, and crossed into the San Luis Valley, where they were taken into custody by a Mexican military patrol on a cheerless winter day in early 1807. After the capture they were escorted south to Chihuahua City, where their notes and maps were seized and they were imprisoned. Eventually the members of the party were

By the early 1830s an enterprising independent trader from St. Louis named Antoine Robidoux had made several trading journeys between western Wyoming locations and Taos. In 1833, he established a fort and trading post near the mouth of what the mountain men called the "Winty," the Uintah. About the same time that the Uintah post was established, Robidoux built another post on the Gunnison, a few miles below its junction with the Uncompahgre, downstream from the present site of Delta. This junction of the two streams was the place where Don Maria de Rivera carved a cross and his initials on a cottonwood in 1761. Captain Gunnison and Lt. Beckwith reported seeing the tumbledown remains of the fort on the Gunnison when they passed that way in 1853.

Hardly ten years after the two Robidoux forts were established the Utes became restive. Their trade had been scant at best; the two posts had served the few whites that passed that way as staging stations on the route between the Green River and the upper Rio Grande settlements. In 1844, the Ute restiveness boiled over into overt action and the posts on the "Winty" and the Uncompahgre were left smoking ruins with murdered defenders. Antoine Robidoux was at Fort Bridger on a trading trip at the time, a fortuitous absence which undoubtedly saved his life.

View of the Roan or Book Mountains, at the Spanish Trail ford of the Green River. (Near present-day Green River, Utah.) (U.S. Pacific Railroad Exploration and Surveys, 38th and 39th Parallels [Gunnison Report]. J. M. Stanley from a sketch by R. H. Kern.)

Robidoux's post on the Gunnison brought the fur trade era as close to the San Juans as it was to get. Taos, the home of Kit Carson, mountain man and scout without peer, served as a way station and resupply point for fur trappers through all of the fur era; however, it was the ultimate outpost of the Spanish Empire in New Spain and, as befitted its station, served rowdy fur trappers disdainfully and with some reluctance.

Joseph Williams, returning from Oregon in 1842, arrived too late at Fort Bridger, Wyoming, to accompany the annual caravan from there to St. Louis. He then diverted south to Robidoux's fort on the Uintah, hoping to catch another trading caravan going south to the Spanish settlements which would afford him protection from Indians on the way.

"We had to wait there for Mr. Rubedeau about eighteen days," says Williams, "till he and his company and horse drivers were ready to start with us." Williams used the eighteen days' wait to catalogue his impressions about the fort. They were caustic at best: "This place is equal to any I ever saw for wickedness and idleness. The French and Spaniards are all Roman Catholics; but are as wicked men, I think, as ever lived. No one who has not, like me witnessed it, can have any idea of their wickedness. Some of these people at the fort are fat and dirty, and idle and greasy." Williams found the delay very trying because of "the wickedness of the people, and the drunkenness and swearing, and the debauchery of the men among the Indian women. They would buy and sell them to one another." It is probable that Williams did not understand Spanish, which fact would have made well over half of the swearing he reports unavailable to him. Toward the end of his diatribe what was really "sticking in his craw," surfaces. He was a Methodist preacher by profession and he remarks sadly, "I tried several times to preach to them; but with little if any effect."

This "den of iniquity," clinging to the north flank of the San Juans, was no better nor worse than several dozen other fur trade posts in other parts of the Rocky Mountains. To survive in the raw frontier of that day a man had either to live a life of animallike, elemental simplicity, without concern for the spiritual consequences, entering into a sort of pact with the devil; or make such a binding commitment to his Maker that none of the worldly diversions of life touched him. Jedediah Smith and the Mormons fit the latter pattern, the denizens of Robidoux's fort on the "Winty" the former. Fur trade posts in their day were probably no worse than most mining boom towns were to become in their time. A raw frontier environment molds raw inhabitants.

NATURAL OBELISKS.

CHAPTER 11

Uncle Sam Investigates

The 38th parallel of north latitude has a special significance for the San Juan Mountains. This imaginary line passes through the northern part of the San Juans. Four of the region's historic mining camps — Lake City, Ouray, Silverton, and Telluride — lie close to the parallel. The fabulously rich Camp Bird, Smuggler Union, and Tomboy mines lie within two or three miles of the line.

St. Louis also lies near the 38th parallel. It was from St. Louis that Lewis and Clark set out to cross the continent. Later, from there, the human wave of U.S. westward expansion set off toward the sunset margin of the continent.

During the early and middle decades of the nineteenth century, St. Louis was the home and political base of Thomas Hart Benton, who served as U.S. senator from Missouri from 1820 to 1851. An ardent exponent of Jacksonian Democracy — he had served with Jackson in the War of 1812 — Benton was a power in the U.S. Senate while the pulse of U.S. westward expansion quickened. He was long the spokesman of the "Western Bloc" in the Senate. Aggressively, Benton championed agrarian interests, free land, or at least cheap land on the frontier, hard money (he was known as "Old Bullion"), and westward expansion.

Thomas Hart Benton was the father-in-law of John Charles Frémont. Benton's position as the leader of the Senate's "Western Bloc" made it possible for him to exercise influence, when necessary, to have his brilliant young son-in-law appointed to the leadership of three U.S. government-sponsored exploring expeditions to the West. Following the first two expeditions, the Senate provided funds for the publication and wide

Opposite: Natural Obelisks, 1848–1849. From John Charles Frémont, Memoirs (Prospectus). This wild, forbidding scene was drawn sometime shortly after the conclusion of the 1848–1849 expedition by Edward Kern, who had been a participant in the disaster. (By permission of the Huntington Library)

dissemination of voluminous and well-illustrated reports, written by Frémont with the collaboration of his wife, Jesse. The extensive readership of these reports established Frémont as the popular, charismatic folk hero of western exploration. He was popularly known as the "Pathfinder"; however, modern scholarship has seen his role more as a superb mapper and surveyor of trails already discovered by other pioneers.

Frémont's first expedition of 1842 mapped the Oregon Trail as far as South Pass and northward into the Wind River Range. The second expedition of 1843 mapped the Oregon Trail to the south of the Columbia River, followed by a detour southward into California.

In 1845, the third expedition mapped the California Trail from the Salt Lake Basin across Nevada and was to plunge Frémont into controversy with the U.S. military authorities in California. Caught in a conflict of authority between Commodore Stockton (Navy) and General Steven Watts Kearny (Army), which was exacerbated by ambiguous orders from the president, Frémont was arrested for disobedience, returned to Washington, D.C., court-martialed, and found guilty of "mutiny, disobedience, and conduct prejudicial of good order and military discipline." Refusing to accept from President Polk an executive remission of his dismissal from the army, Frémont angrily cut himself off from further governmental support of the exploring expeditions which had become the very lifeblood of his existence.

While Frémont, like Achilles, sulked in his tent, Benton was able to recruit support for a private expedition from among members of the St. Louis business community. They commissioned Frémont to explore and map the route for a transcontinental railroad which would have its midwestern terminus in St. Louis, cross the Rockies near the 38th parallel and, keeping to that same general latitude, cross the Great Basin and the Sierras to a Pacific terminal at San Francisco, providing a "middle" route to the Pacific.

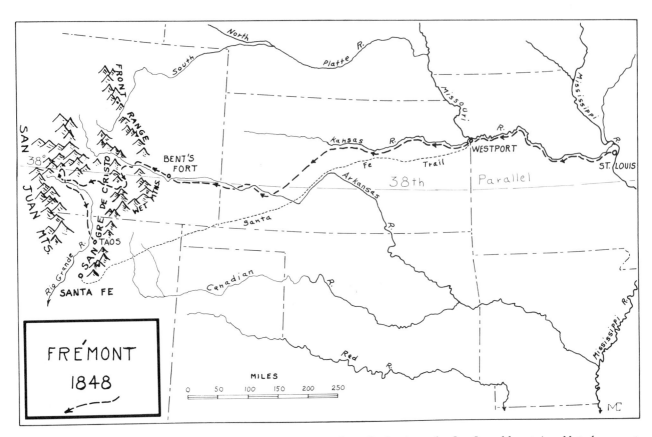

Route followed by John C. Frémont's expedition of 1848–1849 from St. Louis to the San Juan Mountains. Note how route lies near the 38th parallel of north latitude.

The expedition got a late start from St. Louis, did not reach Bent's Fort on the Arkansas until Wednesday, November 15, and left Pueblo for the Hardscrabble and the Wet Mountain Valley at the end of November. Part of the mission of the expedition was to prove the existence of an "all-weather" route. In the face of dire warnings from the old-timers at Bent's Fort and Pueblo against the attempt at a winter crossing, the party pressed on.

The state of Frémont's mind will never be known; later there was much conflicting testimony from the survivors. Frémont's need for a brilliant success must have been very great. He still smarted from the verdict of the court-martial.

The guide, Old Bill Williams, who was recruited at the last moment at Pueblo, when Kit Carson was unavailable, has been blamed by some. Frémont implied, later, that Old Bill had lost his way. Old Bill Williams' partisans, meanwhile, point out that Frémont had rejected Old Bill's strong suggestions that in a winter as severe as this the only feasible route was to skirt the San Juan Mountains to the south.

In the early afternoon of December 3, 1848 the wind-scourged party of thirty-two struggled to the crest of Robidoux Pass (Mosca Pass) in the Sangre de Cristo Range. During the past two days they had come from the east, fighting deep snow and down timber out of

the head of the Huerfano Valley. To the west lay the open sweep of the San Luis Valley. At their feet lay snow-dusted sand dunes, heaped by the prevailing westerly winds. The wind still shrieked through the notches in the Sangre de Cristo Range. Westward, beyond the valley, the leaden sky pressed down on the jumbled crests of the San Juan Mountains. Viewed from a distance of ninety miles, the massive peaks, canyons, and ridges blurred into a treeless white tableland which gave no hint of the monstrous dangers which lay in wait for the exhausted party.

The blizzard-whipped route from Mosca Pass lay around the Great Sand Dunes, which crowd against the east rim of the San Luis Valley, thence into the valley and southwestward to the cottonwood-fringed Rio Grande between present-day Alamosa and Del Norte. In the shelter of the timber along the stream they found some game and made their way westward past Del Norte to the site of South Fork.

The approximate route from there can be worked out from the sketchy records left by men who knew they were slowly dying of starvation and exposure. The expedition beat its way — literally, since they were forced to use wooden mauls and shovels to beat down a path for the mules — through deepening snowdrifts along Alder Creek, north of South Fork. They skirted the edge of Pool Table Mountain, along several steep

The route of the 1848–1849 John C. Frémont party lay up Alder Creek, in the middle distance of this air view, to the crest of the snow-covered divide in the extreme right distance.

mountainsides and at last, above timberline, over a broad saddle cleared of snow by gale-force winds at a little over 12,300 feet above sea level and down the north side of the ridge into the uppermost timber at the head of Wannamaker Creek. Here in the deep snow the party met utter defeat. The mules which had been dying by ones and twos every day had now come to the end of their endurance. Only six or seven of the thirty-four animals which had survived to this point ever left the camp. Starving, they ate each other's tails, while their pitiful braying added a banshee wail to the howling wind.

At last, realizing that the party's fingertip hold on the edge of the San Juans was untenable, Frémont called for retreat. The mules were no longer useful except as food. With superhuman effort the party man-hauled most of its supplies and effects back over the ridge to another more sheltered camp on the head of Embargo Creek, a tributary of the Rio Grande between South Fork and Del Norte. Here they spent Christmas in deep snow and a still deeper premonition of impending doom.

From this camp a party was sent out to search for help from the Spanish settlements down the river at Red River or Taos. Those left behind spent twenty days trying to haul their gear and supplies some fifteen miles down Embargo Creek to the Rio Grande.

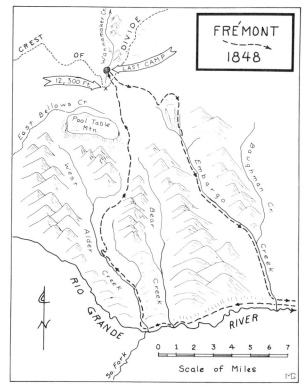

Detail of Frémont route to and from the final camp at head of Wannamaker Creek, 1848–1849 expedition. Planimetry and elevations from U.S. Geological Survey topographic quadrangles.

Air view of the uppermost timber at the head of Wannamaker Creek. Here, in deep snow, the advance of the Frémont party of 1848 came finally to a halt. By that time, most of the mules were dead and the party struggled back over the divide in the left center of the picture and then down Embargo Creek to the Rio Grande. Ten members of the party died during the retreat down the river to the Mexican settlements at Questa, Arroyo Hondo, and Taos.

Before help could return, the retreat had fallen into a disorganized rout. The survivors split into small groups which moved independently down the Rio Grande, all possessions abandoned, save a meager allotment of food, their threadbare clothing, and a blanket or two which were scarcely proof against the bitter cold and snow. Many were too weak to hunt for game or their presence frightened all game from the river valley. Ten members of the expedition succumbed during this retreat.

This debacle, which has been called one of the most appalling disasters in the annals of U.S. exploration, colored the rest of Frémont's life and earned for the San Juan Mountains a notoriety which it didn't deserve.

. . . . .

Eighteen fifty-three saw the beginning of a wave of "government" exploration in the San Juan. Pike's 1806–1807 trip to the edge of the San Juans had been the last government-sponsored effort.

Frémont's first three explorations—along the Oregon Trail, to the Wind River Range, and along the California Trail—had been sponsored by Congress through the mapping agencies of the U.S. Army Topographic Engineers, but they did not touch the San Juan. Frémont's 1848–1849 tragedy in the San Juans had been supported by private subscriptions from among Benton's supporters on the Missouri frontier.

By 1850, the agencies of government saw that the flood tide of western migration and the young nation's commitment to the siren call of "manifest destiny" would soon make it mandatory to build overland links between the rapidly settling Midwest and the Pacific shores. The treaty of Guadalupe Hidalgo, which brought the Mexican War to an end in 1848, opened up a vast new quarter of the U.S. frontier: the Southwest and California. The 1848 discovery of gold in California added urgency to the need for westward routes. The San Juans lay athwart one of the proposed avenues of migration. Frémont's attempt to survey that south central route had been unsuccessful in 1848–1849, but that was no reason to cross it off the list of possible paths to Pacific shores.

The tenth and eleventh sections of the Military Appropriation Act of March 3, 1853, directed "such explorations and surveys as to ascertain the most practical route for a railroad to the Pacific Ocean." In more specific directions, Captain John W. Gunnison was appointed by the War Department to carry out a survey "through the Rocky Mountains in the vicinity of the Rio del Norte, by way of the Huerfano River and Cooche-to-pa or some other eligible pass, into the region of the Grand and Green Rivers, and westwardly to the Vegas de Santa Clara and Nicollet Rivers of the Great Basin, and thence northward in the vicinity of Salt Lake on a return route, to explore the most valuable passes and canyons of the Wasatch Range and South Pass to Fort Laramie."

With admirable devotion to his instructions, Captain Gunnison surveyed the route pretty much as it had been proposed in his orders. As had happened so often in the past, Gunnison was not pioneering new ground; Spanish prospectors and missionaries, fur brigades, even forty-niners had been over the ground before him. Gunnison's guide, Antoine Leroux, was an old mountain man whose services had been secured at Taos by Lt. Beckwith, the expedition's second in command.

Gunnison's major contribution was his accurate mapping of the route and the determination of its suitability for a railroad grade. He succeeded in taking a convoy of six-mule-team army freight wagons along the route, although it was necessary to dig a track at some steep arroyos, let the wagons down steep bluffs by fixed ropes, and hoist them up steep grades by block and tackle and double teaming.

The tragedy of Gunnison's thoroughly professional exploration of a central railroad route across the Rockies lay in his murder by renegade Piute Indians near Sevier Lake in west central Utah on October 26, 1853, after the most arduous part of the survey had been completed. Lt. Beckwith recovered the field notes and instruments and wrote the final report.

Gunnison and Beckwith's route crosses San Juan country from Saguache at the north end of the San Luis Valley to Montrose, in the Uncompahgre Valley. It parallels State Highway 114 west and north from Saguache over Cochetopa Pass to Tomichi Creek east of Gunnison, thence west on U.S. Highway 50 through Gunnison to Sapinero, past Blue Mesa Reservoir, over Blue Mesa Summit to Cimarron, over Cerro Summit, and down Cedar Creek to Montrose, where it meets the old Escalante Trail.

Gunnison left his name on the land: in Colorado, a major tributary of the Colorado River system, a canyon, a county, a town, a national forest, and a 12,000-foot peak in the West Elk Mountains; in Utah, an island in Great Salt Lake, and a town.

. . . . .

Before the next government-sponsored expeditions pressed into the San Juans, the Civil War had run its course, and the vanguard of eager argonauts had raced down the mineral axis of the state to fan out along the creeks and valleys of the San Juan. They did not confine themselves to the lowlands; they were soon clambering up the sides of the mountains into any obscure nook and cranny which looked like it might shelter a lode.

In 1860, Charles Baker led a contingent of gold seekers from the San Luis Valley over Stony Pass onto

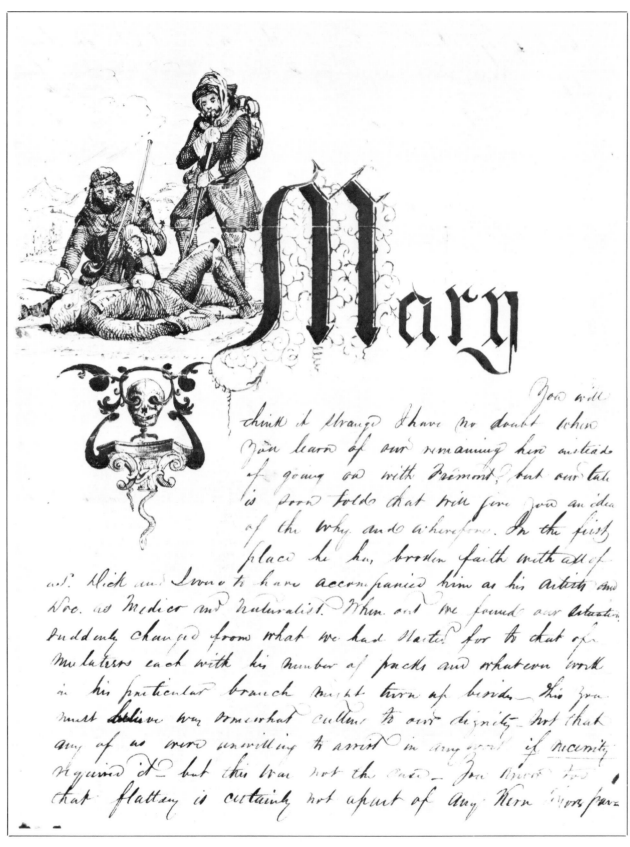

Page 1 of Edward Kern's letter to his sister Mary (Kern) Wolfe, written in January of 1849 at Santa Fe, New Mexico. The three figures at the heading of the letter depict the death of an unnamed member of Fremont's 1848–49 expedition, while the death's head adds a further somber note to the tidings in the letter. (By permission of the Huntington Library)

Peaks of the Sierra Blanca, from near Fort Massachusetts. (U.S. Pacific Railroad Exploration and Surveys, 38th and 39th Parallels [Gunnison Report]. J. M. Stanley from sketch by R. H. Kern.)

View showing the formation of the Canyon of Grand River, near the mouth of Lake Fork with indications of the formidable side canyons. (U.S. Pacific Railroad Exploration and Surveys, 38th and 39th Parallels [Gunnison Report]. J. M. Stanley from sketch by F. W. Eggloffstein.) This view presents a very romanticized picture of the upper end of the Black Canyon of the Gunnison River (called Grand River in the Gunnison Report) near the confluence of the Lake Fork with the Gunnison. This part of the canyon is now under the waters of the Blue Mesa and Morrow Point reservoirs.

Aerial view of Silverton, Colorado, looking north.

the headwaters of the Animas River, at the confluence of Mineral Creek and Cement Creek with the main stream, which came to be known later as Baker's Park. Silverton is now cradled in the mountain-girt bowl. The party "toughed" out the ensuing winter, recovered a minimum of placer gold, and retraced their route to civilization the next summer.

Baker plays an elusive role in the mythology of the San Juan. He has been variously reported as Capt. Baker, as Lt. Baker of the U.S. Army, and as Jim Baker. The route of the party into Baker's Park has been reported both as up the Animas Canyon from the south and over Stony Pass from the east.

The most fanciful tale about Baker was recorded in the *New York Times*, October 25, 1873, which credits him with starting a gold rush to the San Juans in 1860 which petered out almost as soon as it had started. The account says that the duped miners convened a kangaroo court on the spot and brought Baker to trial for spreading false rumors. In his own defense, Baker insisted that the very ground on which the court was sitting contained gold to a greater value than he had ever claimed for it. A gold pan was called for, a shovelful of dirt thrown into it, and washed down expertly with the gold panner's swirling motion. A trace of color worth half a dollar lay in the bottom of the pan at the end of the demonstration. The trace of gold is credited with saving Baker's life.

In 1861, the Baker party, harassed by restless Utes (some of the party lost their lives), made their way out of the San Juans to play their several roles in the gathering tragedy of the Civil War.

After the War, in 1870–1871, despite the overt opposition of the Utes, prospecting parties were back again in Baker's Park. Whereas the Baker party had searched with small success for placer deposits, this new group was more interested in lodes. In Arrastra Gulch, Miles T. Johnson found promising "float" which he was able to trace up the mountainside to its source in the Little Giant vein.

Ore taken from the Little Giant was first ground in a Spanish arrastra, a crude stone crusher, worked like a windlass by burros or mules. The crushed ore was packed on mules to Pueblo, Colorado, for smelting. It is reported that samples of the ore showed from 400 to 900 ounces of gold per ton. By 1872, the Little Giant Mining Company was organized in Chicago. By 1873, a 5-stamp mill had been installed at the Little Giant. That same year, a Judge Green established a small smelter north of Silverton, the new settlement which had begun to grow in Baker's Park. By 1875, the smelter's capacity had been enlarged to twelve tons per day.

Meanwhile, during the first three years of the new camp, 1870–1872, the miners left the diggings during the winter, most returning to Del Norte in the San Luis Valley. The Baker party's winter experiences of 1860–1861 had earned the San Juan winters a bad reputation.

During this time, all San Juan prospectors were trespassing on Ute Indian land, which had been guaranteed to them by the 1868 Treaty. Several times soldiers were sent to escort interlopers out of the mountains, but they always sneaked back. Finally the loud and persistent clamors of frustrated prospectors urged the U.S. authorities to try for another treaty with the Utes which would open up the San Juan mineral lands to exploitation.

. . . .

Before a new treaty could be negotiated, another government exploration was undertaken by the War Department. The account of this investigation is contained in a *Report of a Reconnaissance in the Ute Country, Made in the Year 1873*, by Lt. E. H. Ruffner, Corps of Engineers. The party had the services of a civil engineer, a geologist, and a photographer. Surveying the 107th meridian, west of Greenwich, which marked the east boundary of the Ute Reservation under the provisions of the 1868 Treaty, was the party's most important task. However, they found opportunities to visit mines on the upper Lake Fork of the Gunnison, near Lake City, in Baker's Park, and on the upper Animas River. These were the main foci of San Juan mining activity prior to the expulsion of the Utes, and the primary cause of the tribe's disgruntlement.

A new treaty with the Utes was negotiated in September of 1873, and ratified by the U.S. Senate in April of 1874. Its provisions opened up the mineral lands of the mountains to prospecting and confined the Utes to an east-west strip of reservation along the Colorado–New Mexico border, the Uncompahgre Valley, and the White River Plateau country of northwestern Colorado.

News of the 1873 Treaty touched off a rush of prospectors to the San Juans in 1874. The clandestine mining which had gone on around Silverton in the early 1870s had seldom engaged more than forty to fifty miners per season. By 1880, it is estimated that no less than 7,000 mines and prospects had been located and recorded in the several mining districts of the San Juan. Only a small percentage of these were eventually productive, but they represented the unbounded hopes of their discoverers.

By 1880, mining settlements had been established at Summitville, Gunnison, Lake City, Durango, Rico, Silverton, Ouray, Ophir, Telluride, and a dozen or more satellites which have since fallen into ruin.

. . . .

At the end of the Civil War victorious Northerners and, to a lesser extent vanquished Southerners, stood

Baker's Park and Sultan Mountain. Ernest Ingersoll, Knocking Round the Rockies, *1882.*

ready to turn most of the energy which each had expended in the prosecution of that conflict into the channels of westward expansion. Entrepreneurs on the western frontier stood ready to realize their personal dreams of "manifest destiny." There were mines to develop, forests to turn into lumber, land to break to the plow, stage lines and toll roads to build, railroads to survey and finance, smelters to fire up. Many in the North looked for investment opportunities. In the South, many of those dispossessed during the period of reconstruction, sought avenues for a new start. In that immediate postwar period science was fast becoming the handmaiden of commerce.

The old mountain man could gain some sort of living from the raw wilderness with little more than native cunning to guide him. Not so the postwar settler. The developer of a new railroad or a mine needed maps, geological studies, more sophisticated analysis of minerals, timber, soil.

Almost immediately these new frontiersmen began to call on their government to supply these needs. The government responded by establishing the four "Great Surveys" which studied, measured, and mapped the West from 1867 to 1870. All four were in the business

of gathering geographical and geological information about little known sections of the West. Sometimes their spheres of activity overlapped. Two of the surveys were under the administration of the War Department, two were under the administration of the Department of the Interior. The War Department surveys were under the leadership of Clarence King, a civilian, and Lt. George Montague Wheeler, of the Army Topographic Engineers. The Interior Department surveys were under the leadership of civilians: Ferdinand Vandeveer Hayden and John Wesley Powell. Only two of the four surveys worked within the territory of the San Juan Mountains: The Wheeler Survey, entitled *The United States Geographical Surveys West of the Hundredth Meridian,* and the Hayden Survey, entitled *The United States Geological and Geographical Survey of the Territories.* In 1879, all four surveys were absorbed into the U.S. Geological Survey, which is still in existence.

The Hayden Survey first began work in Colorado Territory in the summer of 1869, but from 1870 through 1872 pulled back out of Colorado to concentrate its efforts on the Yellowstone Park country of Wyoming and southern Montana. But in 1873 parties of the Hayden Survey were back in Colorado in strength.

By 1873, Colorado lay at the threshold of a period of massive development. Three years later it was to become the Centennial State.

In justifying the moving of his survey activities back to Colorado, Hayden pointed out that there was no portion of the continent which promised to "yield more useful results, both of a practical and scientific character. . . . The prospect of its rapid development within the next five years, by some of the most important railroads in the West, renders it very desirable that its resources be made known to the world at as early a date as possible."

By this time Hayden had become an extremely effective lobbyist for his survey, in both the halls of Congress and with the general public. He was to remain so as long as the survey existed.

During the field seasons from 1873 through 1875, the Hayden Survey concentrated on the mountainous portions of Colorado which lie between 104° 31' west longitude and the Utah border. They extended a primary triangulation network into the mountains from a baseline near Denver, fleshing this out with plane table sketches of the hydrology and topography. Their goal was to produce a topographic and geologic

Opposite: Up Arrastre Gulch from the Shenandoah mill, near Silverton. The San Juan's first American gold discoveries were made near the head of this glacial valley.

Left: Detail from the right half of William H. Holmes panorama, "The La Plata Mountains," made from Hesperus Mountain. The figures of surveyor and recorder in the center foreground were modeled from W. H. Jackson photograph No. 1111, made in 1874 on the summit of Sultan Mountain, near Silverton, Colorado. (Credit: Hayden, Atlas of Colorado, U.S. Geological and Geographical Survey of the Territories, 1877.)

Above: Photographer and dark tent on summit of Sultan Mountain, near Silverton, at time picture of surveying figures in Jackson Photo No. 1111 was made. Needle Mountains are on distant skyline, from Arrow and Vestal on far left to Pigeon Peak on right. (Credit: W. H. Jackson, U.S. Geological Survey.)

Right: Topographers at Work, Ernest Ingersoll, Knocking Round the Rockies, 1882, p. 141. The art work in this engraving is less polished than in the Holmes panorama, and the figures have been reversed from right to left, but the origin of the ensemble is plain from the clothing, the instrument tripod, the barometer hanging beneath it, and the map case on the ground.

[It is interesting to note that the three preceding pictures have a kinship which can be traced to a single ancestor: Jackson, page 102 bottom.]

Bottom left: This photograph was made in 1874 on the summit of Sultan Mountain, near Silverton, in the San Juans. The surveyor standing at the instrument tripod is A. D. Wilson. The recorder, sitting on the ground, is Franklin Rhoda, Wilson's half-brother. (Credit: W. H. Jackson, U.S. Geological Survey.) [This photo is the original upon which were patterned the figures in the Holmes panorama from Hesperus Peak, and the picture entitled "Topographers at Work," from Ernest Ingersoll, Knocking Round the Rockies, 1882, p. 141.]

Left half of William H. Holmes panorama, "The La Plata Mountains," which appeared in the Hayden Atlas of Colorado, 1887.

atlas of Colorado Territory, which was eventually published in 1877 at a scale of four miles to the inch, with a 200-foot contour interval on the topographic maps.

In gathering the field measurements which made this atlas possible, the various parties of the Hayden Survey reached more inaccessible parts of the state than had been reached even as late as the 1930s. They climbed scores of mountain peaks, many for the first time, many among the state's 14,000-foot mountains, using their summits as triangulation stations. This often meant climbing the peak carrying a theodolite, a heavy tripod, a cistern barometer, sketch books, plane table, and angle book. Sometimes a storm would drive them from the summit before the work was finished, making it necessay to retreat and return another day. They braved hail, rain, snow, lightning, and dangerous electrical storms. The accounts of the fieldwork contained in the 7th, 8th, and 9th Annual Reports of the Hayden Survey (1873, '74, '75) are fascinating records of the exploration of the high country of western Colorado. From the high summits the drainage was traced on field sheets, the geologists took samples and measured formations, and scarcely a trail or pass was missed as the parties crisscrossed the ranges.

The scientists and technicians who carried out the survey left their names and personalities on the land where they worked. Hayden recruited the best scien-

tists and field men to be found. The roster is distinguished.

From the standpoint of public recognition the name of William Henry Jackson is perhaps foremost. He had joined the Hayden Survey in 1870, during the first year of its work in the Yellowstone region. At that time, and through the succeeding years of a long career, Jackson became the best-known as well as the best early photographer of the West. His wet plate photographs, produced often under great difficulty, of Yellowstone, the Mount of the Holy Cross, the Anasazi ruins of Mesa Verde, and the great mountain landscapes of the San Juan, earned him an enviable reputation and introduced those western wonders to the eastern establishment.

Hayden saw to it that Jackson's pictures played an important place in the Survey's annual reports, where they could influence legislators to appropriate money for next year's fieldwork.

Opposite: Detail from William H. Holmes panorama, "The Quartzite Group — San Juan Mountains," made from summit of Rio Grande Pyramid. [What was called the "Quartzite Group" by the Hayden Survey is now called the Grenadier Range.] Mountain sheep in the foreground provide scale for this mountain landscape. Holmes put figures in the foreground of many of his panoramas for this purpose. (Credit: F. V. Hayden, Atlas of Colorado, U.S. Geological and Geographical Survey of the Territories, 1877.

(Credit: F. V. Hayden, Atlas of Colorado, U.S. Geological and Geographical Survey of the Territories, 1877.)

But Jackson's work was not the only results from the Hayden Survey in the San Juans. In 1872, three outstanding topographers and geologists joined the Survey: crusty Gustavus Bechler, young Henry Gannett, and the brilliantly talented William Henry Holmes. Holmes served both as a topographer and a geologist. Many of his line sketches from nature illustrated geological reports; his topographic sketches did more to reveal the underlying framework of a region's structure than even a photograph could. His geologic reports were innovatively brilliant.

In 1873, Hayden induced James Terry Gardner, who had worked earlier with King's Fortieth Parallel Survey, to become his chief topographer. A. D. Wilson, who had also been with King, joined the Survey in 1874, along with young Franklin Rhoda, and George B. Chittenden. Dr. Frederic M. Endlich was the scientist for the 1874 party and put his name to the scientific sections of the reports.

Frequently the pages of the 1873 through 1875 annual reports provide a personal record of scientific exploration in an undeveloped mountain region. Rhoda describes the first ascent of Mt. Sneffels and its occupation as a triangulation station; he describes an electrical storm which he and A. D. Wilson experienced on Sunshine Peak near Lake City—a tale to chill the most experienced mountaineer. He remarks on the party's chagrin at finding that a sow grizzly with two cubs had been to the summit of Uncompahgre Peak ahead of them. William H. Holmes made a panoramic field sketch of the Needle Mountains from the east, and another of the La Platas from Hesperus Peak which are among the finest scientific mountain illustrations in the literature.

Meanwhile, in the same year, 1874, the Wheeler Survey began work in the San Juans. Lt. Wheeler had carved out for his military survey a monumental task by assaying to produce a topographic atlas of the southwestern United States west of the 100th meridian. He had begun in Nevada in 1869, but the territory to be covered was so vast, empty, and dry that each district covered was given only a hurried treatment. In the best sense of the word the Wheeler Survey was a reconnaissance survey.

The account of that portion of the Wheeler Survey which was carried out in the San Juans is contained in the report of Lt. William L. Marshall: *Executive and Descriptive Report of Lieutenant William L. Marshall, Corps of Engineers, on the Operations of Party No. 1, Field Season of 1876.* Marshall Pass, over which the Denver and Rio Grande narrow gauge line used to climb from the Arkansas drainage to that of the Gunnison, between Salida and Sargents, bears the lieutenant's name. His report covers the field season of 1874 and 1875.

Peaks used as triangulation stations by both the Hayden and Wheeler surveys include Rio Grande Pyramid, Uncompahgre Peak, and Mt. Wilson in the San Miguel Range. Curiously, Marshall reports a "cinnamon" bear and her cub near the summit of Uncompahgre Peak during their ascent in 1874, a few weeks after Rhoda's ascent. One can speculate whether Marshall's "cinnamon" bear was the same as Rhoda's "grizzly," and what must have been her thoughts at having her airy home invaded twice by humans in the same season.

Uncompahgre Peak, San Juan country's highest summit. (H. L. Standley)

CHAPTER 12

Here They Dug Gold and Silver

The San Juan is gold and silver mining country. The skills of four disparate artisans are needed to win precious metals from the earth. The first of these is the prospector. He roams the hill country looking for promising leads. When he finds a likely lode or placer deposit he stakes his claim in accordance with local, state, or federal mineral laws, and records it with the proper authorities. This procedure gives him a proprietary ownership in his discovery. In addition he must fulfill certain other legal requirements in order to retain ownership.

The second artisan is the miner. He is the one who digs the raw ore out of the earth and sends it to a mill or reduction works which recovers its metal content. Sometimes prospectors and miners are combined in one person. The miner is usually a wage earner; he looks upon himself as a "working stiff," although some mining in the West is done on share or other wageless arrangement, particularly during the developmental stage of a mine's history.

The third artisan is associated with both the miner and the prospector. His skills make it possible to extract ore from its resting place with a minimum of trouble, waste, and cost. He has been tainted by formal education. He is the engineer: chemical, metallurgical, mechanical, geological, or civil. He belongs to the professional and managerial class.

The fourth artisan is a business man, speculator, or entrepreneur. Sometimes he is called a promoter, often with a tinge of disapproval. Sometimes all four sorts of developer are combined in a single individual, although more often not.

A promoter buys and sells mines. He puts together properties in such a way as to accumulate capital enough to turn a promising prospect into a working mine. He meets payrolls and interest payments; buys powder, gads, and timber; and shares in profits if they are to be made. The folklore of mining camps has often tarred the promoter with the brush of shady dealing. This sort of story tends to generate more interest than the humdrum truth which might be stranger than fiction. Promoters who had an unshakable faith in a mine or a mining district were often all that stood between obscurity and a bonanza.

All four developers of mining camps have had their part in bringing every working district to full flower. Without the prospector most discoveries would not have been made in the first place. Probably the prospector had itchy feet and was ready to move on as soon as he had made his strike. If he could sell to a promoter, he did and would then hit the trail. It was the promoter, with dreams of something larger, who consolidated a few individual holdings into a viable property; borrowed money from bankers; and hired the miners, the engineers, and the geologists who opened the property to production. At the root of the venture stood the miner, the man who turned the discovery of the prospector and the dream of the promoter into a producing commercial enterprise.

* * * * *

Two basic types of metal deposits have been prospected and mined in the West. One is the lode deposit; in this type the mineral is encased in the rock where it was originally formed in the geologic past by the injection of migrating mineral solutions or molten magma. The second is the placer deposit; this consists of fragments of lode mineral which have been disintegrated by weathering and transported by the erosional

Opposite: Miners loading drilled holes with powder (dynamite) sticks.

A prospector setting out for the high country. (T. A. Rickard, Journeys of Observation, *1907.)*

Arrastra Gulch was named for a Mexican arrastra. A crude mill such as this ground the first gold-silver ore from the Little Giant Mine. (Louis Simonin, La Vie Souterrane, *1867.)*

agents of wind, water, and ice to a new location, at some distance from the site of its original formation.

In most of the mining country of the West the earliest deposits found and exploited by prospectors and miners were placer deposits. The gold found at Sutter's mill at Coloma, which touched off the California gold rush of 1849, was placer gold. It had been injected into fissures in the granitic rocks of the Sierra Nevada, from which it was subsequently weathered and transported by stream action to Sutter's mill race.

John H. Gregory's discovery of the lode deposits at Central City, which initiated the Pikes Peak gold rush to Colorado in 1859, has been described by Young as follows: "Winterbound at Fort Laramie on the Over-

land Trail, Gregory had spent his idle months panning southward between the Cache la Poudre and Pikes Peak, then working up the Vasquez Fork (Clear Creek) of the South Platte. He took whichever fork of Clear Creek showed the best indications, coming at last to a side ravine — now Gregory Gulch — where the color suddenly increased and then abruptly faded out a bit higher up." This led Gregory to suspect "that he had just passed the outcrop of the lode of origin."

In 1870, Miles T. Johnson found the Little Giant vein in Arrastra Gulch, the first lode mine of record in the San Juan, by following promising "float" up the gulch.

Different ore deposits require different mining methods. Lode ore is traced below the surface by tunnels and shafts, blasted free from its matrix, and hauled to the surface for processing.

Placer deposits are found in present or ancient streambeds, usually mixed in sand and gravel with which it has been washed from its original lode. It must be shoveled from the streambed and separated from the worthless gravel and sand, with which it is mixed, in sluice boxes, rockers, and gravity tables.

· · · ·

The stereotype of the western prospector depicts him with his faithful burro packed with shovel, pick, and gold pan; bed roll, beans, and flour. He is hunkered beside a desert dry wash or a mountain stream, swirling a pan full of dirt.

Like sheepherders, prospectors were seldom gregarious; they were used to talking to themselves. They were not above working for wages to get a grubstake, although they preferred to talk a grubstake out of some sympathetic local tradesman or a starry-eyed newcomer. Their most enduring characteristic was the abil-

Fred Helfrich, prospector, seated in front of his hut at the mouth of Noname Creek, Animas canyon.

ity to live in perpetual hope. The next panful of dirt would contain the proof of their faith, the next round of blasting powder would break through to the big bonanza.

Permit me to describe an individual San Juan prospector who will serve as model for his class. His name was Fred Helfrich. He is dead now, but even alive he would not have objected to service as a role model, although his individual characteristics and background may make him idiosyncratic.

He had mined and prospected in many parts of the San Juan, but when I knew him, his theatre of operation was at the mouth of Noname Creek in the Animas Canyon twelve miles south of Silverton. Some merchant of that town was grubstaking Fred.

Fred had an artificial right arm, fitted with a hook. As a young man he had drilled into a "missed hole"

while single-jacking in a mine at Rico, in the La Platas. The arm had been removed just below the elbow; Fred was lucky to have survived.

A missed hole is a dangerous situation associated with blasting in a mine. A charge of dynamite, which fails to go off in a previous round of blasting, is a mortal danger to miners who come to the work face afterward. If they know an undetonated charge is still in the face, they must either remove it, a dangerous and ticklish operation, or set another charge to blow it up. If they don't know it is there, because of a miscount by the previous crew who loaded the charge, the stage is set for tragedy. Fred Helfrich had driven his drill into an undetonated, unreported charge of explosive.

He had adjusted himself well to the use of the artificial limb with which he was fitted, being able to do a remarkable number of the ordinary tasks which are

Narrow gauge train approaching the clearing opposite the mouth of Noname Creek in Animas canyon. Here train crews left supplies for Fred Helfrich in the 1930s.

required of a miner who lives alone in the mountains: cut firewood, cook, wash dishes, even drill holes in his prospect adit with a single jack and hand steel.

The core of Fred's dwelling was a one-room tar paper shack with a single window and a door made from the end of an upright piano box fastened to a rickety door frame with leather hinges. The bottom of the door had swept out a pie-shaped wedge of dirt at the front of the shack. When Fred left to work in his prospect during the day, he jammed the door shut with a bar through a pair of strap-iron loops, after which he stuffed gunny sacks into the chinks between the door and its irregular frame to discourage groundhogs, squirrels, and chipmunks.

The "house" was situated in a pleasant aspen grove beside Noname Creek. Some of the aspens had been cut, windfalls had been picked up, and all of these logs had been piled, jackstraw-fashion, over the top and sides of the tar paper structure, per chance to keep it from blowing away. One could walk along the trail, fifty feet from the shack and never see it. Even close up, it looked like an untidy beaver lodge.

One evening I went up from our camp in the aspen grove just as Fred was returning from his day at his prospect. Raspberries were ripe and Fred had picked a hatful of them along the railroad tracks on his way back to the cabin. (In those days, the narrow gauge Denver and Rio Grande Western pulled a mixed train through the Animas Canyon from Durango to Silverton and returned, three times a week. Silverton got most of its supplies that way. Mountaineers, fishermen, prospectors, and sheepherders rode these trains to any point along the canyon. The train crews dropped off supplies, newspapers, and mail to Fred Helfrich and other canyon dwellers as they went back and forth.)

Fred unbolted the door, took out the gunnysack stuffing, and invited me in. The single windowpane shed about as much light as the translucent walls of an eskimo's snow house.

From the door at one end of the shack, a well-trodden path in the dirt floor skirted a newspaper-littered, double-decker bunk on the near right wall, crossed to an open space in front of a small cookstove at the center of the left wall, and continued to the side center of a bunk against the back wall.

Fred crossed to the small oilcloth-covered table which stood under the shelving to the right of the stove and transferred the raspberries from his hat to an empty gallon fruit can.

I declined his offer of a bowl, having just eaten at our camp. He put part of the berries in a chipped graniteware bowl, sprinkled some sugar over them, and poured on a generous covering of condensed milk.

When the bowl was half-finished, Fred reached up to a foot-thick stack of old, dry pancakes on the shelf above the table, selected one about the middle of the stack, held the cakes above the selected one with the hook on his right arm, and with his good hand deftly jerked out the chosen morsel, which he dipped into the raspberry-stained milk.

All this while Fred had been regaling me with bits and snatches of his past life. When he lit his pipe, a little later, he found that the bit did not clamp firmly between his toothless gums, with which he had been munching the raspberries and pancakes. This sent him on a rapid search of all the shelves, and the pillow at the head of his bunk. Finally he dived headfirst between the bedding to the foot of the bunk and came up triumphantly with the missing plates, which he put in his mouth after wiping them off perfunctorily.

Fred was introduced to the world of work at the early age of fourteen on a Great Lakes sailing vessel, running down lakes with cargoes of wheat which had been loaded at the western end of Lake Superior and were discharged at Buffalo or one of the other Lake Erie ports. He painted for me a vivid word picture of icy decks and frozen spray in the rigging at season's close.

After such early training, three years later, the transition was relatively easy to underground mining in the Calumet and Hecla Mine, located in the copper deposits of the Keweenaw Peninsula on the south shore of Lake Superior.

Fred's mentors in the mine were mostly Cousin Jacks—Cornishmen—who had learned their trade in the tin and copper mines of Cornwall. There were no finer miners transplanted to the New World during the settling of the West. Fred was an apt pupil. When he left the Keweenaw copper belt, after four or five years, he was able to hire on as an experienced miner from the moment he first landed in the San Juans.

Fred's first mining in the San Juans was in the Creede district, followed by experience at Silverton and then to Rico, where he lost the arm.

To my great surprise I next learned that somewhere along the way Fred had absorbed enough information to become a respectable authority on the military campaigns of Napoleon Bonaparte. He undoubtedly made good use of the time needed to heal the amputation and be fitted for and learn to use the artificial arm.

That Fred's erudition came from do-it-yourself reading rather than the halls of *academe* was betrayed a number of times by his inadvertent mispronunciation of common words which would have been spoken differently had he learned them from the lecture podium. He showed no reluctance about using such terms; he always used them in the proper context and with a correct meaning.

But for all of his fractured pronunciations, Fred's

grasp of the nuances of Napoleon's campaigns across the length and breadth of Europe and North Africa was sure. Somewhere he had mastered the general outline of Napoleon's life and had then fleshed this out with a wealth of detail. He had gone to authentic sources. With a little prompting I can remember from his talks such battle names as Marengo, Austerlitz, Jena, Borodino, Leipzig, and Waterloo. Fred also seemed to have a fixation with Marshall Ney. He must have read somewhere a biography of that old soldier's soldier — "the bravest of the brave." A few years later in a college literature course, I read the descriptions of the battles of Austerlitz and Borodino in Tolstoy's *War and Peace.* The chaotic confusion stemming from the titanic struggles of the opposing armies came to life for me — all through the remembered word-pictures of a crippled prospector who once dwelt in a beaver hutch on the banks of Noname Creek.

In the early summer of 1939, train crews noticed that Fred Helfrich had not been picking up his supplies beside the tracks at Noname Creek. Investigation disclosed him ill in his hut. He had contracted Rocky Mountain spotted fever from numerous tick bites. He was taken to Silverton where he succumbed to the fever and other complications. He is buried there in Hillside Cemetery.

Fred Helfrich may not have been the most typical prospector in the West, but a self-taught expertise on the campaigns of Napoleon is no more untypical than a thorough knowledge of central African drums, Egyptian woodwinds, medieval heraldry, the phylum Thallophyta, or the history of the Custer Massacre is un-typical of a bank manager. Expertise thrives where it is found, and who is to raise an eyebrow. A hobby-horse is to be ridden not judged. Fred's story is enough like the tales of many others of his lonely calling, that it can serve as a respectable surrogate, despite its over-gloss of Napoleonic romanticism.

• • • •

Mining is an ancient and honorable craft, although at one time it was the sole province of slaves. It follows a thread through history from the Nubian gold mines of the Egyptian pharaohs, 4,500 years ago; to the silver mines of Laurium, worked during the Golden Age of Athens; to Italy, Spain, Crete, Cornwall, the New World, and thence back to Africa and Australia. Mining has played its part in the social and economic history of mankind: an Athenian slave could be rented to mine silver ore at Laurium for the equivalent of about four dollars per year; miners struck at Butte, Coeur d' Alene, and in the San Juans in the late 1800s and early 1900s for a wage of three dollars per day (thus adding a powerful voice to the rising chorus from the American labor movement); and a contract miner today can make well over a hundred dollars a day in good ground and with a fair contract.

A mineral vein can best be compared to the meat in a ham sandwich: a slice of "goody" squeezed between opposing masses of barren country rock. In the San Juans the late Tertiary mineral veins, which have contributed about eighty percent of the mineral wealth of the region, are arranged in circular patterns around the rims of the great collapse calderas which supplied

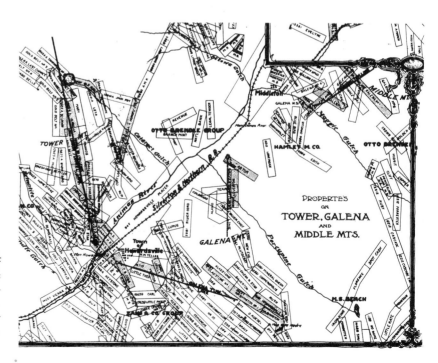

Map of mineral claims on Tower, Galena, and Middle mountains in the vicinity of Howardsville, a few miles up the Animas River, to the northeast of Silverton, Colorado. (From a map prepared by H. S. Sanderson for Report of the North American Mining Co., *Denver, Colorado, December 20, 1927.)*

A Mexican miner picking ore from a rich stope in the Esperanza Mine, northwest of Mexico City. Note the ancient candle holder and hand pick, contrasted with the relatively modern square set timbering, introduced by American and British mining engineers. (T. A. Rickard, Journeys of Observation, *1907.)*

the volcanic material which blankets much of the region. The fissures and faults which were invaded by hot mineral solutions which cooled to mineral veins were usually in a near-vertical attitude so that most veins can be compared to the slice of ham in a sandwich which stands on edge. The mineral-bearing solutions welled upward along these zones of weakness from the magma chambers which had been the source of the great volcanic explosions which once raked the San Juans.

Some veins are relatively short, measured horizontally along their trace at the surface; others may literally run for miles across the landscape, slicing through mountains and coursing across valleys. Sometimes they may cross other veins in bewildering patterns. These contortions may lead to costly litigation over the ownership of veins which intersect, filling the court records in mining country with the expert testimony of mining engineers and the learned arguments of opposing lawyers.

At its most primitive, mining involved picking away at the rock with picks, gads, and shovels. A gad is a long steel bar with a wedge-shaped tip which is used to pry material from the rock face. The pick and long-handled miner's shovel are just as they have been depicted from time immemorial by artists and cartoonists. Ancient miners used to build fires against the working face, trusting to the expansion and contraction of the rock to loosen it. Later, they found the process could be hastened by throwing cold water on the heated rock. This method was still used as late as the early nineteenth century in some Latin American mines. Hannibal is reputed to have used this method

to clear a path for his elephants over the Alps. However, it is said he substituted wine for scarce water — an unspeakably wasteful act, which could only have been the option of a military man.

Today rock is broken by the use of blasting powder. Holes are drilled into the rock in a pattern so that the distance between holes forces all of the energy of the blast to be absorbed in shattering the rock between the holes. Once drilled, the holes are packed tightly with blasting powder which is then detonated. The pattern in which they are drilled, and the sequence in which the individual holes are detonated causes the first few holes to excavate a space in the rock face into which the remainder of the rock can be thrust by the later explosions.

Holes for blasting in solid rock are made with a percussion drill. Before the advent of the compressed-air-driven rock drill in the 1870s, all holes were made by driving a steel drill into the rock by repeated blows from a hand-held hammer. In single-jacking a single miner turned and struck the drill with a four-pound single-jack hammer; in double-jacking two men worked as a team, one turning the drill stem between each blow, while the other struck the drill with an eight-pound double-jack sledgehammer. It was slow, hard work.

Whether the drilling is done by hand or by machine, the hole is chipped out by rotating a chisel-edged drill bit a fraction of a turn between each blow of the hammer. The steel chisel bit chips away slivers of rock at each blow. At one time the chisel bit was forged, sharpened, and tempered on the end of the drill steel by a blacksmith; today the cutting head is a removable

Splitting rock by fire. (Louis Simonin, La Vie Souterrane, *1867.)*

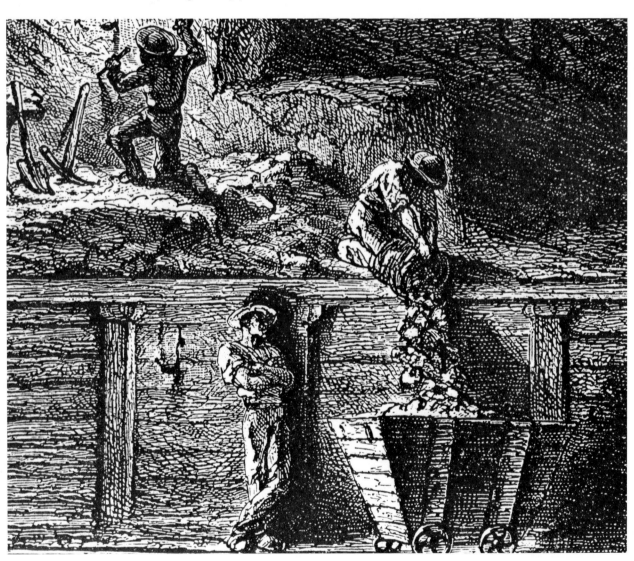

Single-jack drilling and bench mining by descending levels as practiced in the metal mines of Saxony, Rhenish Prussia, and Hungary in the early nineteenth century. (Louis Simonin, La Vie Souterrane, *1867.)*

Drilling a down hole in a shaft or winze by double-jack method. (Louis Simonin, La Vie Souterrane, *1867.)*

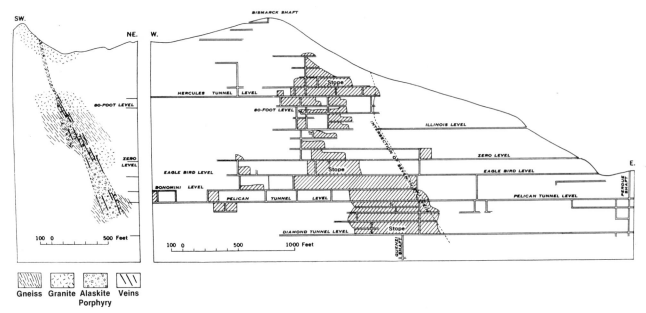

Vertical cross section showing the arrangement of working levels and stopes along the vein in a mine. To the left, at the same scale, is a section at right angles to the trend of the vein depicting the relationships of rock types in which the veins are located. (After Figure 34 and Plate 27, Professional Paper 63, U.S. Geological Survey.)

tungsten carbide bit which screws onto the end of the drill stem. When dull, the bit is removed from the stem and is replaced by a sharp bit. Dull bits are sharpened by machine grinding.

Silicosis, locally called "miner's consumption," a ravaging disease caused by the imbedding of sharp fragments of silica dust in the narrow lung passages of hard rock miners, reached epidemic proportions shortly after machine drilling was introduced. Compressed air drills exposed miners to much more silica dust in shorter periods of time than was the experience with hand drilling. The debilitating disease flared dangerously. The imposition of safety regulations led to the quick development of a drill with a hollow drill steel through which water under pressure could be introduced to the drill bit to wet down and wash away the rock dust and cuttings, at their source, before they could get into the air.

Reduced to simplest terms, mining involves the breaking of rock in and surrounding the vein, and the removal of this broken material to the surface where it can be treated mechanically and chemically to separate vein material from waste rock. The breaking and hauling to the surface is the province of mining; the separation of waste from ore and its treatment to recover the minerals is the province of milling, or as it is sometimes called, *ore dressing.*

If a mine could be viewed from the outside like one of the glass-sided rodent burrows which have become popular displays at many zoos and museums, it would reveal a logical orderliness. All of the parts of the underground workings are arranged in such a way that men, machinery, trackage, air and water lines can be brought to the site of the ore deposit with a minimum of energy loss. If at all possible, haulage drifts, adits, and crosscuts rise gently from the outside to the locations where ore is being mined. Empty ore cars, drilling machinery, powder, timber, and men are hauled up slight grades, while loaded ore cars are held back as they coast downgrade to the outside. The fissures and channels through which groundwater flows downward below the surface, are cut at numerous places by the mine workings. The lowest opening to the surface is usually a drainage ditch. Mines in flat country are kept unflooded by expensive pumping, but in mountain country gravity does the work.

During the height of the San Juan mining boom, most local mines had a set of substantial surface workings. Timber was cleared from the site and used for construction. The principal buildings served the mining activity: snowsheds over adit entrances and trackage, stables, compressor house, blacksmith shop, warehouse, an isolated powder house, a steam power house (or transformer yard after the advent of electricity), water tanks, a boarding house for miners, a machine shop. Isolated locations forced self-sufficiency on most San Juan mines.

If the mine was large enough and the ore was rich enough the owners usually opted for an ore reduction mill. The first ore taken from the Little Giant Mine, near Silverton, was shipped, more than 250 miles by pack mule and ore wagon, to Pueblo, Colorado. The

Surface workings at Camp Bird Mill, southwest of Ouray, Colorado. A much-feared calamity during San Juan winters is fire. This fire, which followed a snowslide on March 17, 1906, destroyed the main Camp Bird mill. (T. A. Rickard, Journeys of Observation, *1907.)*

The Barstow mill in the Red Mountain mining district, between Ouray and Silverton, Colorado, about 1900. (Starns-Orendorf)

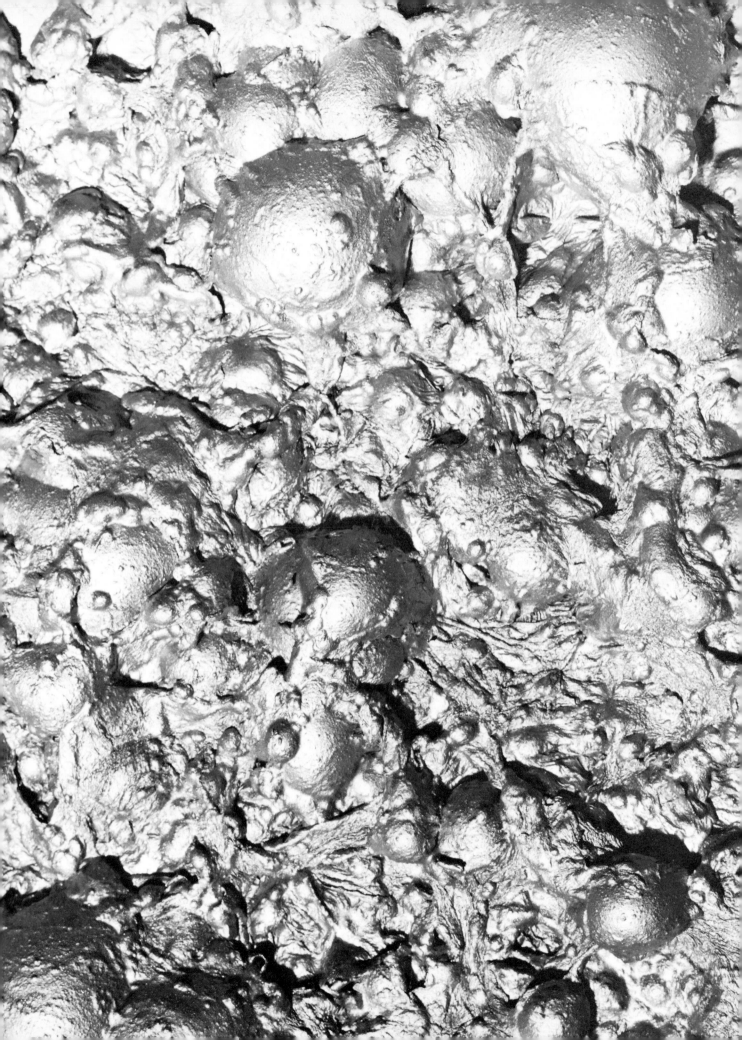

Metal-laden bubbles are here being scrapped by a rotating paddle over the front lip of the flotation cells.

following year, a California stamp mill was hauled in to help cut some of the shipping costs.

Mills were usually sited at the mine; however, if the mine was located on steep and difficult terrain, the mill sometimes had to be placed at a distance. The Smuggler Union Mine, near Telluride, delivered ore down an incredibly steep cirque headwall, by tramway, to the mill at Pandora in the valley bottom. The Sunnyside, up the Animas Valley from Silverton, carried its ore to a large mill at Eureka by tramway. The logistics of haulage, supply, and engineering dictated the location of the mill.

A mill required the shelter of a rather large building which was almost always sited on a hillside so that ore could be fed through the various processes by gravity from one level to another. Broken ore from the mine was dumped in ore bins at the top level of the

Opposite: Close-up of metal-charged skins of bubbles at the surface of the pulp in a flotation cell.

mill. From there it went through crushers, stamp mills (these were later displaced by ball mills and tube mills), and mixed with water to produce a sort of slurry, called pulp. The pulp was then flowed over amalgamation plates, through gravity separation units, and a cyanide plant, or, in more recent years, through a selective flotation unit. Here various metallic components of the pulp were floated to the surface of boxlike cells on the skins of air bubbles whipped up as froth by mechanical beaters in the bottoms of the cells.

All of these processes provided a selectively concentrated product for shipment to the smelter, where the last ounce of metal was separated from the dross by fire. After its final treatment at the mill the remaining pulp ran out to the tailing ponds where the finely ground waste rock settled out and the water was returned to the nearest stream.

The pervading impression of a high basin which cradles a working mine is auditory. The multipitched sounds carry beyond the confines of the mountainsides and are sometimes heard before the source can be seen. The sharp percussion of a stamp mill, or the muffled rumble of a ball mill, join the thunder of underground explosions, the rock-splintering crunch of a jaw crusher, or the more ponderous rumbling of a cone crusher, accented by the clatter of tipped ore cars discharging over the waste dump or into the ore bins. All impart a trembling to the earth, which spreads unease beyond the range of the sound itself. Working with hard rock is a noisy occupation. Huge piston compressors pump great volumes of air into holding cylinders, called receivers, from whence pipes lead it underground to operate the air drills, mucking machines, and small hoists in the crosscuts and stopes. The chunking of the compressors is punctuated at regular intervals when the relief valves on the receivers vent air as it comes to full pressure with an explosive "Choof!"

Underground, the hoarse chatter of drill steel being driven into rock rumbles at a distance, like the mid-range pedal notes of a pipe organ. Shock waves are transmitted great distances through solid rock. If it were not so, the seismograph which picks up the shock waves generated by an earthquake halfway around the world would not be a practical instrument.

One can experience some of the nuances of this subterranean concert by standing or sitting alone in a stope or raise or crosscut, a mile or more underground, and turning off his head lamp. The palpable darkness forces one to depend upon hearing alone as the dominant sense receptor. Dripping water, the sound of one's breathing, the rustle of clothing become acutely magnified. Yet the throbbing mumble of drilling can be both heard and felt as a low-key accompaniment to the closer sounds. One is reminded of the numerous accounts of miners trapped underground by cave-ins who communicated their plight or location by tapping on rails, air pipes, or water pipes.

For all of its engineering orderliness, the underground workings of a mine is one of heavy industry's dirtiest and noisiest environments. The thundering bellow of a stoper or jack-legged drill at close hand is ear shattering. The narrow confines of drift or stope magnify the racket. Escaping exhaust air, having done its work, fills the passage with a palpable fog. Water charged with dust and rock chips, runs from drill holes like suppurating sores. Mud is everywhere, made by water delivered to the cutting head of the drill bit and mixed with seeping groundwater which issues from fissures and seams in the rock. When the miner comes off shift, he removes his digging clothes in a change room, showers off, and changes to outside clothes. Digging clothes are usually so dirty and stiff they will stand alone in the middle of the floor if they aren't hung on a peg.

Two crews drilling in a single heading. Each drill is mounted on the forward extended arm of a drilling jumbo. This gives more maneuverability in a narrow heading than would be provided if each drill were mounted on a single vertical column.

Rust is a lasting impression of the underground world. Rails, pipes, skip buckets, the outside of ore cars, the nonarticulated parts of mucking machines, bolt heads, fish plates — every metal surface exposed to the pervading water and high humidity bears a bloom of red rust. Only cable hoist drums, skip skid plates, the running surface of rails — the metal parts which have to be greased, or oiled, or which rub together in daily use escape the red stain.

In this cacophonous, wet, sometimes cold, sometimes hot, rusty, dangerous world the miner puts in his eight-hour shift. If you ask him why he does it, he will usually reply, "A man has to eat!" Although he curses the system in which he works, and he will change jobs between mines, or even from one mining district to another, at the merest of whims, he takes great pride in the fact that he is one of the industrial world's most highly skilled workers. So long as underground mining has to be done and he keeps his health and vigor, he can find a job. The contract system, for which he and his hard-nosed predecessors fought long ago, and which gives him a certain entrepreneurial freedom, permits the elite of his calling to earn $30,000 or more a year, spiced, of course, with a certain amount of danger. He is as independent as Beelzebub at a church picnic. He refers to himself as a "working stiff"; his underground clothes are "diggers" or "digging clothes"; he "rustles" a new job, and when he quits a job he's gone "deep enough."

His place in American literature has never been as secure and romanticized as that of the cowboy. One wonders why. Perhaps the thread which runs through the explorer, fur trapper, trader, Daniel Boone, yeoman farmer, livestock-rancher, cowboy in the idealization of westward expansion in the United States has been planted indelibly in our psyche. There seems to be more compatibility between the average American and the wide, free, open spaces where antelope, buffalo, cattle, horses, and cowboys roam, than there is with the bowels of the earth where miners toil in dirt and noise.

William Cullen Bryant wrote: "Like a quarry slave, scourged to his dungeon at night." There is something of slavery, the pit, darkness, in the mining environment. The slave miners of Laurium have somehow transmitted their stigma across Europe to the New World over 4,000 miles and almost as many years. Perhaps the lack of trolls, dwarfs, and Fafnir in our western mythology predisposes us against the dark recesses of earth where dragons lurk and treasures are hidden.

A Gardner-Denver mucking machine is here scooping up broken rock (muck) at a heading. In most modern lode mines, air-driven mucking machines have taken the place of the shovel, called by miners a "muck stick," and the wheelbarrow.

CHAPTER 13

Storm and Strife

San Juan County at the turn of the century had not yet been shaken by the labor troubles which had and would soon bring destruction of life and property to western mining camps. But the seeds of storm and strife had already been planted. By the time the upheaval had run its course, on the eve of World War I, it would be called a "Rocky Mountain Revolution."

Its origins can be traced to predawn history when the first human being enslaved a fellow human. This enmity between slave and master had its echoes in the term "wage slave" which spiced the speeches of late Victorian labor organizers and socialist politicians. Holbrook mentions that it found expression in the preamble to the constitution of the International Workers of the World (I.W.W.), which was promulgated by the Chicago founding convention of June 1905: "The working class and the employing class have nothing in common."

The immediate forerunner of the violence which was to grip Telluride from 1901 to 1904, occurred in the Coeur d'Alene mining district in northern Idaho, but the thread goes back further. The first union of western hard rock miners was organized at Virginia City, Nevada, in 1863. Then, in the 1880s, local unions were organized in the Coeur d'Alene district — a local union, there, built the first miner's hospital in the district. In the 1890s compressed air drills were introduced, reducing the number of skilled miners needed per ton of ore produced. The Mine Owners Protective Association of Idaho was organized in the Coeur d'Alene district in 1891. Confrontations between the local unions and the Mine Owners organization led to a lockout in January of 1892. The introduction of non-

union miners led to sporadic warfare through the summer until an uneasy peace was negotiated later in the year.

In May 1893, at Butte, Montana, the Western Federation of Miners (W.F.M.) was organized. Union recruiters spread throughout the western mining camps. For the first time in the hard rock mining industry, many small local unions were gathered together into a single federation.

Friction between the Western Federation of Miners and the Mine Owners Protective Association of Idaho slowly grew in the Coeur d'Alene district until April 29, 1899, when it exploded in violence. Members of the Western Federation of Miners gathered at Wardner, Idaho, across the river from Kellog, drove guards, nonunion miners, and mill men away from their posts and blew up the Bunker Hill & Sullivan concentrator. The damage ran into hundreds of thousands of dollars. At the time, the Idaho National Guard was in the Philippines. After pleas from Idaho's governor, Frank Steunenberg, President McKinley declared a state of emergency. Martial law was invoked, and federal troops arrived four days later. Members of the Western Federation of Miners were rounded up (many had already fled) and were shipped out of the area. A permit system was introduced under which no Federation member could work in the district.

Stewart Holbrook has observed: "The power of the Western Federation in the Coeur d'Alenes was almost wholly destroyed. . . . This nineteenth-century Diaspora of hundreds of miners, with bitterness in their hearts, bore seeds that were to flower with striking malevolence in hard-rock camps throughout the West."

The trail of violence was punctuated during the next few years by murders at Telluride, Butte, in the Bitteroots, San Francisco, and Cripple Creek. In 1904, under the depot platform at Independence, near Cripple Creek, a dynamite bomb was exploded just as the night shift of nonunion miners was assembled

Opposite: A group of miners in front of the Smuggler-Union boarding house at the Bullion Tunnel, Marshall Basin, above Telluride. About 1900. (Denver Public Library, Western History Department)

An aerial view of Telluride, Colorado, showing the relationship between the town at the upper end of the San Miguel valley and the surrounding mountains and basins in which are located the region's principal producing mines.

to catch a train. There were thirteen fatalities, six badly mutilated, and twenty or more who received less serious injuries. On December 30, 1905, exgovernor Frank Steunenberg, who had called upon McKinley to send federal troops during the Coeur d'Alene troubles in 1899, was killed by a dynamite bomb planted at his front gate in Caldwell, Idaho.

The instrument of most of these killings and acts of destruction was an amoral miner, explosives expert, and hired killer named Harry Orchard who, after the Steunenberg murder, was captured and confessed. He spent the remainder of his life in the Idaho State Penitentiary. William E. Borah prosecuted and Clarence Darrow defended "Big Bill" Haywood, George Pettibone, and Charles Moyer in their trial for complicity as the Western Federation's ruling hierarchy who, it was claimed, had hired Harry Orchard as a hatchet man. Darrow won their acquittal, but by then (1906) the Western Federation of Miners was in a state of disarray, from which it never completely recovered. Darrow went on to defend many others, among them an obscure Tennessee schoolteacher named John T. Scopes in the famous "monkey" trial; Borah went to the U.S. Senate, shortly, where he served long and with distinction; Moyer and Pettibone faded into obscurity with the gradual decline of the Western Federation; and "Big Bill" Haywood wielded, for awhile, the levers of power in the International Workers of the World (Wobblies), which had split off from the Federation of Western Miners after the 1906 trial. In 1917, at the beginning of the U.S. involvement in World War I, Haywood was picked up along with several hundred other Wobblies; the organization by then had become overtly revolutionary. They were all charged with sedition. Haywood was convicted and sentenced to Leavenworth Prison. He appealed and was released on 30,000-dollar bail. He skipped bail and reappeared in Russia, where he was welcomed by the new communist regime as a worthy escapee from the pesthole of capitalism. However, he was never afforded the respect he thought he deserved and died in 1928, an embittered, self-exiled man.

. . . . .

Telluride lies at the upper end of the San Miguel River, on the western side of the San Juans. The town itself occupies the narrow, flat-bottomed, glacial-scoured valley, at an elevation of 8,700 feet above sea level. On both sides and at the upper end of the valley, cliffs rise 3,000 feet to the lower lips of a number of glacial cirques which rise to the crests of the range. Telluride's only means of ingress and egress lies either along the twisting canyon of the San Miguel River, through which the narrow gauge Denver and Rio Grande Western Railroad was built in the 1880s and where Colorado State Highway 145 is now found, or up

cliff-hugging trails from the heads of the upper cirques, over 13,000-foot passes and down other passes to other camps such as Ouray or Silverton. Telluride is in what the French describe as a "cul-de-sac"; we use the terms "dead end" or "blind alley."

Most of the producing mines of the Telluride district are located in the upper cirques surrounding the main valley head: Marshall Basin, Middle Basin, Savage Basin, Ingram Basin, Bridal Veil Basin, Jackass Basin, Silver Lake Basin, La Junta Basin. All supplies and building material for the mines, and ore from the mines, had to be moved up or down the switchback trails and roads which threaded the cliff sides between town and the basins in which the mines were located. In a few cases, aerial tramways spanned the elevation difference between valley bottom and cirque lip. Festooning the top of this huge, west-facing amphitheatre was a ridge of 13,500-foot mountains: Dallas Peak, Gilpin Peak, Mount Emma, St. Sophia Ridge, Mendota Peak.

At the time of the 1901-1904 labor troubles, Telluride was a town of 5,000 with the outward amenities of late Victorian, middle-class respectability, overlayed with the garish appurtenances of a boom town mining camp: the well-to-do employer and owner class mixed with miners, native, and foreign born; saloons and gambling houses were placed cheek by jowl with a splendid hotel and a little gem of an opera house; a red light district with cribs and fancy bordellos jammed close to miners' homes.

. . . . .

The characters who took part in the Telluride strike of 1901-1904, were as disparate as a drama of violence demands. They played their assorted parts—heroes, villains, buffoons, goons, philosophers—in deadly seriousness; their stage reached far beyond the confines of the mountain-girt valley. The historical reviews have been mixed, depending on the persuasion of the reviewer. Characters who appeared as heroes in one review, played the parts of buffoons or villains in another. A modern day historian is compelled to steer a chancy course between the reminiscences of mine owners and managers, the strikebreakers hired by the owners, union officers, and the rank and file union members; the active participants are all gone now.

The strike, which was one of the initial causes of the troubles, was called by the Telluride Miners Union No. 63, Western Federation of Miners, on May 4, 1901. Hard rock miners are often "boomers" who move freely from one camp to another as the mood or circumstance strikes them; undoubtedly, some of the miners in the Telluride Union were bitter veterans of the Coeur d'Alene wars two years earlier.

All of the other mines in the Telluride district had gone to an eight-hour day at three dollars per day, except the Smuggler-Union Mine, which used the old Cornish fathom system of contract mining. In this system the ore mined is measured by a cubic measure which is reckoned as 6 feet (a fathom) times 6 feet times the thickness of the ore vein being mined. Unfortunately for the Smuggler-Union contract miners, the Smuggler vein at this location was unusually thick, forcing them to mine extra amounts of ore to produce their fathom. The Smuggler-Union general manager, a hard-nosed Welshman named Arthur Collins, refused to take the case to arbitration, despite the fact that all of the other mines in the district had gone to the three-dollar, eight-hour day. The union struck, and Collins, acting under orders from the owners, brought in strike-breakers (scabs).

Neither side budged until July 3, 1901, when a mob of 250 union miners climbed from the town to surround the Bullion Tunnel, at 12,000 feet in Marshall Basin, as the scabs came off night shift.

A union miner named John Barthell was shot and killed by a mine guard when he stood up to announce to the night shift that they were under arrest. In the pitched battle which followed, two strikebreakers were killed and the mine superintendent was wounded. By evening, cooler heads prevailed; Vincent St. John, president of the Telluride Miners Union, and the San Miguel sheriff arranged a truce but were unable to prevent the strikers from rounding up eighty-eight of the disarmed scabs and marching them over Imogene Pass to Ouray, where they were warned against returning to Telluride. This was the first of many mass deportations of miners out of Telluride during the next three years.

On July 6 Collins was forced to sign a three-year agreement with St. John which provided for a three-dollar pay for an eight-hour shift.

The ensuing winter was a time of natural and man-made disasters. On November 20, 1901, a fire at the Bullion Tunnel of the Smuggler-Union suffocated twenty-four miners. Afterwards, the Smuggler-Union was found guilty of corporate negligence. On February 8, 1902, an explosion at the Japan Mine killed two miners. On March 1, 1902, an avalanche at the Liberty Bell Mine destroyed the boarding house, and nineteen men in rescue parties on the Liberty Bell Trail were killed. Several other miners were killed on other remote slopes.

Later in the spring of 1902 Vincent St. John called together representatives from several other San Juan local unions to consolidate into the San Juan District Miners Union. That spring, the local union built the Miners Union Hospital in Telluride. The Telluride Miners Union seemed to be at the peak of its power. Fearing union domination of the camp, businessmen gathered together into a protective association, follow-ing the example of the Telluride Mine Owners Association.

On August 1, 1902, Eugene Debs, perennial candidate for U.S. president on the Socialist ticket, spoke at the Telluride Opera House. On Labor Day, Edward Boyce, the Western Federation of Miners president and "Big Bill" Haywood, the W.F.M. secretary, spoke at a picnic in the town park. In October of 1902, the Telluride Business Man's Association invited William Jennings Bryan to speak on the evils of socialism. He delivered a carefully edited revision of his famous "Cross of Gold" speech — Telluride was a gold camp!

In November, James Peabody, a business-oriented banker from Canyon City, was elected governor of Colorado.

On November 19, 1902, Arthur Collins, the Smuggler-Union general manager, who had so stoutly resisted the inauguration of the eight-hour day, was killed by a shotgun blast through the window of his home at Pandora, site of the Smuggler-Union mill. Although Vincent St. John was charged with the murder, and fifty-seven other indictments were brought against union members, the charges were not sustained by the evidence. The murderer or murderers were never apprehended.

Now, the fat was in the fire. At this juncture the drama took on the inevitability of Greek tragedy. The great panjandrum of the mine owners and managers was a character straight out of Gilbert and Sullivan: Bulkeley Wells, son-in-law of Colonel Thomas Livermore, owner of the New England Exploration Company, which had only recently purchased the Smuggler-Union for $8 million from a group of English capitalists headquartered in Shanghai, China. Wells was enamored of flashy uniforms; was a militarist at heart; showed pride in his Harvard education; flaunted expensive tastes in wines, food, and women; had reached his position, in part, by marrying the boss's daughter; and was fanatically opposed to unions.

When Arthur Collins was murdered, Wells, who had been managing the Smuggler-Union from Denver, moved to Telluride, shut down the Smuggler for a month in memory of its slain general manager, and initiated an active campaign to rid the mining camp of its union miners. Wells was a general in the Colorado National Guard, and as such had the willing ear of Governor Peabody.

During the next year and a half an active campaign against the Western Federation of Miners broke down the resistance of the union. Hired gunmen were employed to threaten and harass union miners. On two different occasions National Guard units were dispatched to Telluride — November 20, 1903 to February 21, 1904 and March 24, 1904 to April 16, 1904 — each time at the request of Wells and the local business

Aerial view of Aspens at Buckhorn Lakes between Cimarron and Montrose.

A road on Horsefly Mesa, west of Ridgway.

Air view of the upper reaches of the Black Canyon (right).
The Lone Cone viewed from the east, near Dolores Peak
(below).

A shaft house on Red Mountain, south of Ouray.

Abandoned boarding house at Mountain Top Mine, southwest of Ouray.

First Presbyterian Church of Lake City, built by Rev. George Darley in 1876.

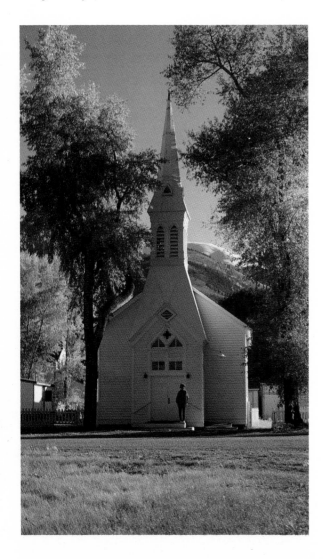

The Alvin McCoy home in Ouray, an outstanding example of Bonanza Victorian architecture.

Sheep camp on Wilson Mesa, west of Telluride (left).
View down Animas Canyon taken near Silverton (below).

Narrow gauge tourist train entering Animas Canyon, north of Durango.

Ouray.

Skiers above Red Mountain Pass.

On October 27, 1902, presidential candidate William Jennings Bryan delivered a heavily edited version of his famous "Cross of Gold" speech from a bunting-draped platform in front of the New Sheridan Hotel on Telluride's main street. (Denver Public Library, Western History Department)

Left: Bulkeley Wells in Colorado National Guard uniform. (Denver Public Library, Western History Department)

Right: Colorado Governor James Hamilton Peabody, about 1902. (Denver Public Library, Western History Department)

129

Above: Twice during the 1901–1904 labor trouble National Guard units were called to Telluride to enforce peace. For the same reason National Guard units were also called to Cripple Creek at the same time. This 1903 picture shows National Guard troopers with a Gatling gun on the main street of Cripple Creek. (Denver Public Library, Western History Department)

Right: This political cartoon appeared in the Rocky Mountain News, Denver, December 16, 1904. Bythat time the close cooperation between Governor Peabody, the National Guard, and the extractive industry owners and managers had raised a smoldering controversy in the state's press. (Denver Public Library, Western History Department)

men's alliance. Ostensibly, the National Guard mission was to protect nonunion strikebreakers from the threats of strikers. The military units built stockades (bull pens) on Telluride's main street, where union miners were incarcerated. When enough "undesirables" had been accumulated, they were herded onto flat cars, or into boxcars, and transported to Ridgway, even as far as New Mexico or Kansas, unceremoniously dumped at track side and told to not return to Telluride. One group was dumped at the top of Dallas Divide, in winter snow.

During the period between the two military occupations, Wells formed a company of local militia from among members of the Citizen's Alliance, mine owners, managers, businessmen, and like-minded citizens, making himself the "law" in San Miguel County. He had a stone redoubt built at the summit of 13,000-foot Imogene Pass and garrisoned it with riflemen to stop all traffic on the trail between Ouray and Telluride — union miners had been infiltrating Telluride by walking over the pass. This guard post, which still stands, was named Fort Peabody.

Although it was no consolation to either camp, the patterns enacted in Cripple Creek were now carried out in Telluride. Strikebreakers were threatened, booed, and sometimes subjected to violence by union men, whereupon mine and mill owners appealed for the protection of troops. Local owners and alliances then promised to buy the scrip which the state issued to pay the cost of the military occupation, which eventually, statewide, was estimated at over a half million dollars.

At one point, Wells distributed a cache of National Guard rifles to his local militia company, unleashing a vigilante mob on Telluride's known or suspected union men and sympathizers.

On April 16, 1904, General Bell, who commanded the second military occupation, turned the district back to Wells. On June 15, 1904, Governor Peabody again declared an end of martial law. The summer saw a continuation of vigilante deportations of union men. Finally on November 29, fifteen months after it started, the strike was called off by the Western Federation of Miners.

On December 1, 1904, Bulkeley Wells agreed to a three-dollar shift and an eight-hour day at the Smuggler-Union Mine and mill. Other mines in the district followed his lead, refusing to hire any man who had ever been a member of the Western Federation of Miners, or the Telluride Miner's Union.

Sporadic incidents occurred after the termination of the strike. It was once said that "skeletons were found in the hills for years afterwards."

Even Bulkeley Wells did not escape entirely the aftermath of the violence in which he had held so prominent a part. On March 2, 1908, he was shaken by the explosion of a bomb, thrown or placed under his sleeping porch bed at Pandora. The mattress had protected him from more serious injury. No one was ever tried for this assault. He was luckier than Idaho's exgovernor Steunenberg in 1905.

Two mementos of the labor troubles of 1901–1904 in the San Juan are still visible: the frost- and snow-riven remains of Fort Peabody at the summit of Imogene Pass, and the monument over John Barthell's grave in the Telluride Cemetery, erected by the Western Federation of Miners.

Grave of John Barthell, Telluride Colorado, Lone Tree Cemetery.

Inscription on monument erected by Telluride Miner's Union, Western Federation of Miners, at grave of John Barthell, killed at Bullion Tunnel, Smuggler Union Mine, July 3, 1901.

CHAPTER 14

From Here to There

San Juan country has an annular transportation pattern. The mountains stand at the center of the region; the primary transportation routes surround the mountains in a ring, like a doughnut on a peg. The next smaller order of transport connections (secondary) probe inward from the annular primary ways to the heads of the mountain valleys, where the mining camps are located. From each mining camp a tertiary, radiating system of roads and trails reaches out to the individual mines and mills, which are located near the tops of the ranges in cirques and on mountainsides.

Towns located on the primary annular ring are Gunnison, Montrose, Durango, and Alamosa (Monte Vista). The mining camps at the heads of the secondary links are Lake City, Ouray, Telluride, Rico, Silverton, and Creede.

During the discovery period a haphazard network of wagon roads and pack trails crisscrossed the mountain zone. Some of these have been resurrected more recently as jeep roads. When the toll road and railroad pioneers got down to business in the 1880s, they became practical. They encircled the San Juan with a narrow gauge railroad, the Denver and Rio Grande Western Railroad, from which secondary lines could tap each of the mining camps. This was as far as they could go.

A miner, a preacher, a mine owner, a geologist, or a prostitute who wished to travel from Ouray to Lake City or from Telluride to Silverton, had two choices: take one of the hill trails which crossed one or more high passes and which were often snowbound in the winter, or travel down the valley to the encircling rail line, and along it to the spur line which climbed the valley to his/her destination. The distance from Ouray to Telluride over the mountains by Imogene Pass is twelve miles; the distance by way of the narrow gauge was fifty-three miles. The disparity in distances by trail and railroad between Ouray and Lake City, and between Creede and Lake City, is more than twice as much.

In only one instance did a primary route cross the range between two mining camps—Ouray to Silverton over Red Mountain Pass; and this had to wait for the motorcar and the state highway system. Otto Mears, the "Pathfinder of the San Juan," was balked in his attempts to drive the narrow gauge track down the Ouray side of the pass farther than Ironton, although he did succeed in building a toll road along the Uncompahgre Canyon, just above Ouray.

• • • •

Whether the burro preceded the mule or the horse as the San Juan's first pack animal we have no way of knowing. The Escalante-Dominguez expedition of 1776 used horses as riding animals and mules as pack animals. It is certain that Mexican settlers who pushed up the Rio Grande and its tributaries in the southeastern San Juan brought burros as well as mules and horses into the country.

The lowly burro was the cheapest and most reliable transportation available to the early San Juan prospectors. The burro could subsist on the land while his master often depended upon a grubstake (usually a month's rations) supplied by some storekeeper in a nearby settlement, exchanged for a 50–50 split of the ownership of any claim which the prospector might discover. When the hard San Juan winter closed in, the prospector and his burros drifted to lower country and did their prospecting there—ready to move back to the high country with the melting of spring snows.

Opposite: Six-horse team and stage coach on Mears' toll road near Ouray, Colorado, about 1900. (Starns-Orendorf)

133

Otto Mears, Pathfinder of the San Juan. (Sidney Jocknick, Early Days on the Western Slope of Colorado, *1870–1883.)*

Above: Otto Mears' toll road two miles south of Ouray, about 1900. Mt. Abram in background, center. The "Million Dollar Highway" was later built along this right-of-way, along the Uncompahgre canyon between Ouray and the Red Mountain mining district. (Starns-Orendorf)

Left: Pack trail to the Silver Lake Mine near Silverton, Colorado. (T. A. Rickard, Journeys of Observation, *1907.)*

135

When a prospect had been developed to the stage of a producing mine, the hauling of supplies and ore was usually turned over to more powerful transport agents — pack mules, teams and wagons, aerial tramways, and trucks.

Burros and mules continued to play a part in the exploitation of the San Juan mining frontier until quite recently. The King Lease of the old Camp Bird Mine used mule transport, winter and summer from the late 1920s until closed by the onset of World War II. One of the most successful packing outfits in the period between 1910 and 1940 was operated by Olga Schaff, later Mrs. W. C. Little, raised on a San Juan foothill ranch by immigrant German parents. Serving mines in the La Plata Mountains, northwest of Durango, she and her husband found that burros could operate over more rugged terrain than either mules or horses and were far tougher. At one time they were packing forty of the little animals.

It was inevitable, however, that the mule would edge out the burro for packing. If the burro was the logical choice for a low-budget prospecting trip, the mule had unique advantages when packing became a high volume business, particularly at the most inaccessible mines in the roughest high country.

In 1917, the writer of a U.S. Army Engineer Field Manual on animal transportation offered the following observations: "The great advantage of pack transportation is its mobility, and this consideration is often paramount. A good pack train, well handled, can make 2 miles to 1 of the best wagon trains on good roads and more on bad ones, and can besides go where there are no roads at all and where the country is so rough that roads can hardly be made and wagons could not pass them if they were made."

Among other advantages of the mule, the writer of the field manual lists, "The mule is tougher and hardier than the horse, less subject to disease or to inflammation from slight injuries, and usually yields more readily to treatment." He offers gratuitously the following counsel: "For indications of disposition look to the head and eye; the latter is especially a good index. Avoid mules with extra long heads; also those with hollow or dish faces. The eyes should be set well apart and stand out prominently. Eyes close together or sunken show a mean disposition. A good mule has a soft kindly look in his eye which is difficult to describe but is easily recognized."

None of your long-faced, beady-eyed, narrow-between-the-eyes mules for this army engineer. One is reminded of Caesar's dour prediction: "Yond Cassius has a lean and hungry look; He thinks too much: such men are dangerous."

The U.S. Army was using pack mules for transport as late as the Korean War in the 1950s. Animal trans-port still flourishes in the more isolated parts of the "Third World."

Most of the large transportation outfits in the San Juans got their start with pack outfits, later graduating to wagon transport, in a few cases to toll roads, and in one case to a miniature railroad system. The names include Buddecke & Diehl, Aschenfelter, Wood, Lavender, Schaff, Thompson, Mears, and other less publicized stage and express lines.

* * * *

Around the turn of the century, the daily shipment of gold bullion from the Tomboy Mine, above Telluride, was running into four and even five figures daily. The danger of theft was very real. Just across the range, the Camp Bird Mine's bullion shipment had been robbed, the driver and two guards killed. Butch Cassidy and his gang had roared in broad daylight down the streets of Telluride, cleaned out the local bank, and escaped to Robber's Roost.

The horns of the dilemma were sharp. To let the bullion shipment go unguarded was to invite theft; to provide a guard advertised its whereabouts and provided an attractive temptation for those inclined toward larceny.

Mine officials racked their brains for some safe means of transport. A mule skinner came up with an inspiration.

For years miners and prospectors had been in the habit of hiring horses and pack mules at Telluride stables, riding to the diggings, then turning the animals loose to return to the stable of their own accord.

A burro pack outfit leaving Ouray with lumber for a nearby mine. Almost always burros were allowed to run free in a loose pack, rather than tied head to tail in a train like mules or horses were. (Starns-Orendorf)

Opposite: The patient burro was usually the pack animal of choice by the early prospectors in San Juan country.

Packer loading sacked concentrates at upper King Lease mill, Camp Bird, Imogene Basin, winter 1932–1933.

Six-horse team and stage coach at tunnel through the remains of Riverside snowslide on Mears' toll road near Ironton Park, about 1900. (Starns-Orendorf)

Mule pack train at the American Nettie Mine, near Ouray, Colorado. (T. A. Rickard, Journeys of Observation, 1907.)

Four hands are better than two when loading a pack animal.

It was common to see unloaded pack mules and horses with empty saddles returning day or night on any of the roads and trails radiating from the mining camp. The animals were trained to return to the stable when they were released. They were accepted as part of the scene.

As the scheme was worked out, the bullion mule went up to the mine from Telluride at the end of the daily pack train, carrying her share of the supplies—timber, powder, food, coal. When the train was unloaded, she was taken from her place on the string and led to the retort room at the mill. There two parcels of freshly retorted gold bullion were dropped into the empty panniers which hung from her packsaddle, one on each side. The parcels were small, though heavy; the panniers seemed empty. The mule's halter rope was tied to the front tree of the pack saddle, and she was given a slap on the rump to start her on her way.

Down the steep trail she went, taking her time, pulling to one side for upbound pack trains, stopping to nibble a tuft of grass, shying away from any downbound miner who might try to catch her for a free ride to town. She could not have traveled more discretely had she known that thousands of dollars worth of gold was thumping against her sides.

When she arrived at the stable, the hostler, who was a party to the scheme, took the two parcels of gold to the railway express car safe. Should the bullion mule loiter, which was seldom, the narrow gauge train was held until she arrived.

For years she carried the Tomboy's riches down the mountain without benefit of escort, faithfully discharging her simple but important duty. Never once was she molested; the Tomboy's gold always went through, mainly because no one ever knew when or how it went. Like Poe's "Purloined Letter" its location was too matter-of-fact to be noticed.

"Without pride of ancestry or hope of posterity" the sturdy, small-hoofed, hybrid offspring of horse and burro saved the day in the rough country which defied roads and most of the other mechanical hauling methods. More than a few isolated communities and mines owed their very existence to him.

Qualities inherited from both branches of his family tree made the mule a more valuable animal than either parent. He possessed the surefootedness, endurance, patience, and sobriety of the burro, and the courage, strength, and vigor of the horse. To these qualities should be added native intelligence, and a steadiness

Opposite: The Camp Bird pack train leaving the upper mill in Imogene Basin with loads of sacked concentrates. Winter, 1932–1933.

140

The small mail pack train at Lower Camp Bird Mill, winter 1932–1933.

under strain which made the animal ideal for the complex packing problems associated with the early mining industry.

The normal load for a pack mule in mine service ranged from 200 to 400 pounds, depending upon the nature of the load and whether the trip was uphill or down. Trails were usually narrow and steep. The mules were tied halter to tail in trains or strings of about fifteen, with a packer on horseback in charge of each string. At sharp bends in the trail, the packer would slow up, and each mule would edge around the corner, being careful not to pull the ones ahead or behind off balance.

It has been said, with some justification, that a good packer and a mule could take a grand piano over the steepest, most crooked trail in the Rockies without a scratch.

The Tomboy Mine once had a new compressor to be installed at the mine. It was shipped to Telluride on a flatcar. There it was dismantled, but even after it had been reduced to its smallest component parts, the largest of these, an iron casting, weighed about 700 pounds. The packers hardly hesitated in accepting this challenge to their ingenuity.

They constructed a strong sawhorse, much like that used by a carpenter, but tall enough to place the crossbar over a packsaddle, while the wooden legs just cleared the ground on each side of the mule. A large-

Opposite: The mailman with a small pack outfit passing a six-horse sled at the narrows on the Canyon Creek road between Ouray and Camp Bird Mill. Winter, 1932–1933. The last three horses in the string, closest to the camera, are being led, saddled, to the mill for miners or other personnel to ride back down the trail to town later in the day.

boned, rugged mule, who had proved his strength and intelligence was chosen for the job. The casting was lifted by chain hoist and lashed to the sawhorse. The saddled mule was led under it, and the whole lashed to the packsaddle.

When the pack animal became tired he could squat and let the sawhorse legs take the weight of the casting while he rested. It took him but a few minutes to learn this trick. The single mule carried the whole weight the entire six miles without a quiver, resting at short intervals as he felt the need.

In response to this type of haulage problem, by the turn of the century, the Ingersoll-Rand Drill Company, one of the largest manufacturers of mine compressors, was building sectionalized models, in which the flywheel was made in seven parts, each frame in three, and each cylinder in one. A 45,000-pound sectionalized compressor would require 150 mule trips, with no single load heavier than 300 pounds.

Odd shapes and sizes of equipment often taxed the mother wit of packers. Heavy, large-diameter compressed air pipe usually came in twenty-foot lengths. Swiveled cradles were placed on the packsaddles, and two mules were used for each length of pipe, one at each end. Getting these ungainly loads around sharp switchbacks in steep trails called for cooperation. Both front and back mules learned to jockey forward and backward until the section of pipe was gotten around the sharp corner.

The heavy track cable for the Liberty Bell aerial tramway, above Telluride, presented another headache in mass haulage. The longest sections of the 1⅛-inch diameter cable were 1,200 feet in length. About eighty mules were rounded up and made into a single pack train. Each mule carried about a 15-foot section of the cable lashed to the packsaddle. The procession crawled up the steep mountainside like a quarter-mile-long centipede — one of the longest pack trains ever used anywhere in the West. Ironically, the willing mules were carrying in the cable for the tramway which was soon to displace them as a means of haulage.

Packers valued the patient beasts which were their means of livelihood. They took care to see that packsaddles were always adjusted to the individual mule — thus preventing sore backs. The breast band and breech band were fitted carefully to keep the load in the middle of the animal's back. Navajo blankets served as favored saddle blankets.

They pulled any mule out of the string at the first signs of lameness. Working mules were given vaca-

Opposite: Camp Bird pack train arriving at the upper mill of the King Lease with loads of dynamite — 50 pounds per box, 200 pounds per mule.

Pack train on Canyon Creek road just below Camp Bird Mill. Crossing a small avalanche track.

tions on rich pasture part of each year, and while working they were grain-fed and stabled comfortably. A good pack mule was nearly always worth more than a horse. The mule could carry more, was tougher and more adaptable, and had a greater earning power than his half brother.

Every mule in the string had a name and responded to it, or at least recognized it. Some names were descriptive, such as Jughead, Blacky, or Whitey. Others were more whimsical. A packer saw nothing incongruous in naming a mule for a good friend or relative. One mule in the Camp Bird string, out of Ouray, a number of years ago, bore a fanciful name which seemed illogical. Repeated questioning of the packer eventually disclosed that the mule was named for a popular waitress in town, who had recently, and apparently with good cause, murdered her husband. It developed that the mule had a vicious habit of trying to kick the packer's head off when least expected.

Late at night in the dead of winter, many years ago, two pack trains and their packers fought through mountainous drifts to the snowbound village of Ironton, between Ouray and Silverton, Colorado. They were carrying much-needed food and supplies. For thirty-six hours they had battled neck-deep snow in a blizzard. Mules and packers were at the point of collapse.

Not until the mules were unloaded, did the packers discover that every stable and barn in the little settlement was full to overflowing. There was fodder but no shelter. The situation was desperate, for to leave the exhausted mules without protection for another night would mean that many of them would die of exposure.

After an hour's search the packers found one two-story building which was temporarily unoccupied—a brothel which had been boarded up by its owner and proprietress during her yearly stay in warmer climes. The building was managed by a local merchant. Over his violent protests, the packers forced the front door and led in their animals. The mules were deployed throughout the building, upstairs and down, in rooms and hallways. Sharp hoofs cut flashy carpets; hay and oats were eaten from washbowls and bureau drawers. The faithful animals bedded down in gaudily curtained boudoirs.

Later the owners of the mules gladly paid for the damage; any one of the animals was worth far more than the price of a fancy lady's cubicle.

. . . . .

The narrow gauge railroad, a solution for the problems of steep grades and narrow valleys, had its origin in the hill country of western and central Europe. It was later introduced to South Africa by the British, where it was known as the Cape Gauge. Still later, the British-built miniature railroad which climbed by spectacular loops and switchbacks to the Himalayan hill station of Darjeeling became a celebrated triumph of the engineer's art.

Colorado was introduced to the narrow gauge by General William Jackson Palmer, whose Denver and Rio Grande Western was first envisioned as a north-south link between the transcontinental Union Pacific, the Rio Grande Valley, and eventually Mexico. It was routed to draw custom from the potentially rich farmland of the Colorado piedmont, the wind-seared ranchlands of South Park, and the fat pastures of the San Luis Valley.

The siren call of San Juan silver and gold diverted the Denver and Rio Grande Western from its planned original route. During its turbulent first thirty years, up to the turn of the century, the toy narrow-gauge Denver and Rio Grande Western encircled and partly penetrated the heart of the San Juan. In spite of reorganizations and takeovers, the battles over disputed rights-of-way, the three-foot gauge track, dumpy little engines, and tiny cars brought the blessings and drawbacks of railroad transport to one of the most rugged regions of the world.

Before the advent of the passenger automobile and the motor truck, the San Juan was "narrow gauge" country. It can still bear that title by virtue of two surviving segments of the former system: the Durango-Silverton route and the Cumbres and Toltec route which crosses and recrosses the Colorado–New Mexico border between Antonito, Colorado, and Chama, New Mexico, on the southeast corner of the San Juans.

Both lines are operated during the summer months, and the Silverton line, which has now passed into private ownership, is operated up the Animas Valley to the mouth of the canyon during the winter months. Complete schedules are published and both runs have become so popular that reservations must be made as much as a year in advance to be sure of a seat during popular holidays.

At the height of the mining boom, both lines, as parts of a single system, were kept open year-round. During the winter, avalanches plagued the Durango-Silverton run in the Animas Canyon, while ninety-foot-deep snowdrifts often closed the Antonito-Chama-Durango run.

The Durango-Silverton line threads a water-level route through the spectacular canyon of the Animas River. The river which carved this cleft between the Needle Mountains and the West Needle Mountains was named by the Spaniards, Rio de las Animas Perdidas (the River of Lost Souls), perhaps in an effort to invest it with a more awesome reputation than its gentler reaches, beyond the mountains, justified. They need not have resorted to such press-agentry. The thousands of tourists per season who make the daily

Narrow gauge freight train on the last grade below the summit of Cumbres Pass, Cumbres and Toltec route of the Denver and Rio Grande Western railroad.

round trip through the canyon enjoy the unique experience of using a nostalgic means of transportation from an earlier era. This is no amusement park, Disneyland, tourist-trap "ride"—the mountain summits rise to 14,000 feet above the canyon, and the river boils through a gorge in billion-year-old granite. Shipments of gold, silver, and concentrates used to come down these rails, while flour, potatoes, bacon, mail, and dynamite used to go up. The trains, as of old, still stop to take on or let off hikers, fishermen, backpackers, and climbers. Scenes are written into Hollywood movies which make use of this authentic narrow gauge "set." David Niven and Cantinflas took perilous passage on the Durango-Silverton run during their dash *Around the World in Eighty Days; Butch Cassidy and the Sundance Kid* blasted open the baggage car and seemed to jump into the Animas River above Rockwood in their escape.

David Lavender has captured most evocatively, in the prologue to *The Rockies*, the sights, sounds, and smells of the narrow gauge journey from Salida to the heart of San Juan mining country at Telluride.

The Cumbres and Toltec Scenic Railroad, which is operated jointly by agencies of the states of Colorado and New Mexico, traverses less spectacular country, with the exception of its airy perch above Toltec Gorge. However, its roadbed has been engineered over such a crooked course that even names such as the "Whiplash" and "Tanglefoot Curve" fail to do it justice. The line stands as an engineering feat of daring ingenuity.

In the early fall of 1883, Ernest Ingersoll, the journalist and naturalist, traveled over the Cumbres and Toltec Railroad (it was then a part of the Denver and Rio Grande Western system) in a chartered train consisting of several cars fitted out for the comfort of the journalist, his wife, and several friends. The private excursion carried them as far south as Santa Fe, as far north and west as Salt Lake City, and into most regions of the Colorado Rockies which were served by rails. The adventure is described in Ingersoll's book, *Crest of the Continent*, which went through at least forty-two editions before going out of print in 1901. Ingersoll's prose is a little rich for modern tastes, but he had a flair for touching a responsive chord in his contemporaries. He describes how the Cumbres and Toltec climbs out of

"Cañon of the Rio de las Animas." (Ernest Ingersoll, The Crest of the Continent, *1885.)*

the San Luis Valley up the eastern flank of the San Juans, as follows:

> To surmount these the track is arranged in long ingenious loops, in one place, known as the "Whiplash," extending into three parallel lines, scarcely a stone's throw apart, but disposed terrace-like on the hillside. . . . The road here is like a goat's path in its vagaries, and wagers are made as to the point of the compass to be aimed at five minutes in advance, or whether the track on the opposite side of the crevasse is the one we have just come over, or are not about to pursue.

• • • • •

Just as the San Juans brought out the best efforts of U.S. narrow gauge builders, they performed a similar service for the obscure designers of the above-ground haulage systems for the mines. By the eve of World War I the San Juan mining activity had reached its apogee. Most of the mines were located in high glacial basins, usually above timberline. To get supplies and equipment in and ore and concentrates out, it was necessary to build cliff-hugging pathways which zigzagged up mountain faces. Sometimes the original trails were later widened to accommodate teams and wagons, but in a great many cases the engineering of a useful road was almost beyond the current state of the art. Furthermore, in order to build a suitable road it was necessary to blast and dig out every inch of the right-of-way from valley bottom to mine adit.

Experiments in Europe had begun on haulage cable-ways which we have come to know as aerial tram-ways; the modern descendants of these systems now grace the slopes of every mountain ski resort in the world. In this sort of rugged country, a mine manager could see economic advantages in such a haulage system. The cableway was supported on towers which might be as much as a thousand feet or more apart. There was no need to dig out a continuous roadway along the intervening mountainside, except for a temporary trace to haul in the material for building the towers. The cableway could be built directly down or up very steep slopes and could be built in short straight segments to accommodate turns. Once in operation, ore could be moved by a continuous stream of buckets downslope from the mine to the mill, and supplies could be moved upslope on the empty buckets.

T. A. Rickard, a noted mining engineer and editor, published a small book in 1903 entitled *Across the San Juan Mountains.* The following excerpt from that slim

Opposite: Denver and Rio Grande Western narrow gauge train entering Animas canyon just above Rockwood on the line between Durango and Silverton, Colorado. (Compare this with the preceding scene: "Cañon of the Rio de las Animas," Ingersoll, The Crest of the Continent, 1885.)

"Animas Cañon and the Needles." (*Ernest Ingersoll*, The Crest of the Continent, *1885.*)

Above: Hauling sacked concentrates down the Canyon Creek road from the Camp Bird Mill to Ouray for shipment by rail to the smelter. (T. A. Rickard, Journeys of Observation, *1907.)*

Left: Miner riding uphill in an empty ore bucket on a tramway somewhere in the San Juan. (T. A. Rickard, Journeys of Observation, *1907.)*

volume outlines the cost-effectiveness of an aerial tramway system:

The cost of a tramway of this kind depends upon the contour of the country traversed, and the distance from the manufacturer who supplies the material. In the high altitudes of the San Juan, say 10,000 feet or over, the cost of material for an installation having a capacity of 200 tons per day of 10 hours would be about $2.10 per foot of tram line, and the cost of freight, plus erection, would be about $1.15 more, so that the tramway one mile long, having the capacity mentioned, would entail an expenditure of about $20,000. Actual expenditures for tramways in this district has ranged from between $2.50 and $8.00 per foot; as a rule the cheap one proves the most expensive on account of the greater cost of maintenance and repairs. The Camp Bird tramway is 8,550 ft. long, with an angle station; the fall, in the length mentioned, is 1,840 ft. and the cost, all told, was $55,094. It is a thorough piece of engineering work. At the present time, it is worked on two 8-hour shifts, with a duty of 210 tons per diem. The operating cost is 17.6¢ and the maintenance 1½¢ per ton. A large amount of material is sent to the mine, as a back load, and the cost of handling this also is included in the figures just quoted.

Most of the later tramways in the San Juan country belong to the Bleichert and Otto systems, in which the bucket is supported by a bail which hangs from bogey wheels which travel on a fixed track cable. The buckets are drawn along by a traveling traction cable. Each bucket, after it is loaded with ore at the mine, is attached to the traction cable by a toggle grip. When it reaches the downhill end of the tramway, the grip is unclamped, the bucket dumped, then passed around to the up-going side to be clamped again to the moving traction cable and pulled up to the mine end of the system. The track cables are anchored at each end, but the traction cable is an endless loop coming down on one side and going back up on the other.

The airy steel strands which spanned chasms and laddered down cliff sides like giant spider's webs were a prominent feature of the San Juan mining landscape. Until a few years ago, two thin steel threads plummeted steeply downward across the Uncompahgre Canyon from the mine to the Banner American mill, just at the north edge of Ouray, Colorado. Rumor has it that an unwary airplane, some years back, fell prey to this gargantuan trap. Whether it did or not, the old track cables were taken down and the up-valley view of Mt. Abram is no longer encumbered by this obtrusive evidence of the region's mining past.

There are numerous other places in the San Juan where these unique haulage systems, now crippled by rust and rotting towers, still span slopes and leap across chasms: at the Buffalo Boy, in Cunningham Gulch, above Silverton; in Governor Basin, below St. Sophia Ridge; at the Mayflower, in Arrastra Gulch, above Silverton; at the Smuggler-Union and Liberty Bell above Telluride. At many sites, where the management prudently took down the cables and salvaged them for scrap steel when the mine went out of production, the gaunt towers now march unencumbered up the hillside. Wherever they are found they testify to the problem-solving genius of the San Juan's early mining engineers and the suppliers of equipment and ideas, locally and at a distance who helped them to dig and mill the gold and silver.

Tramway buckets between Mayflower mine and mill. Looking down the Animas canyon toward Silverton.

High tower, Mayflower tramway near mouth of Arrastre Gulch, near Silverton, Colorado.

CHAPTER 15

Power

In 1888, Lucien L. Nunn, a diminutive young lawyer who was a newcomer to the humming mining camp of Telluride, and an enthusiastic admirer of Napoleon, was retained as a manager by the owners of the Gold King Mine. The Gold King had fallen upon evil times; the property had been attached by court order to pay its debts. Nunn's examination of the books disclosed that the most crippling cause of the Gold King's malaise was the cost of coal for the steam power plant which drove the air compressor, crusher, and stamp mill. The Gold King was located high in Alta Basin on the east side of the Lake Fork of the San Miguel River, between Telluride and Ophir. Coal had to be packed to the mine by mule or burro train at a cost of $40 per ton. For this operating item, alone, the Gold King's costs were $2,500 per month.

Nunn obtained a stay of proceedings in order to win time to investigate alternative sources of power.

These were years of scientific ferment. The advent of the Industrial Revolution, a century and a half earlier, had introduced the concept of mechanical power to the rapidly industrializing Western nations. Direct waterpower had been harnessed to grist mills; the Dutch captured the wind to pump water from the polders they were reclaiming from the sea; the pumps which de-watered mines were being powered by steam instead of plodding men or animals; mobile steam engines, called locomotives, were hauling goods and passengers over steel rails; steam engines supplied motive power for boats, taking the place of sails or tow ropes.

One aspect of the power revolution was receiving special attention during the last two decades of the nineteenth century—the transmission of power from a stationary generating source, such as a waterwheel or stationary steam engine, over a distance to the point of consumption. Among numerous options being considered were compressed air (already being used to drive underground rock drills); high pressure water; cable drives such as the traction cable of an aerial tramway, or the cable cars of San Francisco; belt and pulley systems, such as the forest of overhead pulleys and belts in many factories. By the middle 1880s electrical transmission of power was more than just a gleam in the eyes of dreamers.

The chronology of electrical power transmission is crucial to the history of its development in the San Juan; consider the following dates and events:

1821   Michael Faraday (England) builds an apparatus which demonstrates the principles of the electrical motor.

1833   Thomas Davenport (U.S.A.) invents a crude electric motor for which he obtains a patent but which never has a practical application.

1873   Zenobe Theophile Gramme (Austria) demonstrates the first electrical motor of commercial significance. Direct current. Up to this time electrical motors were curiosities—electricity seemed best suited for lighting.

1881   Gaulard (France) and Gibbs (England) acquire English patents for an electrical distribution system which makes use of alternating current in series.

1882   Thomas Edison (U.S.A) installs the first electrical distribution system for lighting in New York City. This is a direct current system.

1885   George Westinghouse (U.S.A.), inventor of the railway air brake, purchases the patents for the Gaulard-Gibbs alternating current distribution system, which had been developed in 1881.

1886   William Stanley (U.S.A.), a young engineer in the employ of Westinghouse, develops a transformer and an alternating current generator.

Opposite: Power poles and power line on hillside between the Gold King mill and the Ames power plant in the valley bottom. The line shown here is on the alignment of the original powerline erected in 1891, and may even have used some materials from the old line. The pinnacle on the skyline to the right is Lizard Head.

157

1886   Westinghouse and Stanley (U.S.A.) make the first practical demonstration of alternating current power transmission at Great Barrington, Massachusetts. From the generator the voltage was stepped up by transformer from 500 volts to 3,000 volts, transmitted a distance of 4,000 feet, then stepped down to 500 volts again by transformer at the receiving end of the line.

1888   Nikola Tesla (U.S.A.) develops an induction motor to be run by alternating current. George Westinghouse acquires the patent.

[For several years about this time, Thomas Edison and George Westinghouse carried on an acrimonious debate in the popular press over the merits and demerits of direct current and high-tension alternating current as the system for large-scale electrical transmission. The primary advantages of alternating current included the property which permitted it to be increased or decreased in voltage by use of a fixed transformer. Also, alternating current could be transmitted at higher voltages with smaller line losses over smaller wire sizes for a given power factor than was the case with direct current.

Edison and his supporters espoused the cause of direct current, branding high-voltage alternating current as dangerous to the general public, which, of course, it was, despite its other advantages. At one point during the debate, Edison's supporters prevailed upon the New York State authorities to install a Westinghouse alternating current generator to power the state's electric chair at the state penitentiary. But the public mostly ignored this pointed argument.

Westinghouse won the argument in the end. It has been asserted that Edison's lack of theoretical

The Gold King mill between Ophir and Telluride, Colorado. Site of first alternating current electric power transmission. (Denver Public Library, Western History Department)

knowledge of electrical fundamentals led him astray in this case, despite his demonstrated genius in the practical application of science.]

1890–1891   A generator, three-mile transmission line, and 100 horsepower motor were put in use at the Gold King Mine, near Telluride, Colorado. Single phase, 3,000 volt, alternating current system.

1891   First three-phase, alternating current, 100 kilowatt power generators installed at the Lauffen Power Station on the Neckar River, Germany. Three phase, alternating current at 15,000 volts transmitted to Frankfurt, 110 miles away.

1893   A two-phase alternating current generator supplies power for lamps and motors at World's Columbian Exposition (Chicago). Potential of electric power transmission catches fancy of the general public.

1893–1896   Alternating current, hydroelectric power station installed at Niagara Falls. Power transmitted twenty-two miles to Buffalo. Westinghouse alternating current system chosen over direct current system of Edison.

Lucien L. Nunn. (Stephen A. Bailey, L. L. Nunn, A Memoir, *1933.)*

The foregoing chronology highlights two facts. First, it fixes the relative date of the pioneer hydroelectric, alternating current, power transmission venture in the San Juans — 1890–1891. Second, and vastly more important, it makes clear that the development of any technological innovation is usually not the fruit of a single brilliant discovery, but the result of the slow buildup of one discovery upon another, like the placement of one brick upon another in the construction of a wall. Davenport built upon the discovery of Faraday and was followed by Gramme, Gaulard, Gibbs, Edison, Stanley, and Tesla. Nor should we forget that at the proper moment George Westinghouse became an entrepreneur, purchasing patents and pushing their development into practical products.

This whole chain of events became the solution to the Gold King's power problem and at the same time played a part in the worldwide development of electric power transmission.

Other electric power installations had been made in the San Juan prior to the Gold King alternating current venture. There was lighting at Telluride and Ouray and power at the Revenue Mine on the Ouray side of the range, but all of these installations had been direct current and had operated with indifferent success.

In May of 1890, L. L. Nunn wrote his brother Paul N. Nunn, a former midwestern high school principal: "I wish you would investigate the subject of transmission of power by electricity. . . . I am not sure of putting in the plant, but if I do I want you to take charge of the construction, and not let any one know that you are not an old hand at the work."

Paul responded quickly to his brother's request. According to his biography in *Who's Who in America,*

Paul N. Nunn. (Stephen A. Bailey, L. L. Nunn, A Memoir, *1933.)*

Paul Nunn was educated in "pedagogy and technical subjects." He must have been a quick-study because he was not only able to take over the construction and supervision of the "about-to-begin" Telluride Light and Power Company, but several years later he had an important part in the installation of the power plant at Niagara Falls.

Lucien Nunn, meanwhile, was able to persuade the owners of the Gold King Mine that a gamble on electric power transmission was a viable solution to the ailing mine's difficulties. By the summer of 1890 an electrical generator and motor were received from the Westinghouse Company and were installed during the ensuing fall and winter. The decision to opt for the still controversial alternating current system was probably Paul Nunn's. That it was a wise choice was proven very quickly.

The generator was installed in a rude wooden structure at the foot of the lower cirque headwall of the Lake Fork of the San Miguel River, at a site called Ames. In the basin above the headwall, Trout Lake served as a storage reservoir for the water line which dropped 320 feet through penstocks to drive a six-foot Pelton Wheel, which, in turn, drove the single-phase, alternating current generator. From the generator the current was transmitted at 3,000 volts pressure three miles up the mountainside by No. 3 copper wire on Western Union cross arms and glass insulators to the Gold King Mine. The motor which ran the mill was the identical twin of the alternator which produced the power at the Ames plant.

The slender copper strands which connected the generator at Ames to the mill on the mountainside proliferated quickly into a web of power lines which became the expanding power grid of the Telluride Power and Light Company. The strands were marching along mesa tops and hillsides; leaping over 13,000-foot passes; stopping to serve the power needs of the high country mines — the Smuggler, Tomboy, Camp Bird, Liberty Bell, Sunnyside, Silver Lake, Mountain Top; and feeding power and light to the mountain towns — Telluride, Ouray, Silverton, Rico, Lake City, Durango. The Nunn brothers' dream spread beyond the shadows of the San Juans to the Salt Lake Valley. Through their initiative a training institute for electric power transmission technicians was established first at Telluride, later at Provo, Utah, and still later grew into the Telluride Association, a live-in training association for advanced students at Cornell University, Ithaca, New York.

During the first few years, strange and daunting problems faced the infant industry. How to handle the high voltages — 3,000 volts in the beginning grew quickly to 10,000 volts and higher on the transmission lines between generating plant and customer?

The earliest alternating current generator for power service. (Cassiers Magazine, Vol. 27, January, 1905, No. 3.)

Original power station at Ames, Colorado. (Stephen A. Bailey, L. L. Nunn, A Memoir, *1933.)*

Above: Trout Lake.

Left: Trout Lake inlet to the penstock for the pelton wheel which drives the generator at the modern Ames hydroelectric powerplant.

161

The present-day Ames powerplant complex.

Modern hydroelectric powerplant at site of original Ames plant of 1890–1891.

Modern 2400-volt alternating current generator in present-day Ames powerplant.

164

Underground powerplant at Morrow Point dam. This plant, with a capacity of 120 megawatts, is the largest of the three plants on the Gunnison River which comprise the Curecanti Unit of the Colorado River Storage Project. The other two plants are Blue Mesa, with a capacity of 60 megawatts, and Crystal, below Morrow Point, with a capacity of 28 megawatts. (Photo by Vern Jetley, from Bureau of Reclamation, U.S. Department of the Interior.)

Opposite: Morrow Point dam and reservoir on the Gunnison River near Cimarron, Colorado. This dam is a thin concrete arch with center, free-falling spillways — one of the few U.S. dams with this type of spillway. In this picture all four spillways are discharging from the reservoir, filled to capacity. The powerplant at this dam site is underground, inside the right canyon wall at the foot of the dam. (Photo by Vern Jetley, from Bureau of Reclamation, U.S. Department of the Interior.)

Blinding arcs were drawn from switches when breaking or making circuits. One chronicler describes an operator standing on a foot-thick, paraffin-soaked wooden platform, using his hat to whiff out a vicious, six-foot-long arc of dancing current between the plug and jack of a primitive circuit breaker. Thunderstorms are common features of the summer weather in the San Juans; as many as 100 separate discharges of lightning have been counted in a single hour. A lightning strike on a line would not only incapacitate the line itself, but the equipment to which it was connected. Transformers were set afire from the overloads. Switching equipment was burned out at the generator and load ends of the line. Much of the pioneer research on lightning arresters was done on these San Juan power lines. Until nonarcing arresters resulted from the work of a Westinghouse technician on the spot, a set of redundant switching equipment had to be maintained in parallel, making it possible to switch to a new circuit as soon as lightning knocked out the one being used.

In a few short years practical solutions were found to the problems created by lightning, high winds, and avalanches on the mountain passes; long spans over canyons; winter maintenance as snow depths built to forty feet; and the changing demands of the industrial mining equipment which consumed the power.

Paul Nunn went on to take part in the development of the huge hydroelectric power plants at Niagara Falls. The pioneer work at the Ames plant and the Gold King Mine evolved into the Telluride Power and Light Company, then the Western Colorado Power and Light Company, and a few years ago, the San Miguel Power Association, Inc.

Today one can drive down the dirt switchbacks near Ophir to the Ames power station. The rude shack which housed the original generator has been replaced by a sturdy stone structure. From its end sprouts a miniature forest of power poles, festooned with strain insulators, spanning a small transformer yard. Power poles march up the hillside to the south, supporting the three copper carriers of a 44,000 volt line. Another line spans the hillside to the east, in the general direction of the old Gold King Mine, which has long since decayed on the debris-strewn hillside.

Inside the stone powerhouse, a pelton wheel still spins under the impact of water which falls from Trout Lake, driving a dark green generator which has long

since replaced the 100 horsepower, single-phase alternator which started it all.

In the mind's eye it is easy to dance with the agitated electrons along the transmission lines which originate at the Ames station to the power grid which enmeshes the whole San Juan and from thence to the high voltage network which links the Blue Mesa–Curricanti plant to the Glen Canyon plant at Page, Arizona. Only a slight further act of imagination permits one to skip across the remainder of the continent to the Hoover Dam power plant, north to Bonneville and Grand Coulee, and across the international border to Kitimat. Another flight of fancy spans the continent eastward again to the Tennessee Valley, Niagara, and to Churchill Falls, Quebec. With the speed of light we can shift to Skellefteå, Sundsvall, and the Swedish power grid; to the Grimsel in Switzerland; the Dnepropetrovsk plant in the Ukraine; and the great Bratsk system in Siberia — then to Africa: Aswan, Kampala, and Kariba; even to Australia and the Snowy Range.

The lineage cannot always be traced unbroken; nevertheless, each of the world's great centers of hydroelectric power production can seek out its roots on the streams and mountainsides of Colorado's San Juan country.

A footnote to this survey which began in the San Juans is worthy of attention. As the Bureau of Reclamation built the dams and storage reservoirs which are the components of the Colorado River Storage Project, they built hydroelectric generating plants at such dams as Glen Canyon, Arizona; Blue Mesa, Morrow Point, and Crystal, in Colorado; and Flaming Gorge on the Utah–Wyoming border. The sale of this electricity has become an important element in the repayment schedules for the projects.

In 1962, the Reclamation Bureau established the control center for operations and maintenance of the Colorado River Storage electric power grid at Montrose on the north flank of the San Juans. From this nerve center power production is scheduled and dispatched; power trades are made with other networks and grids; and all maintenance of the high voltage lines is carried out. It seems singularly appropriate that the control center for this high tension alternating current power grid should have been located in the foothills of the mountain system where it all began ninety years ago.

Opposite: 230-kilovolt powerline crossing the Uncompahgre Plateau near Horsefly Peak — between Morrow Point substation and the Four Corners powerplant, in northwestern New Mexico. (Photo by Vern Jetley, from Bureau of Reclamation, U.S. Department of the Interior.)

CHAPTER 16

Water in the Valleys—
Herds in the Hills

The livestock came up the long dusty miles out of Nueva Vizcaya. Sometimes they were a walking commissary for the exploring parties which probed northward across the Rio Bravo; sometimes they were foundation stock for the small *ranches* which were spun off from the main northward thrust to build permanent settlements and keep a tenuous hold on the land. By 1609, Peralta had founded Santa Fe. Soon the livestock—sheep, goats, cattle, horses, burros, and mules—were herded northward by their owners into the San Luis Valley and the outskirts of the San Juan.

By this time they had probed into the country. The grass-clothed southern and eastern foothills of the San Juan were far more inviting pasturelands than any of the desert plains along the lower Rio Grande or the *Alto Plano* east of the Sierra Madre in Chihuahua and Durango.

The terrible Pueblo Revolt of 1680 sent the Spanish settlers reeling back southward along their lifeline but left most of their cattle, sheep, and goats in the hands of the Indians. At the time of the reconquest by Vargas, twelve years later, predatory hunting by the Indians had driven most of the livestock into a feral state. However, once the trained hand of animal husbandry was reestablished, the numbers came back with astounding rapidity. Cattle had done better in the wild state than the sheep, which over the centuries had developed a strong flocking instinct and needed the direction and protection of their *pastores*.

Meanwhile as the herds and flocks rebuilt under the nurture of the great landowners and the small

rancheros, the potential San Juan grazing lands remained unused—hostage to the predatory Utes. A few pockets of Mexican settlement had reached out to the fringes of the San Luis Valley, even up some of the streams which issued from the San Juans—but always at the hazard of Ute depredation.

When Frémont's battered winter expedition of 1848 retreated down the Rio Grande they found the first Mexican outposts at Red River and Arroyo Hondo, south of the present Colorado–New Mexico boundary. Three years later, in the spring of 1852, the siren call of California gold set in motion the first livestock drive across San Juan country.

In the spring of that year, "Uncle Dick" Wootton, builder and proprietor of a toll road over Raton Pass, which was later to become the route of the Santa Fe Railroad, assembled about 9,000 head of sheep to be trail-herded to the California gold camps. Gold seekers in the Sacramento Valley were clamoring for meat and wool, not all of which could be supplied locally. The Argonauts of 1848 and 1849 had quickly devoured Sutter's flocks, stripped his fields, and squatted on his property, leaving him financially ruined.

The animals for Wootton's trail herd were purchased near Watrous, New Mexico, and gathered at Taos, New Mexico. Wootton hired fourteen New Mexican sheepherders and eight "American" guards for the expedition. The former knew their business, the latter, recently discharged soldiers and teamsters, were not so reliable. Supplies, transported by mule packtrain, consisted of about a thousand-dollars worth of flour, sugar, beans, coffee, dried meat, and ammunition.

The route led north up the Rio Grande Valley almost to its head, thence over the southeastern foothills of the San Juans to the Uncompahgre Valley between Ouray and Montrose, then down that stream to the Gunnison, thence to the Grand (now called the Colo-

Opposite: Cows and calves in a breeding herd, wintering on the bottom lands along the Gunnison River, near Gunnison, Colorado.

Holding cattle against a drift fence before cutting out beef animals and branding calves dropped during the summer grazing season. Cement Creek, near Gunnison, Colorado.

Opposite: Sheepherder with his dogs in Yankee Boy Basin, at the head of Canyon Creek, near Ouray, Colorado. This picture was made in the 1930s when grazing allotments were still held by sheep growers in this part of the San Juans. The area is now in the Uncompahgre Primitive Area, from which grazing has been excluded.

rado River) to the present site of Grand Junction. The remainder of the route crossed the Wasatch Mountains south of the Salt Lake Valley, thence along the *California Trail*, and over the Sierras to a winter camp north of Sacramento.

With two goats to lead the way and a single dog to encourage stragglers, Wootton was able to deliver more than 8,900 sheep to his Sacramento buyers the next spring—a remarkable record for the time and considering the route he had followed. It is said that his gross return on the venture exceeded $50,000, a princely sum in those days.

As could have been predicted, the Utes objected strenuously to the sheep crossing their San Juan sanctuary. Near the head of Cochetopa Creek, somewhere southwest of Cochetopa Pass, a local chief, Uncotash, and his band tried to scatter the sheep by rifle fire. The ruse was not successful; sheep have a strong flocking instinct which only drove them together under the protection of their herders. At this point, realizing that the chief's requests for a passage fee—a sizeable cut of the flock—would lead to more extravagant demands, Wootton ended the discussion by wrestling the chief to the ground and putting a knife to his throat. While his braves looked on helplessly, Uncotash compromised for flour and ammunition.

This first large-scale incursion of livestock into the San Juan did not lead to the permanent establishment of an industry. Chief Ouray spent a young period in his life as a sheepherder in the Rio Grande Valley. Cattle were brought into the country to provide the ration allotments for the Utes at the Los Pinos Agency. But contact and even familiarity with livestock did not turn the Utes toward ranching as an alternative lifestyle. The introduction of the livestock industry had to await the expulsion of the Utes and the firm establishment of white settlement.

A number of factors have been suggested as responsible for the introduction and growth of agriculture in San Juan country. Among these factors can be listed the removal of the Utes in 1881; the subsequent mining boom, which created an expanding local market; and the silver panic of the 1890s, which drove many miners from the diggings to the agricultural valleys surrounding the mountains. Further, there was an introduction of irrigation to the arid valley lands, and the discovery that the integration of the mixed-crop, irrigated agriculture in the valleys with natural summer grazing in the mountains provided a more profitable, balanced operation than could be realized with either alone.

Opposite: Ewes and lambs on summer range near timberline.

John Wesley Powell. (U.S. Geological Survey)

Finally, the introduction of specialty, cash crops such as fruit, potatoes, head lettuce, pinto beans, malting barley, and sugar beets speeded the agricultural growth.

In 1879, John Wesley Powell, the venerable, one-armed explorer of the wild canyons of the Green and the Colorado rivers, published his *Report on the Lands of the Arid Region of the United States.* At the time, Powell was the most experienced, trained expert in the country. In this report he pointed out the fundamental difference between those arid lands of the West which could not be irrigated because of a lack of water and inaccessibility—they were thus subject to pastoral use into the foreseeable future; and those arid lands to which water could be diverted for irrigation, permitting crop agriculture. Powell saw clearly that public land policy needed to be changed to take into account the vast environmental differences between these two types of land. Conventional wisdom, since before the enactment of the 1862 Homestead Act, held that the ideal size of land holding for the average farm family was 160 acres. This became the legal size of a claim under the Homestead Act. Powell showed that the 160-acre size was too large for irrigated land, while it was far too small to sustain a single family under

pastoral use. He suggested 80 acres as a viable unit under irrigation and 2,560 acres—four full sections—under dry land pastoral use. To legislators tinged with the "yeoman farmer" populist leanings of the late nineteenth century, this was dangerous heresy.

In spite of Powell's professional stature and his persuasiveness, Congress was never able to break out of the 160-acre syndrome, which had been established when dealing with better-watered, midwestern and eastern lands. The failure of Powell's recommendations established a pattern which later made it extremely difficult to intermesh the agricultural system which developed on the irrigation projects established in the marginal valleys of the San Juan with the grazing economy which had already gained a foothold before irrigation came.

The lineage of San Juan irrigation can be traced back to the Middle East and the Mediterranean coasts of North Africa. Ancient irrigators in the Tigris-Euphrates and Nile valleys bequeathed their skill to the Phoenicians, who slowly spread it westward along the North African coast. Islam embraced this boon to food production in the desert world, carrying it across the Pillars of Hercules to Spain. The twelfth-century Arab geographer, Al-Idrisi, recalling his student days in Spain, wrote nostalgically, "The gardens of Toledo are laced with canals on which are erected water wheels used in irrigating the orchards, which produce in prodigious quantity fruits of inexpressible beauty and quality."

From Spain irrigation techniques accompanied the *conquistadores* to Mexico and spread northward into the arid lands of New Mexico and Mediterranean lands of California.

To be strictly accurate, the first irrigation in San Juan country was practiced by the ancient Anasazi people at Mesa Verde, who built primitive terraces and water diversion channels to bring moisture to their corn, squash, and bean plots on the mesa tops.

The white man's first permanent irrigation in Colorado was initiated by Mexican Americans in the San Luis Valley, when the San Luis People's Ditch in the Culebra Valley was started on April 10, 1852. This is on the east side of the San Luis Valley, opposite the San Juan Mountains. This pioneer irrigation system is still operating today.

Following the lead of their Mexican American neighbors, many of the earliest settlers in the mountain valleys built irrigation diversion dams and feeder canals for their small garden plots, and sometimes their hay fields as they scrambled to fill the produce and fodder needs of the exploding mining camps.

Meanwhile, on the Eastern Slope of the state an edifice of water law was being slowly erected. Anglo Americans had no experience yet in regions where there wasn't enough water to go around. The first

Irrigation in the San Luis Valley, near the site of Colorado's first Spanish irrigation.

Anglo settlers brought with them the common law doctrine of riparian rights. Cummins mentions that this gave "the riparian (bankside) owner a right to the flow of water in its natural channel upon and over his land, even though he makes no beneficial use thereof." Such a system was unworkable where placer miners needed a supply of water, although they might be located on benches and mesa tops away from stream channels, and agricultural land was located at a distance from flowing water. Furthermore, in arid lands few streams carried a supply of water great enough to satisfy all of the needs which arose within its drainage basin. A system of priorities and allocations had to be devised for the equitable distribution of the scarce commodity.

During the period between 1861 and 1901, forty years which were crucial to the orderly settlement and development of the arid West, a series of constitutional enactments and legal cases were carried up to and through the Colorado Supreme Court, establishing the right to divert water from a stream for beneficial agricultural use and confirming the doctrine of appropriation of water based on prior right. *"Priority of Appropriation* shall give the better right as between those using the water for the same purpose." This system of

prior appropriation of water became known as the "Colorado system," and was eventually adopted by the other irrigation states of the Rocky Mountains and the Southwest. Historians are quick to point out that this system of water allocation borrowed some of its provisions from the Code of Hammurabi issued in Babylon about 2200 B.C.

The Colorado Supreme Court, in 1882 in *Coffin* et al. v. *Left Hand Ditch Company*, held that "Imperative necessity, unknown to the countries which gave it birth, compels the recognition of another doctrine in conflict therewith. And we hold . . . the first appropriator of water from a natural stream for a beneficial purpose has, with the qualifications contained in the constitution, a prior right thereto, to the extent of such appropriation."

Even before the founding of these protective legal precedents, farmers who flooded into the valleys surrounding the San Juans as soon as the Utes were removed in 1881, began the cooperative construction of diversion works and canals to bring water away from the perennial streams to the dry land benches.

An outstanding example was the Uncompahgre Valley; which, from the verge of the mountains between Ouray and Ridgway to the "desert" below Delta, became the scene of feverish water development. The first irrigation in the valley — for hay fields — dates from 1875, while the Utes were still present. The upper Gunnison River and its tributary, Tomichi Creek, saw the early diversion of water for hay fields. The numerous tributaries of the Rio Grande which drain the southeastern flanks of the San Juan experienced the rapid borrowing of Mexican irrigation techniques from the other side of the valley and from further downstream. The lower Animas Valley above Durango, as well as the La Plata, the Mancos, and the Dolores saw the diversion of water to early hay fields and vegetable crops before the water was lost in the labyrinthine canyonlands beyond the mesa margins.

One place to trace the development of irrigation agriculture at the margins of the San Juans is the Uncompahgre Valley, which flows northward from the San Juan front to become one branch of the upper Colorado River system. There, the pioneers learned very quickly there was too much good land and too little water. Before the turn of the century, all of the useable water in the river and its small tributaries had been appropriated, while uncounted acres of potentially good land cried for water.

All this while, fifteen miles to the east of the Uncompahgre, deep in a granite gorge, the Gunnison River carried untapped, unappropriated water downstream to a junction with the Uncompahgre at Delta — too far downstream to vitalize the flagging hopes of the farmers further upstream, near Olathe and Montrose. The high ridge between the two streams seemed an insuperable barrier — unless? Could a tunnel divert water under the ridge from the Gunnison to the Uncompahgre? Was the bed of the Gunnison higher or lower than that of the Uncompahgre? Where could the money for a tunnel be found if it were feasible from an engineering standpoint? They would never know if they didn't try!

In the winter of 1882–1883, a survey crew had found that the canyon below Cimarron was impractical for a further extension of the Denver and Rio Grande Western railway. In 1900, William W. Torrence, superintendent of the Montrose Electric Power and Light Company led a party of Montrose and Delta farmers and ranchers, and the Delta County surveyor, into the canyon to run a level line. They were balked by the boulder-choked middle reaches of the canyon.

A year later, in April of 1901, another effort was led by A. Lincoln Fellows, irrigation engineer and resident hydrographer of the U.S. Geological Survey at Montrose. The U.S.G.S. had appropriated funds that year for a survey of the canyon and the proposed tunnel sites. W. W. Torrence, who had led the previous year's party, volunteered to accompany Fellows. This time, after heroic efforts, the attempt was successful.

It took the two pioneers nine days to traverse the whole length of the canyon, but not without being forced to let the stream carry them under a jam of huge boulders at one place, and at another capturing, bare-handed, and killing a mountain sheep with a pocket-knife when they had lost their food supplies. This epic passage proved the feasibility of the proposed tunnel.

After failure to raise sufficient local capital for a short tunnel at Red Rocks Canyon, and obtaining only token support for the proposed undertaking from the Colorado state legislature, the newly born Reclamation Bureau of the Department of the Interior, created by act of Congress on June 17, 1902, undertook the project. It was one of the first five major engineering works undertaken by this new agency, which was to become eventually the West's premier builder of dams, storage reservoirs, irrigation projects, and hydroelectric plants.

Within six months of the project's start, in January 1905, the original contractor on the tunnel had to be relieved because of financial difficulties. From this point on the Reclamation Bureau assumed the task of completing the tunnel and the distribution system.

On September 23, 1909, after a construction cost of twenty-four lives and $4,418,434.51, President William Howard Taft opened the headgates which let the first water flow through the six-mile-long Gunnison Tunnel, from the Black Canyon to the Uncompahgre Valley. There, through a canal distribution system, water was carried to about 70,000 acres of rich farmland; euphoric early estimates had placed the figure at twice that much.

Thus was inaugurated the Uncompahgre Valley Project. The federal government had now gotten into the planning, construction, management, and social engineering of western irrigation, hydropower production, and public recreation — an intrusion which was to generate controversy in the years ahead. But its controversial role was lost sight of in the flashy celebration over the magnitude of the new project and the potential of the newly minted acreages. One chronicler, Richard Beidleman, remarked that in the future "some . . . will remember a moment . . . when the valley traded its desert for an Eden. At the touch of a President's hand, the head gates of a new tunnel, the longest in the West, had swung open, releasing the turbulent waters of the Gunnison River from the forbidding chasm of the Black Canyon into what William Howard Taft called the 'incomparable valley with the unpronounceable name.' "

Many years later as the pay-back period on project costs had to be extended and additional debts were incurred to reclaim water-logged, salt-encrusted, wasteland by costly drainage works, project farmers began

East portal of the Gunnison Tunnel. From this point in the upper Black Canyon water diverted from the Gunnison River is transported by a six-mile bore under an intervening mountain ridge to the Uncompahgre irrigation project.

Cultivating head lettuce in the San Luis Valley.

Opposite: Gated aluminum pipe distributes irrigation water into individual furrows.

Center pivot sprinkler system watering a barley field in the San Luis Valley. The water for this irrigation system comes from an underground aquifer, which is recharged by runoff from the eastern flanks of the San Juan Mountains.

to take a more realistic view of the cost-benefit ratios of the undertaking.

Meanwhile the desert bloomed. It still blooms, on all except those marginal lands, out at the farthest reach of the lateral ditches, where the soil is often too clayey and poorly drained to be thrifty.

Specialty crops came to the valley—fruit orchards on the gravelly mesa tops; potatoes on the sandy soils of the higher parks—an 800-bushel club flourished for awhile (800 bushels of potatoes per acre). There is head lettuce, onions, and sugar beets for a factory at Delta, and Moravian barley for a national brewer on the Eastern Slope.

• • • • •

A persistent problem which has plagued the Uncompahgre irrigation project is the integration of irrigated crop agriculture in the valley with grazing in the foot-

hills and the mountains. This is the same problem which Powell foresaw in 1879. The acreage of irrigated land necessary to support a farm family with specialized crop agriculture is not the same acreage required to produce primary and supplemental feed for grazing animals which are on the public domain during the summer months.

"Diversification" has been a long-standing recommendation of county agricultural agents in the mountain West. The word has gone out, over and over, "Don't be at the mercy of the market for a single cash crop!" If wheat is depressed, perhaps alfalfa will be up. The bad year for sugar beets may not be a bad year for onions or potatoes. Above all else, integrate livestock with crops for a balanced production schedule.

But this is easier said than done. It is seldom compatible to produce an irrigated cash crop and run a successful cattle or sheep outfit in the same operation.

180

Even the federal agencies which administer the lands falling under the two types of use, look upon them in different ways. Grazing on government land is controlled by the Bureau of Land Management (BLM) on general public domain and the Forest Service in national forests. One agency is in the Interior Department, the other in the Department of Agriculture. Policies for lands on federal irrigation projects are administered by the Reclamation Bureau, an agency of the Department of Interior.

The Bureau of Reclamation still adheres to the 160-acre rule. In this case, as an agency of the federal government, it advanced the money for a costly tunnel and distribution works. When the water users were not able to pay on schedule, it has had to reschedule the repayment of that original debt. The cost of the project has still not been amortized, although it is fair to say that over the years the estimates of costs have always fallen short of actuality and a great many unforeseen costs have been added to the estimated tally. Small wonder that some small-scale farmers feel that they have fallen into the clutches of a loan shark, which is far from the truth, because the debt has been either interest free, or at an unrealistically low interest rate. The Bureau looks for repayment eventually from the small farmers engaged in cash crop production on the project. Even forage crops are classified by the Bureau in the same category as alfalfa for cash sale to stock raisers.

The Forest Service considers the lands which it administers, as its roadside signs advertise, "Land of Many Uses." Under this multiple use concept national forests are required to return yields, directly or indirectly, from sale of timber, fees from grazing permits, to serve as watershed, to serve tourism, and at the same time produce intangible "values" such as natural beauty, wilderness, open space, and wildlife habitat.

On both Forest Service and BLM lands grazing is controlled by a system of grazing allotments which translate into permits to graze specified portions of the range. By virtue of prior use, custom, and maintenance of a base of operations, ranchers have acquired grazing rights by which they are allotted a specified number of Animal Unit Months (AUM) in designated grazing areas. The AUM is the measure for the amount of feed, of whatever kind, necessary to maintain one cow or five sheep for one month. The livestock rancher pays a fee per cow month or sheep month for his grazing privileges. The grazing on each national forest is governed by an advisory board of ranchers who use that range.

The overlapping governmental control of different aspects of resource utilization in the Uncompahgre Valley is responsible for many of the difficulties in integrating the irrigated agriculture of the valley with the dry grazing lands of the foothills and mountains. During the past sixty years of the project there has been a decrease in the number of cattle and an increase in the number of sheep on adjacent ranges. The symbiosis between crop agriculture and livestock raising which the planners envisioned when they sought initial support and funding for the infant project has not yet arrived. However, each year brings adjustments which make the system more viable. There has been an increase in the number of farmers who run a few cattle or sheep, but not anything like the number needed to offset the breakup of the large cattle outfits after the initiation of the Uncompahgre Irrigation Project. Neither fish nor flesh, nor good red herring, the project knows not whether to be a center of irrigated specialty crop production or the hub of a cattle and sheep empire. It has not yet learned how to be partly each.

In spite of the difficulties in integrating livestock raising with irrigated agriculture on large irrigation projects, cattle and sheep ranching still flourishes in especially favorable parts of the San Juan environment. These are places where livestock raising got an early start, and where the irrigation was tailored specifically to production of wet pasture and hay on the home ranches. Most of these ranches have early water rights, and the diversion works were built by the individual appropriators. Home ranches were established or consolidated early enough to have escaped the 160-acre rule. Irrigation is a part of the seasonal support system of the ranching activity, rather than a cash-crop enterprise.

Such operations are found on the upper Uncompahgre, above the Uncompahgre Irrigation Project, along the two tributaries of Cow Creek and Dallas Creek; on the Big and Little Cimarron rivers before they join the Gunnison at the Black Canyon; in the Gunnison Valley and its principal tributaries, the East River, Taylor River, Ohio Creek, Quartz Creek, and Tomichi Creek; on the upper Rio Grande and the principal tributaries which drain the west side of the San Luis Valley; on those tributaries of the San Juan River which drain the south flanks of the San Juan Mountains; and along the streams which dissect the mesa lands to the west of the San Juan Mountains.

Most of these operations have been successful because the home ranch could grow enough hay to winter a breeding herd, was sheltered enough to offer some spring and fall pasturage, and had sufficient summer grazing allotments on Forest Service and Bureau of Land Management land to carry the herd.

Although the pattern tends to vary from one operation to another, depending upon whether the ranch is a cattle or a sheep outfit, or both, it follows a seasonal regime which is geared to the climate and the natural vegetation succession. Winter feeding of hay takes place outdoors in the hay meadows at the home ranch. The hay stubble provides some grazing before

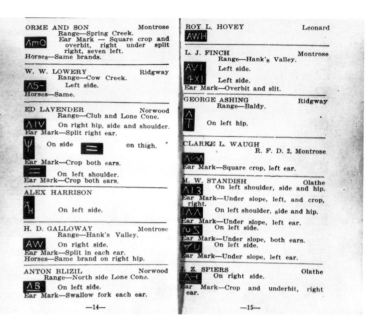

Right: Pages 14 and 15 from the Brand Book of the Uncompahgre Valley Cattle and Horse Growers Association, 1927. The book contains the ranges, addresses, earmarks, and brands of each member of the association. The book also contains the constitution and by-laws of the association. Ed Lavender, listed at about the middle of page 14, was the stepfather of David Lavender, the well known Western author and historian.

Branding a summer calf at the fall beef roundup—Cement Creek, near Gunnison, Colorado.

Fall beef roundup — a summer calf being brought to the branding fire. Cement Creek, near Gunnison, Colorado.

Sheep shearers at work.

Opposite: Freshly sheared sheep.

Sheep in Chicago Basin, Needle Mountains. Grazing is now excluded from the Weminuche Wilderness of which the Needle Mountains are a part.

and following the feeding period. Calving takes place outdoors, generally in early April—sometimes when there is still snow cover. With sheep, lambing usually occurs in early May.

In the spring animals are gradually moved to higher, dry rangeland as soon as it is ready for grazing. Ewes will have been sheared before they are moved from home pastures. Meanwhile, irrigation is begun on the meadowlands. During the summer some cattle are carried on irrigated pasture, others on partially forested hill rangeland, and later some are put on Forest Service grazing allotments in the mountains. Still later sheep are taken to tundra grazing allotments on the mountaintops. The national forest lands lie generally below the timberline, which occurs at about 11,500 to 12,000 feet above sea level in this latitude. Since the heart of the San Juan lies above 11,500 feet, there are extensive areas of high basins and mountaintops which are administered by the BLM. Although, today, large acreages of this land are being withdrawn from grazing and put into Wilderness and Primitive areas, sheep are still grazed in many parts of this high mountain world.

Meanwhile, the hay in the irrigated meadows is cut, raked, and stacked. Following the short grazing season on the high mountain tundra, sheep are moved downward to the valley floors again; a reversal of the up-migration begun in the early summer. The cattle which have been grazing on national forest allotments are next taken from the forested mountain slopes to the partly forested foothills, and eventually back to the irrigated hay fields in the valleys. After the animals have been returned to the home ranch, the marketing of lambs and feeder calves takes place. Breeding stock is pastured on the hay meadows until winter snowstorms start the feeding cycle again.

Transhumance is the term applied to this type of seasonal, altitudinal grazing pattern. It traces its origins to circumMediterranean lands and Biblical times. It depends upon high mountain pastures for summer grazing, sheltered fields for wintering and the production of winter feed, and stock driveways along which animals can be moved readily from one grazing or feeding zone to another. Altitude differences and the vegetation zonation brought about by those differences are the principal ingredients of the regime. This system seems to have come into San Juan country from Iberia by way of Mexico.

Fat lambs at loading pens awaiting shipment to market.

CHAPTER 17

Village, Ranch, Mine and Open Space

Let us assume that John Charles Frémont could be brought back after 135 years to the summit of Mosca Pass, from which he first saw the storm-scourged San Juans on a cold December day in 1848. Today, as he squints through the blowing snow, he can barely recognize the slight changes which have been wrought by the passage of the years. The "everlasting" hills change slowly. The natural world is measured by a scale of space and time so much more vast than the yardstick used for human works and affairs, that mere man is engulfed by the stage setting in which he acts out his petty dramas.

The modern roads, fields, fence lines, and settlement clusters of the San Luis Valley, at Frémont's feet, look no more like a human-dominated landscape now than did the Missouri River Valley landscape near St. Louis, from which Frémont had departed on his westward wayfaring 135 years earlier. The population densities of the two places are comparable across that span of time; two or three persons per square mile would have sufficed for either, with many a square mile empty of all human effluvia.

One is almost persuaded that a cunning guide of today might lead our resurrected Frémont along the crest of the Continental Divide over its whole San Juan length, from Marshall Pass to the New Mexico border, without encountering the works of man. Of course, the guide would have to lead Frémont, blindfolded and at night, across the pavement at North Pass, Cochetopa Pass, Spring Pass, and Wolf Creek Pass, but other than at these highway crossings and power line cross-

ings of the divide, man has made little mark on the high country. The narrow-gauge railway crossing at Marshall Pass has long since been ripped up and has made a start toward revegetation, although the grade serves now as a vehicular divide crossing. Indeed, our clever guide would be aided and abetted in his ruse by the fact that an 80-mile stretch of the Continental Divide, from its great western bend near Stony Pass, above Silverton, to Wolf Creek Pass, near Pagosa Springs, serves as the backbone of the Weminuche Wilderness, 433,745 acres of forest and mountain country, preserved and restored to the state in which Frémont and the other pathfinders found it a century and a half ago.

Much of the zone along the Continental Divide was only lightly scratched by prospectors during the silver rush because it was not heavily mineralized and it was relatively inaccessible from the mining centers. Because of the long winters and short grazing season, cattle and sheep had made only a slight mark on the high tundra meadows by the time the wilderness was set aside. Restoration, when the Forest Service established the Wilderness Area, in the last few decades, was moderately easy.

The point we are making speaks to the tremendous difference in scale between the great mountain masses and far-reaching carpets of forest which occupy most of San Juan country, and the puny marks of man's parceling, digging, cutting, and cultivating. The San Juan landscape reveals a dichotomy: (1) a great cosmic sweep of raw nature, measured on a space and time scale of leagues and millennia, showing man-made scars in only a few places; and (2) a human microcosm, spread over the natural landscape in a thinly articulated network.

If one looks at a topographic map of almost any part of San Juan country, even areas which were most

Opposite: Teacher arriving at school early in the morning with a pail of drinking water.

189

heavily mined, he will be struck by the high percentage of the total map area which is covered by the green tint of forestland and the tightly contoured mountain slopes above the treeline. The network of roads, dotted trails, buildings, and mine adits takes up an infinitesimally small part of the total area. Although men picked, blasted, and shoveled mightily at the mineral deposits, the extent of the activity was confined mostly to narrow veins and took place underground. The most conspicuous evidences of mining activity are the waste dumps where unprofitable rock was strewn on the hillsides and the tailings ponds where waste pulp from the flotation mills has settled out of the water in which it was suspended during its journey through the mill. Even the gridwork of streets in the little mountain towns such as Telluride, Ouray, Silverton, and Lake City is squeezed between steep mountain slopes, so that the whole extent of urban human activity occupies a small percentage of the area displayed on the total map sheet.

. . . . .

San Juan country's population and settlement pattern is an annular one. The major trading towns, which surround the mountainous heart of the region, are Alamosa, Monte Vista, Del Norte, and Saguache on the east; Gunnison and Montrose on the north; Cortez, Dolores, and Mancos on the southwest; and Durango and Pagosa Springs on the south. These peripheral settlements have the largest San Juan populations and serve as supply and trading centers for the agricultural and ranching lands which surround them, as well as for the nearby mining towns at the heads of the mountain valleys. The 1970 and 1980 population figures for these supply centers are:

Settlement	1970 Population	1980 Population
Alamosa	6,985	6,830
Monte Vista	3,909	3,902
Del Norte	1,569	1,709
Saguache	642	656
Gunnison	4,613	5,785
Montrose	6,496	8,722
Cortez	6,032	7,095
Dolores	820	802
Mancos	709	870
Durango	10,333	11,426
Pagosa Springs	1,360	1,331

The principal mountain towns all started as mining camps. The current slump in the metal market has now robbed them of most of their original economic support. They are listed below with their 1970 and 1980 populations:

Camp	1970 Population	1980 Population
Creede	653	610
Lake City	91	206
Ouray	741	684
Rico	275	76
Silverton	797	794
Telluride	553	1,047

Today, although all of these camps except Telluride have less than 1,000 full-time inhabitants, in their heyday, from 1880 to 1900, most of them had several thousand inhabitants. In 1880, Silverton, with a population of 5,040, was the third largest city in Colorado, behind Denver and Leadville. Substantial houses and brick and stone mercantile establishments testify to these earlier times.

The still smaller settlements of San Juan country, numbering about thirty, fall into two categories: mining camps located higher in the mountains than the major camps listed above at the sites of individual mines or clusters of mines—a number of these small camps have withered away to ghost towns, and small crossroads trading centers in agricultural and ranching areas. Among the small mining settlements can be listed Ophir, Eureka, Howardsville, Gladstone, Sneffels, Summitville, Platoro, and La Plata. Agricultural trading centers include Center, Hooper, and Moffat in the San Luis Valley; Olathe and Colona in the Uncompahgre Valley; Norwood, Nucla, and Redvale in the San Miguel area; and Hesperus and Bayfield in the south.

Of the fifteen counties, all or parts of which lie within San Juan country, five have less population today than they did in 1900. These are San Miguel, Ouray, San Juan, Hinsdale, and Mineral. All were the sites of big-producing mining camps for several decades up to 1900.

. . . .

Culture crept into the San Juan right from the first, along with the necessities of popular sovereignty and self-government. While the rudiments of law, order, taxes, and public good came to the high country, they were accompanied by what the "common folk" call "the finer things of life"—churches, schools, theatres, newspapers, libraries, and self-improvement ventures. No clutch of miners in a cirque head could escape the tent saloon with a plank between two barrels as a bar, nor the itinerant preacher or priest who would sweep it clear of its bottles and cups and consecrate it as an altar on the Sabbath.

In 1876, George Darley, serving first as carpenter and later as minister, built with his own hands the first church on the Western Slope of Colorado at Lake City.

This Presbyterian church, which is still standing, was dedicated only two years after the founding of Lake City. The Cousin Jack miners from Cornwall, the Keweenaw, and Grass Valley brought "shouting Methodism" with them to the new mining country. The Irish brought Catholicism, and soon after the founding of Ouray and Silverton shepherds were assigned to the little flocks and small Catholic churches were built there.

Printing presses and fonts of hand-set type were freighted into the high country settlements almost as soon as the town streets were platted. The early newspapers traced faithfully the chronological and social history of the communities which they served, and more than one fostered a spirit of local boosterism which provided an astringent quality to frontier living.

Ouray County was the first county created after Colorado statehood—the date was January 18, 1877. Before it was split into its component parts of Ouray, San Juan, La Plata, Montezuma, San Miguel, and Dolores counties, the county seat for the single large county was in the far northeast corner at Ouray. This galled, no end, the miners at Rico who had to file claims and transact other business at Ouray. The *Dolores News* of January 22, 1881, page 3, contained the following bitter complaint:

> When we have business to transact in relation to mining matters, we must put our hard tack in our pockets and strike out through eighty miles of forest and the county won't even lend us an axe to blaze the trail. When we get to Ouray the citizens find out you are from Rico and they begin to bleed you. They will first steal your horse and then sympathize with you and tell you they are sorry you should be so treated in this hospitable town. They will charge you $30.00 a week for day board and when they have detained you as long as they think you will stand it, they recover your horse and charge you $5.00 a day for his board and $50 reward. You will then turn over the horse for damages, and start for home afoot. Before you get a mile out of town, a committee appointed for the purpose, knocks you down and takes away all the cash you have; after casting lots for your clothes you are allowed to go on your way.

During these same years the *Ouray Solid Muldoon* was published by the redoubtable David Frakes Day (Dave Day).

The *Solid Muldoon,* over the years of its existence, took on all comers and was to gain a reputation which reached far beyond Ouray's mountain-girt bowl. It is said to have been quoted by papers in cities as far distant as New York and London. There is debate today and was during its flamboyant heyday, about the "cultural" ingredient of the *Solid Muldoon.* Day was a vocal Democrat who seldom lost an opportunity to puncture the pretensions of mine owners, managers, merchants, and assorted supporters of the Republican establishment. In many ways he was a sort of early

David Frakes Day. (Denver Public Library, Western History Department)

day forerunner of H. L. Mencken, with a sense of scatological scorn for pretension and the foibles of *"boobus Americanus."* The self-appointed guardians of community morals tended to view him with unbridled alarm. Some quarters of Ouray society heaved a sigh of relief when Dave Day moved his theatre of operations to Durango and there vented his spleen indiscriminately on Republicans and Indians who were another of his pet peeves.

William Rathmell, an early day resident of Ouray, who knew Dave Day well, has recorded: "In his home, Dave Day was one of the most entertaining characters that anyone ever met, never indulging in any conversation that could, by any stretch, be classed as vulgar. His wife, one of the most lovable women that one can imagine, was educated and an entertainer, and could always be depended upon to give the guests a real treat. . . . Mrs. Day was a leader in society and was generally present when an impression was sought with a celebrity."

As prosperity came to the mine-owning and managing classes, "conspicuous consumption" began to creep into the mining camp way of life. Wives conspired with local carpenters and builders to erect homes which would display, both inside and out, the new affluence of the owners. An art historian has termed the resulting architectural style, "Bonanza Victorian," and has discovered examples in most of the western mining camps between the Front Range and the Pacific shores. The San Juan had its share of "Bonanza Victorian" architecture.

Not all of the conspicuous consumption was indulged in by those who went from rags to riches in San Juan country. British and eastern investors actively sought promising mines to develop. Two outstanding examples were the Smuggler-Union, near Telluride, and the Camp Bird near Ouray. The Smuggler-Union was owned and operated by a group of English bankers headquartered in Shanghai, China, who sold it about 1900 for eight million dollars to the New England Exploration Company, controlled by the Boston family of Colonel Thomas Livermore. The Camp Bird, in which Thomas Walsh "struck it rich," was sold later to an English company, Camp Bird Ltd., which operated it until 1918 or 1919 with imported managers and engineers.

These outside investors brought a way of life to the San Juan which was foreign to the rough miners who had stampeded to the region initially and had made the first strikes. Some of them were modest and hid their light under a bushel; others flaunted the wealth and position they had acquired elsewhere.

None was more conspicuous than the dashing son-in-law of Colonel Thomas Livermore, Bulkeley Wells, who was sent to manage the Smuggler-Union after the former manager, Arthur Collins, was assassinated in 1902, during the Telluride labor strife.

Bulkeley Wells was a controversial figure. The stories about him are legion; there was no unanimity about his personality, even among his closest associates. A Harvard graduate in 1894, a year later he married Grace Daniels Livermore, and by 1896 he was in the West looking after the widely dispersed Livermore mining interests. A flamboyant and handsome man, he was equally at home in the drawing rooms of Back Bay Boston, the salons of Europe, New York's Delmonicos, General Palmer's home, Glen Eyrie in Colorado Springs, the Denver Club, or Telluride's Pacific Street.

Memorable features of Wells's sojourn in the San Juans were the impromptu picnics which he presided over for a number of years. They were planned meticulously, were served on fine china with the whitest of napery and with wines of the best vintage, and were likely to be served with jellied consommé chilled to perfection in a mountain stream or a snowbank. Wells was even known to produce on demand a wildfowl basted in the proper wine.

In his introduction to *Bostonians and Bullion, the Journal of Robert Livermore, 1892–1915*, Gene M. Gress-

ley recounts the following tale about Bulkeley Wells which shows the gauge of the man as well as the culture which was introduced to the San Juans by the new entrepreneur-investors-managers who came to the mining country after the initial discoveries:

> One mining engineer acquaintance of Wells remembered an incident illustrative of Wells' epicurean nature that took place over fifty years ago. Meeting him on a platform of a small Colorado railroad station, Wells invited the friend to accompany him in his private car on the tiny narrow-gauge railroad. As they were slowly wending their way along the pinched-in mountain valley, Wells suddenly pulled the bell cord to summon the conductor. When the conductor arrived, Wells ordered him to stop the train immediately. He then climbed down from his car and walked to the bank of a little mountain stream, where he gathered some wild mint. Returning to the car, he proceeded to mix a round of mint juleps for the entire party.

Another example of conspicuous consumption was "Waldheim," erected by Edward G. Stoiber, the owner of the Silver Lake Mine, at the mouth of Arrastra Gulch above Silverton. In the '90s and early decades of the present century, its high-ceilinged, third-floor ballroom throbbed to the cadences of periodic dances for the young. Its mistress, known with some affection tinged with awe as "Captain Jack," tooled expertly along the mountain roads and town streets in a shiny buggy pulled by a matched pair of spirited bays, urged to greater efforts by a vocabulary as colorful as any mule skinner's. At Christmas she loaded her handsome sleigh with presents for every child in Silverton, and she personally delivered them to every house.

Ouray, Telluride, Silverton, Lake City, and Durango each had half a dozen or so examples of the new architecture. The hotels and some of the commercial buildings began to display similar tendencies in their interior woodwork. The solid walnut panelling and stair banisters of the old La Veta Hotel in Gunnison, the high-ceilinged rooms and fretted woodwork in the Beaumont at Ouray, the Sheridan in Telluride, the Strater in Durango, all testified to the atmosphere of the "good old days." The little jewell of a bandbox-sized theatre—"Opera House"—in the New Sheridan at Telluride was a perfect setting for the best travelling troupes that the Gay Nineties could produce—Denver, Kansas City, Chicago, San Francisco, or Leadville did not boast finer.

An item in a May 1896 issue of the *Ouray Herald* alerts the community to the following cultural event:

> The popular young romantic actor, Mr. John Griffith, will play an engagement at the Opera House, May 25, 1896, in Henry Irving's version of Goethe's masterwork, "Faust." He will essay the role of Mephisto, claiming originality both for his conception and enactment.
>
> Nature has been very kind to Mr. Griffith, his handsome mobile face, his dark, flashing eyes, his tall, lithe,

strong and graceful figure will fit him for the task of representing the "Prince of Darkness."

The production is staged with a magnificence that borders on the sublime, every attention being given to the most minute detail, so that this weird spectacle will remain a pleasant memory in the minds of the beholders.*

Another item from the same issue of the *Ouray Herald* touts the Bon Ton, Ouray's largest restaurant:

There is not a better restaurant in town frequented by a better class of people. . . . Female help is exclusively employed, and it is supplied with the best the markets afford of everything.

Mrs. K. Heit, proprietress of the Bon Ton has been in the restaurant business in Ouray for eight years. She came originally from Chicago. Her rate for single meals is 35¢ but a reduction will be made for patrons who wish to secure board by the week or the month.

None of the mining towns, so long as a work force of unattached males labored in the high country, went without a "red-light district." Second Street was the "row" in Ouray, Pacific Street in Telluride, while Blair Street served a similar function in Silverton. In Ouray both sides of Second Street were lined with establishments bearing such catchy names as The Club, The Morning Star, The Clipper, The Monte Carlo, The Bird Cage, and The Temple of Music. The gaudier establishments on the "row" usually supported a parlour, complete with a "professor" at the piano, a small dance floor, a corner bar, and flamboyant wall decorations. Sometimes beyond the larger establishments, the "row" strung out in a thin line of one-room "cribs," whose proprietors, during working hours, sat at street-level windows, soliciting. The married women of the community looked upon this social arrangement with disapproval, but so long as men alone had the vote and miners outnumbered burghers, these amenities were maintained. The denizens of these segregated parts of town knew their place and seldom intruded on the lives of those who dwelt further up the hill.

◦ ◦ ◦ ◦

In no part of the cultural realm did the San Juans shine more brilliantly than in that of education. In the beginning, in a hard frontier environment, the schoolteacher exercised a stabilizing influence on a turbulent era while carrying the three "Rs" to the very summits of the ranges. As soon as a town was established, if any school-age children were in camp, the beginning

of a school system was inaugurated. Most of the towns soon supported a school system which provided all of the grades through high school. In 1876, the year the town of Ouray was incorporated, it had 214 buildings, a population of 400, and a school with forty-three students. At the isolated mines and cattle-ranching locations the traditional one-room country school was provided by local school boards. The isolation, avalanche dangers in the high country, and sometimes obstreperous conduct of the pupils made it hard to keep a teacher more than one school term and often not even that. On the other hand, there were some dedicated teachers, both men and women, who stayed at their posts year after year so long as there were pupils to teach. Their loyalty could not have been purchased with the pay, which was pitiably low, nor the amenities, which were almost always totally lacking. Perhaps they got their reward in the feeling of pride which resulted when a bright student went on to college and made his or her mark in the scientific or professional world, or climbed through the labyrinthine chain of command to the helm of some business or industrial establishment. College professors, doctors, lawyers, clerics, merchants, engineers, state and national legislators, U.S. Congressmen, a state governor, a president of the state university, a chief justice of the state supreme court, among numerous others of equal eminence, received their initial education in one-room or town schools of San Juan country.

Ruth Rathmell—formerly of Silverton, Ouray, Montrose, and now Durango—has recorded the following story of the Cow Creek School, which was related to her by her father-in-law, William Rathmell, who once taught there. Cow Creek is east of Ridgway, in cattle ranching country. The boys in the area attended school only in the middle of the winter, having to take part in the fall roundup, putting up the third cutting of hay in the fall, helping to plant crops in the spring, and irrigating. The Indians had only been moved to the Utah reservation seven years previously. The labor needs of a frontier ranch took precedence over the less pressing requirements for an education. Consequently many of the male students were pretty well grown up before they had enough formal schooling to satisfy the state authorities. Any teacher who aspired to teach in such a situation usually found his or her hands full. In the spirit of good clean fun, with their practical jokes, they had run off several teachers. "One young school mistress left in hysterics after they stood her on her head in a corner of the room."

On a blustery autumn afternoon in 1888, the school had reached another of the periodic interregnums which it suffered because of the exuberance of its older male students. While the school board was at its wits end, the president was approached at his home by

---

*Author's note: I must register a disclaimer of any relationship with the Mr. John Griffith alluded to in the clipping. His name is spelled without a final *s*, and mine is. To strengthen the disclaimer, anyone familiar with my physiognomy, frame, and disposition knows that nature has not been so kind to me as it was to Mr. John Griffith in 1896. I would seem to be better fitted to play the part of Sir John Falstaff than that of the "Prince of Darkness," if I had an ounce of acting ability, which I haven't.

Students leaving Camp Bird school at noon, followed by the teacher.

a small, modest man, who asked to be considered for the job. The school board president considered him skeptically.

"You know the trouble we've had here this past year?" he demanded. The applicant said quietly that he did. The board president said bluntly, "We have some good-sized boys in this school. Excuse me, but you don't seem very well equipped to handle them!"

"All I'm asking," said the mild gentleman, "is a trial. If I can't manage the job, you won't owe me a dime."

Somewhat reluctantly the member agreed. "Show up Monday morning and we'll see."

News travels swiftly over the oak-brush telegraph. Next Monday morning the one-room, frame schoolhouse was filled to overflowing with a mixed bag of students ranging in age from six to twenty. The small, soft-spoken teacher sat at his desk. As he nodded a greeting to the assembling students, the older boys exchanged knowing glances, sizing up the little man's possibilities. With an outward show of docility, they squeezed, with difficulty, into the biggest desks and sat down.

"Nine o'clock!" suddenly the teacher's voice boomed out with an unexpected note of command, "I think all of you know I'm the new teacher. This is my job and I aim to keep it." With a sudden movement of his right hand he produced a six shooter and laid it on the desk. A gasp of astonishment went around the room. In another instant, his left hand produced a companion gun which he laid beside the other. The room quieted into absolute silence.

"Now then, in case you think I can't handle these — observe the knot in the board just over the back window." All eyes turned at once in that direction. The entire assembly jumped at the thunderous report of a pistol. When the smoke had cleared, a bullet hole appeared dead center in the dark brown half-dollar-sized knot.

"I aim to teach you young ones the best I know how," came the calm voice of the small man at the

194

The "facilities" out back at the Camp Bird school.

desk. "You can't teach where there's unruliness and confusion. We'll have neither here! Write your names and the grade you last attended on the sheet of paper I will pass around. School's in session!"

This was reported to be one of the most successful terms ever taught at Cow Creek. The pupils not only respected the quiet gentleman, they came to love him dearly. Despite their protestations, when the end of the school year arrived, the modest little man packed his few belongings in his duffel bag and moved on "farther west" never to be heard of again.

. . . .

At the height of the mining boom schools were built and used at many isolated mine locations to accommodate resident children. In most cases, the mine owners and operators were the sole employers in the district and provided a local tax base for the support of the school, the mine owner or manager sometimes serving as the local school board president with one or more parents as a supporting cast. Sometimes one of the mothers of school-age children had a teaching degree or had had previous teaching experience. If such a teacher was not available, the next best bet was a young woman who had grown up in one of the nearby mining camps and knew firsthand the sort of conditions she was likely to meet. The isolation, the primitive winter conditions, and the numerous calls for the exercise of innovation and self-reliance, demanded too much from most young women with a big city background and a freshly minted teaching certificate.

Two such schools were kept open in the high country at relatively recent dates. One was located at Sneffels, an extinct settlement near the site of the Revenue and Atlas mines; the other at the Camp Bird mill. Both were up Canyon Creek southwest of Ouray: the Camp Bird mill six miles from Ouray at about 9,500 feet above sea level; the Sneffels school about eight and one-half miles from Ouray at 10,500 feet above sea level. This is high country. Snow was deep from October to May. Avalanches were common. The schoolhouse at Sneffels was demolished by the Torpedo-Eclipse avalanche several winters after it was last used for classes. The school at the Camp Bird mill sat beside an avalanche track which was known as the Schoolhouse Slide. Before it was occupied the last time it was moved to a safer location.

Two of the young women who taught at these schools live in Ouray, today. Barbara McCullough

Students and teacher engaged in a snowball fight at recess time. Camp Bird school.

Camp Bird school. Drying socks, pants and mittens at the pot-bellied stove.

Spencer taught at the Camp Bird school on the eve of World War II; Verena Rucker Jacobson taught at the Sneffels school for several years in the late 1920s.

Each of the former teachers has memories associated with the school where she taught. The following observations come from both. Interestingly, neither dwelt much on the hardships of shoveling snow, carrying coal and water to the schoolhouse, sweeping out, building a fire in the potbellied stove at dawn's early light so the room would be warm enough by the time the pupils arrived, or the isolation of being cut off from most of the rest of the world. Their memories were mostly associated with the good fellowship in the boardinghouse dining room when eating with the mine crew; the home atmosphere of living in the household of the student's parents; an occasional horseback ride to town; and the progress made by several of the better students. The rewards were mixed in with the difficulties.

These mountain schools ran regular terms from September to June, although the term was sometimes shortened in the spring if all prescribed work had been completed. This meant that the middle of the term came at the height of the San Juan winter. Snow might be anywhere from three to ten feet in depth. A trail had to be shoveled or tramped out to the schoolhouse at the first snowfall and kept open with each succeeding snowfall. The schoolhouse was heated by a potbellied stove in the center of the room. Overalls and socks which got wet on the way to school were hung around the stove pipe to dry during the school session. Drinking water came by dipper from a pail in the corner of the room, or, occasionally in a more technologically advanced situation, through a spigot from a stone crock. Coal and kindling for the stove were kept in a covered box just outside the door. The teacher's extra duties included starting the fire before the students arrived, bringing a can or pail of drinking water, and sweeping and dusting the schoolroom after the students had gone for the day.

As in all one-room schools, students recited by grades and worked at reading or doing arithmetic

Camp Bird school interior. Teacher tutoring one student at her desk while two other students work at their desks.

problems when it was another grade's turn to recite. Where there were only four or five students in the whole school, some grades had no students while others had only one. Many of the precepts which would last a student for a lifetime were learned while sitting at the side of the teacher's desk.

Mining camps were usually compact communities, so it was customary for students to go home for a hot lunch at noon; no one had to walk more than several hundred yards. At recess time students and teacher bundled up enough to withstand the weather, went outside, and engaged in snowball fights, ball games, sledding, or whatever energy-releasing activity would arrest the onset of cabin fever, which was a constant danger during San Juan winters.

Mary Kuchs Griffiths attended the Sneffels school with her older sister and two brothers during the years from 1925 to 1930. Verena Jacobson was the teacher at that time. Mary's father was the postmaster and proprietor of the Sneffels store. During the first part of the period there were children from other families at the school.

Mary remembers a lot of hard schoolwork, including the memorization of such gems as Lincoln's Gettysburg Address, the Declaration of Independence, the Preamble to the Constitution, along with such old chestnuts as "The Charge of the Light Brigade," "The Boy Stood on the Burning Deck," and "Under the Spreading Chestnut Tree." This material was for recitation at programs presented by the students for admiring parents and any itinerant miner or mule skinner who could be dragooned into attending a Christmas, Easter, or Washington's birthday affair.

But not all was memorization or exercise drills. Schoolwork was left at the schoolhouse door for the teacher lived and boarded in the Kuch's home, which made her both a teacher and a friend, and there was a whole big unknown world to be explored when school was not in session, especially during the summer months. In those years sheep were grazed each summer above timberline. Mounted on stick horses, the children pretended to herd sheep while the bands of ewes and lambs went by on their way to pasture in the high basins. Once a horse, which had been ridden by a miner to the Revenue Mine and turned loose to return to the Ouray stable (a common practice) was captured and hidden in a willow clump below the schoolhouse, fed grass, and ridden clandestinely, unknown to the children's parents, until Johnny Donald, the stable owner, came up to inquire if anyone had seen the animal.

Many hours were spent riding down the last section of the Torpedo-Eclipse aerial tramway cable on an improvised tram bucket with a makeshift wooden seat —

an exhilarating but dangerous pastime which almost wiped out the entire student body the day Margaret, the oldest and the brakeman for the clumsy contraption, caught her clothes on a protruding bolt head and was only able to leap to the ground in the nick of time to arrest the downward flight of the carriage.

Bill Kuchs, now an engineer for North American Aviation in southern California, remembers vividly the day his Flexible Flyer sled bore him with uncontrolled speed over the frozen crust and into the gorge of upper Canyon Creek before his mother's horrified eyes. With the greatest of good fortune, he and the sled landed on a pile of avalanche debris left on the gorge side, from which his distraught father was able to rescue him. The sled went into the storage closet for the remainder of the season.

If the mountain schools were fun for the children, they were no less so for the teachers. Although Barbara McCullough Spencer had lived in Ouray most of her life, she remembers still the school terms of 1939–1940 and 1940–1941, when she taught at the Camp Bird school. She was later, for a number of years, the Ouray postmistress, a position from which she has recently retired. A letter from her captures some of the flavor of being the Camp Bird "school marm."

April 18, Ouray

Dear Mel and Barbara:
. . . They [students] were all charming children. That's the trouble with being young — it seems I didn't appreciate then the beautiful qualities I remember in those children now. There was no need for "discipline," that bugaboo of young teachers. And we had good times. You ask about the grades taught — In the two terms, I taught all 8 grades — and the little ones learned from the big ones. But, as usual, the teacher learned the most. . . .

Frank Bell got some of the men to lay a water pipe so I could carry fresh water into the school. We kept it in a big earthen-ware crock with a spigot — sorry — no dipper. The — ah — facilities were out in the back — of course. We had electric lights — and the piano which I put [there?] gave us lots of up-town points. I built the fire in the big stove. Have you *priced* those big stoves lately? It probably has something to do with a law of physics, but I could never understand how *one* bucket of coal became *two* buckets of ashes. And I knew we were in the path of a murderous slide. Every so often, I'd tell the children how to react if the slide did run. Next year they moved the schoolhouse closer to the housing area.

How we were looked after at the Camp Bird! The warm room, bridge games sometimes with Mrs. Charles Bell, Mrs. Chuck Bell, Mrs. Josh Billings, Mrs. R. F. Dunn and others as the personnel moved into camp, and out.

And the good food. What great cooks they were — and what pleasant companionship at the table with

Mike Driscoll asking someone to pass "the black bottle" and 'lowing that since "it wasn't fly season," he believed he'd have "another piece of that good raisin pie."

I rode in a "car pool" on Friday evenings to town and back up on Monday mornings with never a qualm over the snow crouched above us or the abyss below. But one time, the slides did run. Boley [Fellin] couldn't get through with his team, let alone the freight truck, and Ed Freeman and I had to go up on horseback. My feet nearly froze into solid lumps. We had to dismount at the Waterhole [a notoriously bad avalanche track] and walk the rest of the way—and I hadn't had enough breakfast. Couldn't take 2 steps without stopping for rest—right under the slide—where 4 men were killed 10 years later—and Ed, bless his courageous and gallant heart, waited for me each time.

You know how beautiful the little town was in the snow at night. No street lights—only the lights from the little homes—looked like a village where Christmas toys were made. The clean, crisp air and the sun after a new snow, making it look as tho' the hills were covered with pink whipped cream. I loved it all, even unto the smell of Xanthates [an oderiferous reagent used in the flotation mill]—and do you remember Franklin Bell saying when he got dressed for town, he slicked his hair down with "Crater Compound," [a heavy black grease used to lubricate the drive gears of the ball mills]? . . .

The school ran another year or so and then they found it more economical to "bus" [loose term] the children to town.

I'm so glad I was the Camp Bird school marm. Wouldn't have traded it for anything. I remember buying a fine big axe to chop the firewood, and walking up Main Street with it over my shoulder. Now, that turned a few heads.

Cordially,
/s./ Barbara

• • • •

Two college-level institutions lie within the boundaries of San Juan country: Western State College, at Gunnison, and Fort Lewis College, which was moved from Hesperus to Durango a few years ago. Both colleges have beautiful mountain country campuses and draw their student bodies from far beyond San Juan country; they are a part of the Colorado state higher educational system.

Two other colleges in the Colorado state system lie very close to, but not in San Juan country: Mesa College, at Grand Junction, and Adams State College, at Alamosa.

Opposite: Barbara McCullough Spencer, Camp Bird teacher, sweeping the floor after students have left for the day. Note the curtains at the windows, the National Geographic map thumb-tacked to the wall, and pictures on the wainscoting.

CHAPTER 18

On High Hills

A thin line must be drawn between the climbing of a mountain summit for the sport and exhilaration of the accomplishment, and scaling a mountain in order to make surveying observations, or to trace a geologic formation across its summit. Both types of climbing have flourished in the San Juan. Mallory's time-worn dictum that a mountain is for climbing "because it is there," isn't always completely satisfactory.

• • • •

The history of mountaineering in the San Juan has gone through at least four phases. If we leave Indians out of the reckoning—so little is known about their mountaineering proclivities that we are in no position to judge—the first phase of San Juan mountaineering occurred during the initial years of the mining boom. It included such early climbs as those made by prospectors in tracing out promising veins; the scientists of the Hayden and Wheeler surveys, who climbed many of the high peaks in the San Juan to occupy them as triangulation and plane table stations; Sunday excursions by miners, storekeepers, managers, surveyors, and assorted townspeople; and vagrant wanderings by sheepherders. Prospect diggings can be found at the very tops of some of the San Juan high peaks, and numerous cairns on ridges can be ascribed to sheepherders.

The topographers and geologists of the Wheeler and Hayden surveys, in 1874, climbed Uncompahgre, Sneffels, Sunshine, Redcloud, Mt. Wilson, and Handies Peak among the 14,000 footers, and several scores of lesser peaks which they used as secondary plane table stations. When the mining boom was going full blast,

Opposite: Mel Griffiths cutting steps across east couloir on north face of Mt. Sneffels, 1930.

even after the turn of the century, it was not uncommon for outing and picnic parties to ride horseback or muleback as close as possible to one of the high peaks from which the erstwhile mountaineers, male and female, scrambled as best they could to the summits of their objectives.

On page 18 of Wright and Wright, *Tiny Hinsdale of the Silvery San Juan,* appear two pictures of parties on the summit of Uncompahgre Peak. The costumes set the time as about 1900. Outing parties frequently set off for Uncompahgre from either Lake City or Capitol City on Henson Creek. One picture shows a sizeable party arranged in front of the remains of the old stone summit shelter which had been erected by the U.S. Army Signal Corps unit which experimented with heliograph communication there in the 1880s. The caption under this photograph contains the information, "Mrs. W. P. Hunt—seated between the two piles of rock—was the oldest woman ever to climb the peak." The other photograph shows several members of the party dangling their feet gingerly over the sheer north face of the peak, and bears the caption: "On top of Uncompahgre. From where this picture was taken one can look straight down several thousand feet."

The sort of mountaineering which was carried out by prospectors and mining engineers during this earliest phase of San Juan climbing has been described engagingly by Robert Livermore, a young mining engineer who worked at the Camp Bird in 1903:

> I liked best the outside work, when in summer we toured the surrounding country surveying claim lines or triangulating contours. I earned the name of "the mountain goat" by my agility in scaling cliffs and planting marker flags in lofty spots. Up above us there were little flats, glacial cirques, real mountain meadows, usually with a small lake in the center, simply ablaze with flowers, the beautiful columbine, painter's [sic] brush, and many alpine varieties unknown to me.

An alpine tarn near timberline in Ice Lake Basin, at head of South Mineral Creek west of Silverton.

Opposite: Aerial view looking south from alpine meadows near head of Blue Creek, south of Cimarron, Colorado. Uncompahgre Peak in right center (14,309 feet above sea level). Glaciated valley of the East Fork of the Cimarron River at right flank of Uncompahgre Peak.

Lizard Head from the north. The ascent of this peak in the San Miguel range was first made by Albert Ellingwood and Barton Hoag. Its summit is still considered to be the most difficult to reach in Colorado.

Sometimes in one of these, out of sight of the transit man below, I would lie on the mossy sward, smoke a pipe, hear the bees humming, the sweet call of the white-crowned sparrow, and watch the cottony clouds go by in the sparkling blue air, for the moment my own master.

Some of the work took us to the tops of the ranges, locating the outcrops of the veins or finding boundaries, where we could climb about on peaks and ledges where a misstep would have meant disaster, where snow lay deep on the north slopes, and ptarmigan, unafraid, walked barely aside, like pigeons on the Common at home. Once, nightfall caught us still on the wrong side of the range, clinging like flies to the steep mountainside. The sun setting behind Potosi lit up the peaks and left the gulches in deepest gloom, so that when we reached the top of the divide we walked along a knife-like ridge in sunlight with black gulfs yawning on either side. A month before I would have been scared by a lively imagination, but by then I was seasoned mountaineer enough to enjoy the experience.

· · · ·

The second phase of San Juan mountaineering is confined to the relatively short period between 1920 and 1929. Climbers from the East and the Midwest, who had experienced mountaineering in New England, Europe, particularly the Alps, began to bring some of their skills and initiative to the Colorado Rockies. All of the highest San Juan summits, the Fourteeners, had already been climbed; indeed, some of them, like the highest of all, Uncompahgre Peak, had become "an easy day for a lady," if the record is clear.

In 1920, technical climbing was brought to the San Juan in a single virtuoso performance by Albert R. Ellingwood. It was technical climbing of a high order of skill. Ellingwood, a professor of political science at Colorado College, Wake Forest, and later an associate dean at Northwestern University, had been a Rhodes Scholar after high school and undergraduate work at Colorado College, Colorado Springs. While at Oxford, he had been introduced to safe technical rock climbing with rope and piton. He had attended Merton College, Oxford, from 1910 to 1913. Godfrey and Chelton, who have traced the history of Colorado rock climbing in their carefully researched and superbly illustrated book, *Climb*, speculate that Ellingwood, while at Oxford, probably climbed "in Wales, the Lake District, and the Alps in the summer." He later showed a familiarity with routes which had been done by pioneer rock climbers at Wasdale Head in the Lake District. Back in Colorado Springs, Ellingwood pioneered in 1914 and 1915 a number of short technical climbs on the soft standstones near the city. His name was given to Ellingwood's Route on Keyhole Rock and what was later called the Old Climber's Route on Greyrock. By modern standards, these routes are still classed as of a high order of difficulty. Ellingwood was

now ready to try his skills on the difficult ridges and faces of the high mountains of the state.

He chose Lizard Head, in the San Juans, as his first goal. A 400-foot tower of rotten volcanic breccia surmounting a ridge east of Mt. Wilson, in the San Miguel Range, the 13,113-foot peak, "even today, is considered to be the most difficult summit to reach in Colorado," according to Godfrey and Chelton. The heart of its difficulty is the extreme rottenness of the poorly consolidated rock which makes up the final spire.

I once tried to describe the ascent of Lizard Head to another climber by the following analogy: "The peak is so rotten that you have to hold it together with one hand while you climb it with your free hand and your feet." Ellingwood had put it this way: "Pebbles rained from its sides as readily as needles from an aging Christmas tree."

Perhaps I can convey some of the anxiety which such a climb on rotton rock creates by relating an incident which occurred in 1931 when I led the party on the sixth recorded ascent of Lizard Head. Preparing to lead up the first pitch, and knowing my mouth was dry to begin with, I popped two sticks of gum in my mouth, hoping to keep the saliva flowing. When I reached the tiny ledge, eighty feet up from the bottom which offers the first stopping point and a meagre station from which to bring up the second man, the chewing gum was coated on my teeth and gums and stuck to the roof of my mouth so tenaciously that it took me the rest of the day to get it unstuck. It would be hard to imagine a more telling testimony to my state of sheer terror.

Godfrey and Chelton have said, "Ellingwood's ascent in 1920 with Barton Hoag was a landmark in Colorado climbing history . . . [their] climb . . . with hemp rope, nailed boots, and only three soft iron pitons for protection has become legendary."

Another San Juan climb of note was Ellingwood and Hoag's ascent of Pigeon Peak in the Needle Mountains ten days before their successful ascent of Lizard Head.

Climbs in other parts of the state which compare with San Juan routes during this period include the 1924 first ascent of the Ellingwood Arête on the Crestone Needle, in the Sangre de Cristo Range; Prof. J. W. Alexander and Jack Moomaw's first and second ascents of the east face of Long's Peak by way of Alexander's Chimney in 1922; the same route's third ascent the same year by a party led by Carl Blaurock; and the 1927 ascent of Stettner's Ledges on the east face of Long's Peak by the Stettner brothers, Joe and Paul.

· · · ·

To put the third phase of San Juan mountaineering in proper perspective we must go back more than a hundred years.

On September 12, 1876, William Henry Holmes, the brilliant geologist/artist of the Hayden Survey (*The United States Geological and Geographical Survey of the Territories*) climbed Hesperus Mountain, in the La Plata Mountains of southwestern Colorado.

While at the summit of Hesperus, Holmes made preliminary notes and sketches from which he later prepared, in his Washington office, a drawing which was reproduced as a chromolithographic panorama depicting the view to the southeastward of the mountain summit. This appeared in the *Hayden Atlas of Colorado*, published in 1877. Near the center of this panorama is an imposing, jagged, dark peak which Holmes labeled, Mt. Moss, named for Capt. John Moss, a crusty old pioneer of the region and one of the founding fathers of nearby Parrott City.

However, the name of Mt. Moss did not long remain on the summit which Holmes had designated. The first U.S. Geological Survey maps of the La Plata Mountains, printed twenty or so years later, apply the name of Moss to another prominent peak, a quarter mile to the southeast and thirty-two feet higher.

The dark peak in the middle of the Holmes panorama remained unnamed until 1976, a hundred years after it sat for its first portrait. During the intervening years, it provided a strong, silent bond between the geologist/artist who first sketched it in the field, a Colorado College professor who proposed a name for the "dark, jagged peak in the middle," and a young engineering student, whose name was eventually given to the peak.

From the summit of Hesperus Mountain, on that day in 1876, Holmes could look down on the piñon-juniper-clothed tableland of the Mesa Verde, whose canyons and overhanging cliffs sheltered the massive apartment complexes of the Anasazi, abandoned in the 1290s. In 1874, two years before his sojourn on Hesperus, Holmes had accompanied W. H. Jackson, the Hayden photographer, down Mancos Canyon. Holmes made very detailed sketches of Anasazi granaries and small cysts on shelves in the canyon walls. But he and Jackson did not see any of the large communal cities such as Cliff Palace, which waited for discovery until 1888.

From Hesperus, to the west, just at the limit of seeing, the blunt conical summits of the Henry Mountains were barely visible, marked by tiny summit clouds on the horizon beyond the Colorado River canyon. They bore the name of Joseph Henry, the American physicist who had been the first secretary of the Smithsonian Institution. Already, Holmes had described the geologic processes which produced the intruded, domed structures to which G. K. Gilbert, a year later, gave the name "laccolith" in his classic study of the Henry Mountains. Holmes didn't yet know that a few years later one of the five peaks of

the Henry Mountains would bear his own name—Mt. Holmes.

Holmes's immediate interest lay to the east and southeast. Hesperus was one of the primary triangulation stations of the Hayden Survey in Colorado. He wished to show its relationship to the main mass of the San Juan Mountains, particularly the other triangulation stations—Mt. Wilson, Mt. Sneffels, Rio Grande Pyramid—the framework upon which the maps of the Hayden survey atlas was being constructed.

Holmes's panorama depicts the view to the southeastward from the summit of Hesperus Mountain. It takes in a horizontal field of view of about 135°, extending from Banded Mountain on the left (it had not yet been named) to Spiller Peak on the right.

Holmes had a passion for detail; he was a superb draftsman. He drew each landscape as he saw it. His concern for accuracy and detail resulted in the depiction of every slope and pinnacle in precise delineation. Because of his training in geology he was able to emphasize the elements of the landscape which best explained its morphology and origin. At the same time he did not hesitate to exercise artistic license if it did not compromise the topographic accuracy of the sketch.

He sometimes placed distant human figures in his panoramas to enhance the feeling of depth and size. A Holmes panorama (in the 1877 Hayden atlas), made from the summit of Rio Grande Pyramid, looking toward the Needle Mountains, contains several mountain sheep on crags in the middle distance.

Scale is provided, in the Hesperus Mountain panorama, by climbing human figures on the ridge between Hesperus and the peak in front of Mt. Moss. Closer, in the foreground, stands a bearded surveyor in a shin-length coat. He is apparently reading the horizontal circle of a theodolite mounted on a tripod, between the legs of which hangs a cistern barometer. Almost underfoot, the recorder sits on the stony ground, writing in the field book which is perched on his knees.

The realism of this surveying ensemble is obvious when one realizes that it was patterned after a photograph made by William Henry Jackson, the Hayden Survey's great photographer, in 1874, two years before the Hesperus scene was sketched. Jackson made his photograph on the summit of Sultan Mountain, south of Silverton, Colorado. The subjects were the topographer, A. D. Wilson and his recorder, and half-brother, Franklin Rhoda. The figures were added to the Hesperus Mountain panorama when Holmes was preparing the finished drawing for publication.

The addition of human figures to a scientific panorama of this sort did nothing to detract from the honesty of the scene. Such touches helped to make the awe inspiring landscape comprehensible to the uninitiated eastern viewer. Thus did Holmes and the Hayden Survey play their part in the opening of the Rocky Mountain West to scientific inquiry.

· · · · ·

The third phase of San Juan mountaineering, which occupied the years from 1929 to about 1960, was most strongly influenced by the efforts and personality of a single individual, Dwight G. Lavender, and the loosely knit organization known as the San Juan Mountaineers, of which he was the initiator and guiding force.

During this period, the Denver-headquartered Colorado Mountain Club scheduled outings into several parts of the San Juans, giving climbers from other parts of the state, and from other states, an opportunity to sample San Juan climbs. Localities visited during the period, and since, have included the Uncompahgre-Wetterhorn locality near Lake City; the San Miguel Range west of Telluride; Chicago Basin, Ruby Creek, Noname Creek, and Balsam Lake in the Needle Mountains; the Mt. Sneffels region near Ouray; and Ice Lake Basin, near Silverton. Although most climbers on these

outings were interested in bagging one or more of the region's 14,000 footers, a select few, following the example of Albert Ellingwood, turned their attention to lower, more difficult, unclimbed peaks and routes. Dwight Lavender was one of these. He combined a lively interest in pioneering first ascents and new routes with an academic's diligence in recording the past climbing history of his chosen arena of activity. By the date of his untimely death in 1934, he had compiled an enviable record of climbs, research, and writing, to say nothing of his advancement toward his educational and professional goals.

Born in Telluride in 1911, Dwight had spent his formative years there. With his older brother, David, he engaged in numerous youthful hikes, climbs, escapades, and adventures on the mine trails, in the basins, and on the glaciated slopes above the town. Later he continued his schooling in Denver. There, while in East High School, he was introduced to the mountaineering activities of the Colorado Mountain Club.

On the 1929 Colorado Mountain Club outing, held in the Uncompahgre-Wetterhorn section of the San Juan, Dwight and David Lavender had come back into their boyhood stamping grounds. The 1931 outing was

Climbing gear of the early 1930s at a lunch stop at the foot of Lizard Head. The shoes in the center of the picture are rope-soled and are being dampened with snow to make them hold better on smooth rock.

Twin Thumbs from the head of Noname Creek in the Needle Mountains. Dwight Lavender is figure at lower right margin.

even more at "home" for them, since it was held in the San Miguel Range, near Telluride.

By this time the boys' step-father, Ed Lavender, was operating sizeable cattle holdings in the west ends of San Miguel and Montrose counties, and the family spent June, July, and August at their summer camp at the foot of the Lone Cone, south of Norwood. Ed Lavender was also one of four owners of the King Lease of the old Camp Bird Mine which was recovering pockets of ore passed over by the former and current owners of the mine.

One of the finest books ever written about the contemporary and just-gone ranching and mining frontiers of the West is David Lavender's *One Man's West.* It describes, lovingly and graphically, the experiences he had as a young man working at the Camp Bird Mine and on the Club Ranch during the sere gray days of the "depression."

Opposite: Dwight Lavender rapelling down the east face of Teakettle in the Sneffels sector of the San Juans. (Lavender-Griffiths)

During the 1929 Colorado Mountain Club outing, Dwight Lavender and his young friend Forrest Greenfield, besides climbing the Fourteeners, made several climbs of lesser peaks on the Cimarron Ridge. Following this, Dwight struck up a correspondence with Chester Price, a Montrose youth who had left his name in the register on the summit of Uncompahgre Peak, inviting correspondence with anyone interested in San Juan climbing. Chester's family were sheep ranchers in the Cimarron Valley between Montrose and Gunnison.

As a result of the correspondence, Chester spent a week visiting in the Lavender home in Denver the following winter. During this visit the boys laid plans for an early trip the next summer into Navajo Basin, at the foot of El Diente and Mount Wilson, in the San Miguel Range near Telluride. This was looked upon as a reconnaissance for the 1931 Colorado Mountain Club outing, which was to be held in the San Miguel Range. On this trip, Dwight, Chester Price, and Forrest Greenfield made what they thought was a first ascent of El Diente, named the peak, and added it to Colorado's list of 14,000-foot peaks. Dwight was to

find later that their climb of El Diente was not a first ascent, it having been climbed earlier by Percy Thomas and W. G. Douglas in 1890, from a start near Dunton. Dwight had uncovered the account of this climb in an 1890s issue of the *Alpine Journal* of London.

As early as 1928 or 1929, Dwight had begun systematically collecting basic historical information about mountaineering in the San Juans. He had searched mountaineering and other outdoor journals, foreign periodicals, the reports of the U.S. government surveys during the last few decades of the nineteenth century, and local newspapers. He began to carry on a voluminous correspondence with all known climbers in even obscure corners of the San Juan.

My own association with Dwight resulted from his meeting and climbing with Chester Price in 1929 and 1930. From the summer of 1931 onward until his death in the fall of 1934, I shared in most of Dwight's San Juan climbing experiences.

By the fall of 1932, Dwight had visited and climbed in almost all parts of the San Juans and had gathered enough material to provide the information base for a "guidebook." With characteristic energy, Dwight did not wait to find a publisher for the work; he forged ahead on his own. Carleton C. Long researched and wrote Part II of the guide which covered the Needle Mountains and the La Plata peaks, while I provided a very short summary of climbs to that date in the Black Canyon of the Gunnison.

The material, which Dwight had been assembling since 1929, was coordinated with the material supplied by Long and Griffiths and produced in typescript book format during Dwight's 1932–1933 fall and winter terms at Leland Stanford University. How he kept up with his studies at the same time is difficult to understand. I never did know whether or not Dwight did the typing himself. The sketch maps, which are sprinkled throughout the text, were hand drawn by Dwight in multiple copies. The photographic illustrations were all taken from cuts which had been published previously in the Colorado Mountain Club's journal, *Trail and Timberline.*

The finished *San Juan Mountaineers' Climber's Guide to Southwestern Colorado* represented an incredible amount of work. It has never been published. However, among the four or five carbon typescript copies which were made, one was placed in the library of the Colorado Mountain Club, where it has been available to climbers who are planning trips in the San Juans.

Left: Two climbers on summit of the Penguin, one of the group of pinnacles on the northwest side of Mt. Sneffels.

Group of three young mountaineers at the head of Navajo Basin in 1930, after successful ascent of El Diente (14,159 feet above sea level). Left to right: Dwight Lavender, Chester Price, and Forrest Greenfield. Lavender and Price, especially Lavender, were responsible for the organization of the San Juan Mountaineers. (Lavender-Griffiths)

213

214

Lunch stop. Just below the summit of Kismet, in the Mount Sneffels group, after the first ascent. Left to right: Dwight Lavender, Gordon Williams, Mel Griffiths.

Opposite: Crossing the bergschrund on small glacier at the north foot of Kismet Peak. Mt. Sneffels in the background. Dwight Lavender giving Lewis Giesecke a foot up.

Dwight Lavender did not live to enjoy the fruits of his labors. In the fall of 1934 he was an early victim of poliomyelitis, only a week or so after returning to Stanford for his first year of graduate work.

Robert M. Ormes, the third member of the trio, was born and raised in Colorado Springs, where his father was the librarian at Colorado College. Bob began his distinguished climbing career under the tutelage of the great pioneer Colorado mountaineer, Albert Ellingwood, who made the first ascents of Lizard Head, Pigeon Peak, in the Needle Mountains, and the Ellingwood Arête of Crestone Peak, all climbs which Bob duplicated at a later date. Now in his seventies, Bob still leads hikes and climbs in the Colorado Springs region, and for many years has been an active member of the Ad-A-Man Club, which makes an annual New Year's Eve climb of Pikes Peak. In addition to numerous articles, maps, and other books, Bob is the author of *Guide to the Colorado Mountains*, which is now in its seventh edition.

During the sixties and seventies, Bob Ormes was the chairman of a Colorado Mountain Club committee on the names of Colorado Mountains. Among other activities this committee investigated and recommended new names to the U.S. Board on Geographic Names, Washington, D.C. This board, under the aegis of the U.S. Geological Survey, Interior Department, supervises the naming of natural features such as lakes, ranges, mountains, rivers, and peaks, which appear on official U.S. maps such as U.S. Geological Survey topographic quadrangles, Coast and Geodetic Survey charts, and maps which appear in the United States Atlas.

Sometime in the early 1970s, Bob Ormes circulated the following memorandum to his fellow members of the Colorado Mountain Club committee on mountain names:

> The rough part of the La Plata Range has a peak about ¼ mile northwest of Mount Moss which it seems to me deserves a name. The San Juan Mountaineers designated it Peak L. [Actually Ll] It is described as incredibly festooned with monzonite pinnacles. Two possibilities suggest themselves: Monzonite Peak and Lavender Peak, the latter to honor the deceased member of the trio of San Juan Mountaineers who conducted measurements and explorations all over the San Juan and produced the Climber's Guide to that area. Dave Lavender [Dwight's older brother] is the author of *Bent's Fort* and other popular western historical studies; their father [step-father] Ed Lavender was a colorful early day stockman.
>
> I'd be interested to hear from the committee if you have a vote—either no or yes, with a preference.

The committee vote was in favor of the Lavender designation, and the recommendation went forward to the Board of Geographic Names, along with the names for several other Colorado mountains.

On October 28, 1975, Ormes was notified by Donald J. Orth, Executive Secretary, Domestic Geographic Names: "At its October meeting, the Board on Geographic Names approved the names, *Precarious Peak, Long Trek Mountain, Lavendar Peak, Lakes Peak,* and *Half Peak*. These decisions will be published in Decision List 7504."

Jerry Hart, a Mountain Club committee member from Denver, discovered that Dwight's name had been misspelled, "Lavendar." It was too late to stop its printing in Decision List 7504. This error was rectified in Decision List No. 7603, which reads, in part:

> *Lavender Peak:* peak, elevation 4,011 m. (13,160 ft.), 0.81 km (0.5 mi.) SE of Hesperus Mountain; named for Dwight Garrigues* Lavender (1911–1935) [1934], mountaineer and author of a climbing guide to the San Juan Mountains: Montezuma Co., Colo.; 37° 26' 30" N, 108° 04' 49" W; 1975 decision revised. Variant: Lavendar Peak (former decision).

While searching for material for his "guidebook," Dwight Lavender must have admired W. H. Holmes's panorama from the summit of Hesperus Mountain; perhaps he felt the strong bond between mountain lovers which spanned the 100 years between their times. It is one of life's ironies that Dwight didn't then know, nor would ever know, that the dark peak in the middle of that panorama was destined for a better name—*Lavender Peak*.

The "Climber's Guide" may have been the principal justification for the decision of the U.S. Board on Geographic Names, however those of us who had climbed with him and had been members of the San Juan Mountaineers could list innumerable other accomplishments for which he was just as deserving. Among these might be listed: participation, often as leader, in a score or more of first ascents and new routes in the San Juans and the Wind River Range in Wyoming; numerous articles on climbs or technical climbing matters in *Trail and Timberline, Appalachia,* and the *American Alpine Journal*; organization of a "San Juan Mountaineers' Geological Survey" which made a supplementary triangulation survey among the major summits of the Sneffels area and, by a line of levels, linked a San Juan Mountaineers' bench mark in Yankee Boy Basin to a U.S. Coast and Geodetic Survey bench mark at the Camp Bird mill; and numerous experiments on the forging of pitons and ice axe heads in the shop of the Engineering School at Leland Stanford University.

As memory brings back the numerous climbing experiences which led us over new routes and to the sum-

---

*Dwight's middle name was that of his maternal grandfather, Judge James E. Garrigues, a justice of the Colorado Supreme Court from 1911 to 1921, and chief justice from 1919 to 1921. It will be further noted that the year of Dwight's death was erroneously given as 1935, whereas the correct year was 1934.

d.d. Head waters of the Rio La Plata
Drainage of the foreground belongs to the Rio Mancos

The central part of the William H. Holmes panorama, "The La Plata Mountains," from the Hayden Atlas of Colorado, *U.S. Geological and Geographical Survey of the Territories, 1877. The peak labeled "C" in this panorama was named Lavender Peak in 1976 to honor Dwight G. Lavender, who produced the* San Juan Climbers Guide to Southwestern Colorado, *and pioneered mapping, exploration, and technical climbing in the San Juans. (F. V. Hayden,* Atlas of Colorado, *U.S. Geological and Geographical Survey of the Territories, 1877.)*

mits of unclimbed peaks in the Sneffels Range, the San Miguels, the Needle Mountains, I marvel that Dwight was able to pack so much of it into the few short years which were allotted to him.

Although it was dominated by his presence, the third phase of San Juan mountaineering did not come to an end with Dwight Lavender's death in 1934. Members of the San Juan Mountaineers, as well as others, continued to explore the ranges, follow new routes, and make first ascents: Needle Ridge, Chimney Peak, Jagged Mountain, the Index; the east face of Monitor Peak, the north face of Pigeon Peak; winter ascents of Sneffels, Mount Wilson, Arrow, and Vestal. Indeed, there are still new faces and routes to be conquered in the San Juans.

• • • •

The fourth phase of San Juan mountaineering is almost anticlimax. There are no snow and ice climbs in Colorado comparable to those found in the Alps, the Himalayas, or among the Alaskan giants—except those found on an occasional winter climb.

The San Juan climbs which gave their stamp to phase four were rock climbs. They occurred during the period from about 1960 to the present. The chief accomplishments have resulted from the introduction of advanced climbing techniques brought to Colorado in the immediate post-World-War II era: the principal of the "dynamic belay," introduced from California, which enabled the second man on the rope to adequately protect the leader on long rope run outs; new nylon climbing rope which was elastic yet strong enough, combined with a dynamic belay, to afford the leader real protection in case of a fall; expansion bolts which could be placed in drilled holes for direct aid over sheer, smooth, and overhanging pitches; light alloy pitons and aluminum alloy carabiners (snap rings); stirrups (*etriers*) introduced from Europe; and the prusik knot and jumars for climbing a fixed rope directly.

Tent on summit of Mt. Sneffels (14,150 feet above sea level). San Miguel range faintly visible on left skyline. A surveying crew of San Juan Mountaineers camped for several days on the summit of Mt. Sneffels while Dwight Lavender turned angles for a triangulation network.

Opposite: Ice climbing in the central couloir on the north face of Mt. Sneffels.

The view to the south from the summit of Jagged Mountain in the Needles. Windom Peak (14,087 feet above sea level) on the left center skyline is separated from Sunlight Peak (14,059 feet above sea level) on the right, by a narrow, jagged ridge of granite pinnacles.

Opposite: Pinnacles on the west flank of Mt. Sneffels. View from the base of The Hand. Dallas Peak is the notch-topped summit on the skyline. Below and to the left of the summit of Dallas, a little higher than halfway between top and bottom of the print, is the steep-sided cone which Dwight Lavender named Wolf Tooth.

Climbing into the base of a prominent chimney on the east face of Wolf Tooth.

Climbing in chimney on the east face of Wolf Tooth.

223

Outfitted with an adequate poundage of hardware and the necessary footage of rope and line for this type of direct aid climbing, teams and even solo climbers were prepared to "engineer" their way up sheer and even overhanging walls.

Most of these new climbs in the San Juans have taken place on the sheer walls of the Black Canyon of the Gunnison: the north and south walls of Chasm View, and the Painted Wall, where over 2,000 feet of sheer and overhanging granite and pegmatite-injected gneiss has challenged the most accomplished rock climbers in the state. The rock is relatively solid, has a good fracture system, and is appropriately vertical.

As one who did most of his climbing during the third phase of San Juan mountaineering, when it was "inappropriate" for the leader to fall, I find these "new" climbs and climbers puzzling. I had never heard of a dynamic belay until my climbing days were mostly over. I find it slightly unnerving to drive out to Chasm View in the Black Canyon Monument and watch two or three puppet-sized figures suspended on thin nylon spider webs, working their slow way up the smooth vertical face of the opposite canyon wall. On some of these climbs which take several days, the climbers are prepared to spend the night suspended in a cocoon of rope snapped by a carabiner to a wafer-thin piton pounded into a hairline crack in a vertical face. I can remember with distaste an occasional nocturnal vigil on an uncomfortable rocky ledge, on the side of some San Juan Peak, but seldom was this by choice.

Not all of the "new" rock climbing is direct aid climbing, where pitons and expansion bolts are used as direct aid (a sort of ladder) for surmounting a difficult pitch or overhang. In the past ten or fifteen years, more and more skilled climbers have come to what they call "free climbing." The rope and the hardware is kept below and behind the climber for protection in case of a fall. The overriding philosophy is "if you can't climb it without direct aid, don't climb it." The practitioners of free climbing are usually magnificently trained and conditioned athletes who are able to climb pitches and even overhangs which would not have been attempted without direct aid a few years ago.

I must confess a feeling of greater kinship with the "free climbing" tradition than with the "direct aid" school, which would force a way to the top by whatever means required. Besides, the "direct aid" school tends to leave a lot of untidy hardware behind, pinned into the face of their mountain. In these days of environmental concern, that is a form of littering. Perhaps San Juan mountaineering has now come full circle. It would seem that the prospector, Indian brave, or government surveyor who climbed the peaks in pursuit of a personal goal or in his line of work would recognize a greater kinship with the free climber of to-day than with the "rock engineer," who drills and pins his way to his goal.

* * * * *

The history of skiing and winter sports in San Juan country is both parallel and divergent from the development of mountaineering.

During the mining boom, roads and trails between high altitude mines and the nearest camp were kept open year around in order to keep a crew working during the hard winters. At some of the mines there were Norwegian and Swedish miners who had brought from the old country a long heritage of skiing. Their long, narrow cross-country-type skis (up to eleven feet long) with leather thong bindings (locals called these skis "snow-shoes") were soon making tracks beside the trenched mule trails from the mines.

Standard skiing technique was to ride these clumsy boards with a single six- or seven-foot pole upon which the skier rested his weight while dragging it on the inside of a turn, wrestling the skis around. When going straight down steep slopes, the skier rode the pole like a stick horse, dragging it behind as a brake.

Few non-Scandanivian miners took to skiing, but their example introduced all to the mobility afforded by these ungainly appendages. They were a particular boon to mail-carriers who had to cross the ranges in winter time.

During his tenure at the first church on the Western Slope at Lake City, it was decided that the Reverend George Darley should cross to Silverton to meet with the Presbyterians in that camp and hold services. He started on May 17, 1877, in the teeth of a violent spring storm, on horseback. On the early morning of the eighteenth, Darley got breakfast at a cabin far up the Lake Fork above Lake San Cristobal. The Reverend Sheldon Jackson, Darley's superior, continues the story:

> While there Gus Talbot, who carries the mail over the mountains on snow-shoes and has seen a hundred avalanches thunder and crash across his trail, came along with the mail, having traveled sixteen miles since one o'clock that morning. By seven A.M. they reached Burrows Park, ten thousand five hundred feet above the sea. This was as far as they could ride. From there on they must walk on snow-shoes. At the park were a number of miners waiting to cross the range, but, as the storm was still raging, none of them dared make the attempt. A consultation was had. It seemed madness to venture. But the mail-carrier was determined to make the attempt, and Mr. Darley caught the spirit. Said he: "Darley, I have carried the mail across here for years. Again and again I have crossed when I could not see as far as the point of my snow-shoe. You have faced the storm twenty-two miles yesterday, dare you face it twenty-three miles farther with me?"
> With the calmness of men who understood the perils before them, they started—Gus Talbot with forty

Mel Griffiths at the summit of Mt. Sneffels during first winter ascent of the peak, February 1934.

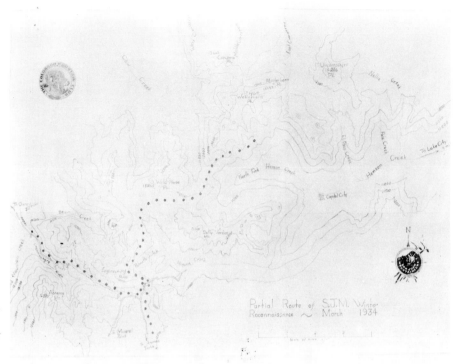

Map of winter reconnaissance, March 1934, made by Gordon Williams and Mel Griffiths from Ouray to the head of the north fork of Henson Creek, near Lake City. Map plotted by Dwight Lavender.

pounds of mail on his back and Mr. Darley with his blankets.

The upshot was that they got lost in the storm after crossing the divide, and after tumbling over a cliff in the deep snow drifts they finally staggered into Animas Forks.

Sixteen downhill miles later, in Silverton, the next day "Gus Talbot, the plucky mail-carrier, told the people that they could 'tie' to George M. Darley, for, out of more than one hundred men he had piloted across the range, the Presbyterian preacher was the only one that had the grit to keep with him all the way."

Skiing for sport in the San Juans did not truly arrive until the 1920s, when it was done in conjunction with sledding by school children on the streets of mining camps or on nearby hills.

Alpine-type skiing came to the high country around Ouray, Telluride, and Silverton in connection with winter ascents of some of the higher peaks. One winter, three of us spent three or four months at the Crawford sawmill at the north base of Mt. Sneffels. From there we made ski climbs in Blaine Basin, Blue Lakes Basin, and a winter ascent of Sneffels itself. Later that winter, Gordon Williams and I skied from Poughkeepsie Gulch over Engineer Mountain Pass, across American Flat to the base of Uncompahgre Peak and back into Silverton by way of Animas Forks.

The development of winter sports centers in the San Juans had to wait until after World War II had run its course.

Large infusions of development money and a good measure of local faith and effort have permitted Telluride, Purgatory, and Crested Butte (which technically does not lie in San Juan country, although it is in Gunnison County) to capitalize on some of the finest weather and skiing terrain in the world.

At least one of these centers will someday develop into a world-class resort.

• • • •

Beginning in 1979, the MOUNTAINFILM festival has been held in Telluride, Colorado. It is described as "A Celebration of Mountain-Related Film Art." It more than lives up to its billing.

For the three days of the festival (usually at the Memorial Day weekend) mountain-related films from all over the world are shown to packed houses in the little opera house at the New Sheridan. It is an occasion for mountaineers from many countries to meet, exchange reminiscences, and view the films of the year which have been gathered from far and wide.

Participants who have attended the two or three other mountain film festivals in Europe and Canada, have pronounced the Telluride festival the best of the lot. It is gratifying and appropriate that San Juan country should be the setting for such an international event.

EPILOGUE

Here and There

I t is unfortunate that the love-hate relationship between man and nature, through most of human history, has been an adversary one. Nature must be conquered. Raw materials must be cut and mined from the environment. Animals, birds, and fish caught and killed to replenish the larder or provide a product for market. Only at rare intervals in this eternal dance of death and destruction has the occasional individual or organization paused long enough to contemplate the natural environment with a benign, thankful, or coldly scientific eye.

At the Atlantic shore the Old World immigrant took axe in hand, set his face westward, and chopped his way through the wilderness, making a home, clearing fields, planting a subsistence crop, congregating with his peers in rural villages. The term "frontier" was synonymous with the cutting edge of the struggle between man and nature. It took 200 years to push that cutting edge from the rocky New England coast to the bluffs and mud flats of Puget Sound.

As in a prolonged military campaign, pockets of enemy resistance were left behind, to be surrounded by the successive waves of the great westering. The San Juan country became one of these pockets where a mopping-up action was required decades after the initial waves had overrun the outposts.

The conflict between man and nature still looms large in the San Juans; the pioneer fringe — the cutting edge — still lies across the high peaks and forests. The individual skirmishes which have marked the past and continue today, punctuate the struggle. These little dramas are as diverse as the actors and the aspect of the natural landscape which they illuminate.

. . . .

As tourism becomes a stronger segment of the regional economy, particularly with the decline of mining, the conflict between man and nature goes on between a new pair of antagonists — a flatlander who has

seldom been previously exposed to the essential fragility of the high country environment and an environment which has not yet recovered from the shock waves of the mining boom.

The impact is not always destructive. A group of Future Farmers of America from the Uncompahgre Valley or the San Luis Valley, can traverse a section of the Weminuche Wilderness for a week with saddle horses and a pack outfit and bring away only pleasant memories and leave behind no debris to mark their passage. The same can be said for a troop of well-indoctrinated Boy Scouts, Girl Scouts, or a clutch of Outward Bound participants. However, this happy state of affairs is not so likely to be true of the daily passages of tourist-laden jeeps through parts of the high country. Cliffhanging mine roads crosscross the high basins and ridges. The four-wheel-drive vehicle has made these high places accessible now to the armchair tourist, if his lungs and heart can take the altitude. Furthermore, the tourist with a valid driver's license can hire a drive-it-yourself jeep in most of the mountain towns, thus escaping the supervision and aid and comfort of a driver familiar with local conditions, restrictions, and customs.

. . . .

A stretch-frame jeep, its four bench seats crammed with tourists, arrives at the site of the Tomboy Mine above Telluride. This above-timberline basin, once filled with mine and mill structures which throbbed with activity, has now fallen prey to winter snows and summer rains. The jeep driver announces this as a half-hour stop. By the time the words are out of his mouth, the passengers have swarmed over the already-devastated hillside, like scavenging ravens at a town dump, looking for spikes, bolts, shards of chinaware, bottles, any shred of rusty metal, brick, or crockery which will serve as a memento of their adventure in the high country.

·····

The average native resident of San Juan country is a rancher, miner, merchant, farmer, salesman, teacher, construction worker, service industry employee, clerk, typist, mechanic. Statistically, a higher percentage of this number is likely to be self-employed than among the population at large. He sometimes bears the scars of pioneering in a sparsely settled and remote region. He is more interested in local happenings than in the earth-rumbling occurrences which punctuate the news in the broad world beyond the ranges.

Describing the innate provincialism of Alaskans, John McPhee said: "If Boston was once the most provincial place in America (the story goes that after a six-megaton bomb exploded in Times Square a headline in a Boston paper would say, 'HUB MAN KILLED IN NEW YORK BLAST'), Alaska, in this respect, may have replaced Boston."

San Juan country seems to occupy an intermediate station, closer to Boston or Alaska than to San Francisco or New York. The tide of Back-Bay Boston capital investment in San Juan mining ventures at the turn of the century, may have tinctured San Juan intellectual isolationism. The price of wool, potatoes, onions, yearling calves, fat lambs, and grain on the country's commodity markets, and gold, silver, lead, zinc, and copper at the smelter, commands more attention in the San Juan than the progress of the latest disarmament talks in Helsinki or Geneva. This is not to say that the average San Juan native is boorishly provincial. His tussles with an uncompromising "world" has taught him to look first toward the segments of the external environment which are most likely to affect hearth and home. Only later does his attention extend to more esoteric matters.

·····

The awesome proportions of the generation gap were brought home by a recently scanned paragraph from a leading western newspaper. The item was embedded in a man-about-town type of column, and I'm morally certain the author meant to be humorous:

"Out on West 54th Street in Table Mountain there's an eatery which advertises 'Oven-Fresh Hot Pasties.'

"I wonder if they stick better when they're hot?"

To permit a misconception of this magnitude in a widely read newspaper of an old dowager mining town is beyond the bounds of good taste. My initial interpretation classifies the columnist as a member of the younger generation and an outlander, to boot. The point of his humor seems to derive from his assumptions that "pasties" are legally indispensable items of camouflage sometimes worn by topless waitresses and strippers.

Unless my credentials in an older and slower generation are spurious, what the eatery's proprietor was advertising was a type of meat pie much esteemed by Cornish miners. It is sad to note that the heritage of the Cousin Jack miner has apparently survived scarcely more than two generations since its first imprint upon the western mining frontier. In the heyday of Butte, Wallace, Central City, Aspen, Telluride, Ouray, the Comstock, Grass Valley, and the Mother Lode, the Cousin Jack miner who went down the shaft without a fresh-baked pasty in his lunch bucket or jacket pocket was a deprived man.

The pasty—pronounced with a short "a" to rhyme with "blast"—crossed the Atlantic in the nineteenth century with the Cornish miners who immigrated to U.S. hard rock camps—the copper ranges of Michigan, lead mines at Galena, copper workings at Butte, silver at Coeur d'Alene, and the gold camps of Central City, Cripple Creek, Ouray, Telluride, Grass Valley, Placerville. Any similarity between a Cornish pasty and the frozen meat pies dispensed by quick food counters or by working wives is coincidental.

Pasties in the old mining camps were encased in a durable crust which was strong enough to dam up the insides without the necessity of being baked in an individual pannikin. Jennie Wright put her pasties together with a final Cornish twist or crimp which would have eluded the skills of an accomplished pretzel bender, and which kept the contents safe through the vicissitudes of baking and the journey underground to the working face.

Some unsung Cornish miner's wife must have created the first pasty as a convenient way of getting her man's meat and potatoes to the underground place of consumption. It could be carried expeditiously in a pocket or lunch pail. Wrapped in a few layers of cloth or paper, its contents stayed warm for a long time. It was both tasty and nourishing whether hot or cold.

Its manufacture was simplicity itself. A translation of Jennie Wright's recipe would have gone something like this, if she had ever written it down. The dough for the crust was usually more short than standard biscuit dough but was not so short as pie dough. When mixed this was patted out to a thickness several times greater than pie dough. It was then cut into six- or eight-inch squares, each one of which was intended to encase a pasty. The remaining ingredients, which made up the filling, consisted of irregularly chopped chunks of trimmed veal, pork, onion, turnip, and potatoes, salted and peppered to taste. None of the inside ingredients was cooked ahead of time, nor was any moisture added to that already contained in the natural ingredients. A portion of the prepared inside filling was placed in the center of each square of dough and then imprisoned by catching up the four corners and crimping them at the center. Three or four slits were made in the top of the dough to permit steam to escape. The pasty was baked in a moderate oven for an hour or perhaps a little more at higher elevations, where many western mining camps were located.

When other ingredients such as pilchard, herring, mutton and goat meat, were easy at hand, they were used, albeit reluctantly. Even when times were hard, the contents of a pasty seldom wandered far afield from the basic ingredients.

Many a pasty was heated in a lunch bucket supported by three spikes driven in a timber over a miner's candle. But an equally large number were eaten cold, with the consumer none the worse for it.

To know that an honest Cornish pasty had been confused with something to paste on the outside of the anatomy instead of the inside, would have been a sore blow to the likes of Cornish-born Bob Fitzsimmons who lifted the world's heavyweight boxing championship from "Gentleman Jim" Corbett in 1897, or the countless hardworking "Cousin Jennies" who followed their men to the New World and made certain that their lunch buckets were appropriately filled.

All of which illustrates how fleetingly time flies as our Western heritage is buried in new folkways. It is a sad thing to see the pasty, which once enjoyed an honored place in the miner's lunch pail, transmuted by the alchemy of time and misapprehension into camouflage for working girls. *O tempora! O mores!*

* * * *

In spite of the stamp of provincialism suggested for San Juan country, the region has produced its fair percentage of individuals committed to the life of the mind. The *Denver Times*, July 28, 1901, contained the following book review:

Spirit of the Mountains

Alfred Castner King has lived among the wonderful works of nature in the heart of the Rocky Mountains, and has breathed inspiration from his surroundings. What he has seen he has also felt, and these feelings he has expressed in the form of verse, collected in a little volume just published by the Fleming H. Revell Company, New York. The work is entitled *Mountain Idylls* and contains about sixty poems, most of them on subjects suggested by the grandeur and beauty of the mountains. The book contains seventeen half-tone illustrations of Colorado scenery, principally from the San Juan country.

The verses have much merit and indicate the soul poetic of the writer. Mr. King resides at Ouray, and has written these verses since the light of the Colorado sun was banished forever from his eyes by a premature mining explosion a year and a half ago.

* * * *

Two miles below Ouray, on a shelf above the Uncompahgre River, the grade of the long-abandoned narrow gauge railroad line hugs a red sandstone bluff. Between the grade and the river two rounded knobs

offer enough space for a pair of vacation cabins, each a modern A-frame with firewood ricked under the eaves.

The downriver cabin of the two bears this sign at the roadside:

CALCULUS CASTLE
DR. JOHN SLYE

$$\chi = -b \pm \frac{\sqrt{b^2 - 4ac}}{2a}$$

* * * *

The influx of part-time residents and full-time retired residents to San Juan country during the past twenty years has moved the region steadily toward a certain elitism which it did not seek. A random roll call would cite the following: an airline president, the president of one of the nation's largest general aviation sales organizations, a former Pulitzer Prize-winning journalist, a Texas legislator, a dozen or more retired or semiretired college professors or deans (this does not count any of the resident faculty of Fort Lewis College, Western State College, Mesa College, or Adams State College), a working airline captain who commutes from the Western Slope to his work out of Denver, and assorted geologists—oil, mining, government, active, and retired.

* * * *

Alex and Dorothy Brownlee's modest, rambling home is hidden by a spruce grove. Unless you have been led to it, you would never find it, although it is within a mile of Ouray. Alex and Dorothy are retirees from the University of Chicago, where his teaching career was in the field of statistics, while she pursued a research career in biochemistry and microbiology. Outside of the fact that Dorothy presents an occasional invited paper at a scientific meeting and Alex serves as a consultant to projects going forward at distant research institutes, their quiet lives seem undistinguished.

Not so! Neither has fallen into the lethargic retirement inactivity which so often overtakes one just cut free from wage-earner status. Dorothy has taught herself to play the harpsichord on an instrument which Alex built for her. She also plays recorder in a local ensemble made up of other retirees and townsmen. To this she has added active greenhouse gardening—she sometimes plant-sits for vacationing friends—weaving, and needlework. The books and records on the shelves, the scientific journals and art reproductions on the walls attest to a way of life and style which was brought to their new home from the academic background from which they retired. She and Alex both attend special interest meetings in distant towns and states and have seldom let a year pass without visiting one of the European cultural centers. Some time ago

Alex showed me a hardbound Russian translation of one of the standard books on statistics which he had written a few years ago. He hasn't received any royalties, nor is he likely to, but at least the Russians have paid him the sincere flattery of pirating one of his books.

All this is only a prelude to serious retirement living. Back of the house, Alex has built an astronomical observatory complete with a sixteen-inch reflecting telescope and a protective dome. Setting circles have been fashioned from plywood arcs upon which are mounted steel tape measures, marking off degrees, minutes and seconds of declination and hours, minutes, and seconds of right ascension. The sturdy fork of the mount was built of four-by-six timbers salvaged from the Ouray city dump.

On moonless nights, winter and summer, Alex makes exposures on photographic film at the prime focus of the telescope. Getting a good negative of a faint object may take several hours of patient tracking as the object moves across the sky, painting its faint light on the film. His special targets are galaxies. His astrophotographs are exceptional—they pass the test of close visual comparison with photographs made at major observatories such as Palomar, Kitt Peak, and Yerkes. From time to time one or more of his photographs is published in one of the astronomical journals.

To come into Alex and Dorothy Brownlee's home and enjoy their hospitality and the *ambiance* which surrounds their past academic and artistic pursuits is to escape into an intellectual realm not often found on what remains of the Western frontier. They are not alone; the number of their kindred spirits is increasing in the high country.

· · · ·

A monumental social document came out of the Great Depression—the photo collection of the Farm Security Administration. Individual pictures in this collection of almost 150,000 photographs, housed in the Library of Congress, have been called by Edward Steichen, one of the twentieth century's master photographers, "the most remarkable human documents ever rendered in pictures." Another observer has said these are "pictures that altered America."

As the Depression deepened in the early 1930s, farmers as a group were hard hit. Prices had tumbled, mechanization was driving the small farmer from his land or into tenancy, and the most severe drought in decades settled in the Midwest and the high plains. The exodus, so hauntingly depicted by John Steinbeck in *The Grapes of Wrath*, had already begun from the parched grainfields and cotton land of the South and the mid-continent to the beckoning shore and the great central valley of California.

Franklin D. Roosevelt, in April of 1935, established the Resettlement Administration, which was soon renamed the Farm Security Administration, to relocate dispossessed farmers. Rexford Guy Tugwell, Columbia University economist, was placed in charge of the undertaking. Aware of the controversial nature of the proposed resettlement, and realizing that it would be necessary to persuade the public of the need for such massive federal help for the rural sector of the economy, Tugwell turned for help to one of his fellow faculty members at Columbia.

This colleague, Roy Stryker, was an engineer and economist, and an unlikely candidate for the task of convincing the nonfarm segment of the country's population that farmers needed special and urgent federal help. Some observers in inner administration circles were surprised that Tugwell did not turn to one of the great public relations or advertising firms for the selling job. That he had chosen wisely was soon apparent.

Roy Stryker was still a country boy at heart, despite years of intense college training and several decades of residence in New York City. He had been raised on a ranch near the headwaters of the Uncompahgre River on the north edge of San Juan country. From this "homeland" he had gone forth to do battle with the world.

Stryker chose the photograph as his persuasive tool. He once described it to me thus: "The photograph, that little rectangle, that's one of the damndest educational devices that was ever made." He brought together a company of men and women photographers, and soon-to-be photographers, whose names would become legendary in the annals of documentation: Dorothea Lange, Arthur Rothstein, Russell Lee, Marion Post Wolcott, John Vachon, Carl Mydans, Walker Evans, and even the artist Ben Shahn, who, at the start, hardly knew one end of a camera from the other, but who, once he had mastered the rudimentary operating fundamentals of a Leica, began to produce sensitive photographs of dispossessed farm people.

Roy Stryker was not a photographer himself. He once said, "I wouldn't know how to take a picture of my aunt." But he did know how to quiz, prod, probe, hector, challenge, suggest, and inspire his team into producing the sort of spare documentary photographs which became a powerful evocation of our country's time of trial during the Depression. Roy once told me that one of his first tasks was to instill in each of the photographers a sense of the man-land relationship in America. To help them toward this insight, he gave each a copy of J. Russell Smith and M. Ogden Phillips's *North America*, a 1,000-page, economics-oriented geography text, the senior author of which was one of Stryker's Columbia colleagues. He insisted that they read it. As the photographers familiarized themselves with the meaning of environment and man-land dynamics from the Smith and Phillips text, as they received encouragement and probing questions from Stryker, and as they absorbed some of the earthy humanity from their farm subjects, they began to produce photographs which taught the nation the plight of a dispossessed rural population.

When his college teaching days were over, Roy Stryker returned to the Uncompahgre Valley from which he had gone forth. He later moved to his retirement home in Grand Junction, where he worked with his beloved photographs until the day he died.

* * * *

In these many subtle ways has San Juan country shed its influence and made its environmental impact on past and present. We can only guess at what the future will bring. The San Juan environment and the people who call it home have, in a unique way, made it a very, very special sort of place. Many of those who have come to love San Juan country have felt a holistic kinship between man and nature which suggests that belief in the progress of mankind, which was so much a part of nineteenth century philosophy, and which was thought to have been extinguished by World War I, World War II, the death camps of Auschwitz and Buchenwald, the violence of Hiroshima, Vietnam and Iran. It may not be dead after all. San Juan country still has brittle blue winter skies, golden sunsets, and shimmering flames on frost-touched aspens—a sustaining ecosystem in grandest terms.

BIBLIOGAPHY

PROLOGUE
San Juan Country
The Miera map mentioned here is reproduced in:

Bolton, Herbert E. (1950) "Pageant in the Wilderness, the Story of the Escalante Expedition to the Interior Basin, 1776," *The Utah Historical Quarterly*, Vol. XVIII. Salt Lake: The Utah Historical Society.

A general discussion of the landforms which shape and surround San Juan country are found in:

Hunt, Charles B. (1967) *Physiography of the United States.* San Francisco and London: W. H. Freeman and Company.

CHAPTER 1
The Landscape
An excellent introduction to the geology of Colorado is found in:

Chronic, John and Halka (1972) *Prairie, Peak, and Plateau, a Guide to the Geology of Colorado.* Denver: Colorado Geological Survey Bulletin 32, Colorado Geological Survey.

For a detailed discussion of San Juan geology see:

Atwood, Wallace W. and Kirtley F. Mather (1932) *Physiography and Quaternary Geology of the San Juan Mountains, Colorado,* U.S. Geological Survey Professional Paper 166. Washington, D.C.: U.S. Government Printing Office.

CHAPTER 2
Skin Game
"How the Rhinoceros Got his Skin" is found in:

Kipling, Rudyard (1978 Edition) *Just So Stories, for Little Children.* New York: Weathervane Books.

The modern concept of plate tectonics is described in a number of recent books and periodicals, among which can be listed:

Sullivan, Walter (1974) *Continents in Motion: The New Earth Debate.* New York: McGraw-Hill Book Co.

Continents Adrift, Readings from Scientific American, with Introductions by J. Tuzo Wilson (1971). San Francisco: W. H. Freeman.

The structural elements of the Uncompahgre Arch, the fractured mineral belt, and the San Juan uplift are discussed and illustrated in:

King, Philip B. (1959) *The Evolution of North America.* Princeton: The Princeton University Press, Chapter 7, Part 5.

The detailed geologic history of the San Juan region is covered in a number of monographs, among which can be listed:

Atwood and Mather (1932) cited among sources for Chapter 1.

Larsen, Esper and Whitman Cross (1956) *Geology and Petrology of the San Juan Region, Southwestern Colorado,* U.S. Geological Survey Professional Paper 258. Washington, D.C.: U.S. Government Printing Office.

Barker, Fred (1969) *Precambrian Geology of the Needle Mountains, Southwestern Colorado*, U.S. Geological Survey Professional Paper 644-A. Washington, D.C.: U.S. Government Printing Office.

Steven, Thomas A. and Peter W. Lipman (1976) *Calderas of the San Juan Volcanic Field, Southwestern Colorado*, U.S. Geological Survey Professional Paper 958. Washington, D.C.: U.S. Government Printing Office.

CHAPTER 3
The Mills of God

The recent study of rock glaciers cited in this chapter is:

White, Paul Gary (1973) *Rock Glaciers in the San Juan Mountains, Colorado*. (Unpublished Ph.D. dissertation), Department of Geography, University of Denver.

Other monographs dealing with rock glaciers in the San Juan region include:

Atwood and Mather (1932) previously cited in Chapters 1 and 2.

Howe, Ernest (1909) *Landslides in the San Juan Mountains*, U.S. Geological Survey Professional Paper 67. Washington, D.C.: U.S. Government Printing Office.

Cross, Whitman and Ernest Howe (1905) *Silverton Folio*. U.S. Geological Folio No. 120. Washington, D.C.: U.S. Government Printing Office.

CHAPTER 4
Water, Snow, and Ice

The Atwood quotation is from Atwood and Mather (1932) already cited in the bibliography for Chapters 1, 2, and 3, p. 42.

A fundamental physical geography text which will provide the reader with the basic background information on water and glacial erosion is:

Strahler, Arthur N. (1969) *Physical Geography*. New York: John Wiley and Sons.

CHAPTER 5
A Self-made Climate

Mark Twain's speech about New England weather is from:

Bartlett, John (1955) *Familiar Quotations*. Boston: Little Brown and Company.

For a general discussion of Colorado and San Juan climate, the following sources are recommended:

Siemer, Eugene G. (1977) *Colorado Climate*. Fort Collins: Colorado State University.

Berry, Joseph W. (1960) *Climates of the States, Climatography of the United States, #60–5 Colorado*. Washington, D.C.: United States Department of Commerce, Weather Bureau.

Peattie, R. (1936) *Mountain Geography, A Critique and Field Study*. Cambridge, Mass.: Harvard University Press.

Atwood, W. W. (1927) "Utilization of the Rugged San Juans," *Economic Geography*, 3: 193–209.

The quotation from the "historical climatology" section of the "final report" is taken from:

Steinhoff, Harold W. and Jack D. Ives, Editors (1976) *Ecological Impacts of Snowpack Augmentation in the San Juan Mountains, Colorado*. Final report to Bureau of Reclamation, San Juan Ecology Project, prepared by personnel from Colorado State University, Fort Collins; Institute of Arctic and Alpine Research, University of Colorado, Boulder; and Department of Biological Science, Fort Lewis College, Durango.

CHAPTER 6
Catastrophe

Incidents in connection with the Wolf Creek Pass avalanche have been taken from local and regional newspapers at the time.

An invaluable compilation of statistics on avalanche occurrence in the central San Juans is to be found in:

Armstrong, Betsy R. (1976) *Century of Struggle Against Snow: A History of Avalanche Hazard in San Juan County, Colorado*, Occasional Paper No. 18, 1976, San Juan Avalanche Project, Institute of Arctic and Alpine Research, University of Colorado, Boulder, Colorado.

——— (1977) *Avalanche Hazard in Ouray County, Colorado, 1877–1976*, Occasional Paper No. 24, 1977, San Juan Avalanche Project, Institute of Arctic and Alpine Research, University of Colorado, Boulder, Colorado.

The discussion of avalanche characteristics is based on Chapter 2: "Nature and Causes of Avalanches in the San Juan Mountains" in:

Armstrong, Richard L. and Jack D. Ives, Editors (1976) *Avalanche Release and Snow Characteristics*, Occasional Paper No. 19, Institute of Arctic and Alpine Research, Report to the Bureau of Reclamation by INSTAAR. Boulder: University of Colorado.

The description of the Camp Bird Avalanche of 1936 is based on the author's having been in the rescue party, digging for victims, and from interviews with survivors. An account of the avalanche can be found in:

Griffiths, Mel (1956) "White Terror at Camp Bird," *Empire Magazine*, The Denver Post, Feb. 26, pp. 12–14.

Armstrong, Betsy R., *Century of Struggle Against Snow*.

The incident in which miners from the Virginius Mine were buried in an avalanche is from:

Gibbons, Rev. J. J. (1898). In *The San Juan, Colorado, Sketches*. Chicago: Calumet Book and Engraving Company.

CHAPTER 7
Life on an Ash Flow

The birth of Surtsey is discussed under several headings in *Encyclopaedia Britannica*, 15th Edition.

Vertical zonation of vegetation is discussed in most elementary botany and ecology texts. Two works which focus on Colorado mountain flora and fauna are:

Rodeck, Hugo G., Editor (1964) *Natural History of the Boulder Area*. Boulder: University of Colorado Museum, Leaflet No. 13.

Moenke, Helen (1971) *Ecology of Colorado Mountains to Arizona Deserts*. Denver: Denver Museum of Natural History Pictorial No. 20.

CHAPTER 8
Wildlife

This chapter contains personal and regional reminiscences; it is not meant to be a scientific treatise. With a little searching the reader will find that the biological literature contains hundreds of specialized studies of genera or species, peppered with Latin names, and focusing on restricted localities. Titles appear such as: "Analysis of a Pika Hay Pile," "Vernal Behaviour of the Yellow-bellied Marmot," "Mountain Lion Eats its Kittens," "List of Mammals Collected by Mr. Charles P. Rowley in the San Juan Region of Colorado, New Mexico, and Utah, with Descriptions of New Species (1893)."

This is not to belittle such studies, they are the lifeblood of all scientific disciplines; without them humankind would not have come as far as it has from the stone age cave.

The nonspecialist reader will derive most pleasure from such guides as:

Peterson, Roger Tory (1961) *A Field Guide to Western Birds*. Boston: Houghton Mifflin Co.

Armstrong, David M. (1975) *Rocky Mountain Mammals*. Rocky Mountain Nature Association, Inc., and National Park Service, U.S. Department of Interior.

Griffiths, Melvin, "Branding the Bums," *Western Sportsman*, March, 1940.

A work which supplies much information on animal ranges in Colorado is:

Armstrong, David M. (1972) *Distribution of Mammals in Colorado*. Lawrence: Monograph #3, Museum of Natural History of Kansas, University of Kansas.

Ouray County Plaindealer, Aug. 24, 1978 (newspaper).

Most of the ideas on game management in this chapter have been suggested by personnel in the Colorado Division of Wildlife. The author of this book takes responsibility for all omissions and misinterpretations.

CHAPTER 9
Native Americans

The following materials will help the layman to envision the prehistoric peopling of southwestern Colorado:

Wormington, H. M. (1966) *Prehistoric Indians of the Southwest*. Denver: Denver Museum of Natural History Popular Series, No. 7.

———(1957) *Ancient Man in North America, 4th Edition*. Denver: Denver Museum of Natural History Popular Series, No. 4.

Rippeteau, Bruce Estes (1979) "A Colorado Book of the Dead: The Prehistoric Era" *The Colorado Magazine*, Fall 1978. Denver: The Colorado Historical Society.

Haynes, C. Vance, Jr. (1966) "Elephant Hunting in North America," *Scientific American*, 214, No. 6 (June 1966) pp. 104–112.

Wheat, Joe Ben (1967) "A Paleo-Indian Bison Kill," *Scientific American*, 216, No. 1 (Jan. 1967) pp. 44–52.

[The Haynes and Wheat articles, cited immediately above, are also contained in *Early Man in America*, Readings from *Scientific American* (1973). San Francisco: W. H. Freeman & Co.]

Indians in Colorado and in North America during historic times are covered by:

Hughes, J. Donald (1977) *American Indians in Colorado*. Boulder: Pruett Publishing Co.

Kroeber, A. L. (1963) *Cultural and Natural Areas of Native North America*. Berkeley: University of California Press.

General material on the Utes in western Colorado, including the Meeker Massacre, can be found in:

Rockwell, Wilson (1956) *The Utes a Forgotten People*. Denver: Sage Books.

Emmitt, Robert (1954) *The Last War Trail*. Norman: University of Oklahoma Press.

Parkhill, Forbes (1945) "The Meeker Massacre and Thornburgh Battle." Denver: Denver Posse of the Westerners.

Jocknick, Sidney (1913) *Early Days on the Western Slope*. Denver: The Carson-Harper Co. [In 1968, this classic of Western Slope history was republished by the Rio Grande Press, Inc., Glorieta, New Mexico 87535, in a facsimile edition.]

Information on Chief Ouray's burial can be found in several sources. See:

Rockwell, Wilson (1956) cited earlier in this chapter.

Wiegel, Mrs. C. W. (1928) "The Re-burial of Chief Ouray," *The Colorado Magazine*, The Colorado State Historical Society, Vol. 5, October, pp. 165–173.

Griffiths, Mel (1982) "The Ultimate Compromise," *American Heritage*, Vol. 33, No. 3 (April/May) p. 112.

CHAPTER 10
The White Man Arrives

Quotations from the translated diary and itinerary of the Escalante Expedition, including an historical introduction by Bolton, a translation of Miera's report, and a copy of his map are contained in Bolton (1950) already cited in the bibliography for Chapter 1.

Zebulon Montgomery Pike's brief sortie into San Juan country can be traced in:

Hollon, W. Eugene (1949) *The Lost Pathfinder, Zebulon Montgomery Pike*. Norman: The University of Oklahoma Press.

The story of Antoine Robidoux's two forts on the Uinta and the Gunnison found in:

Hill, Joseph J. (1930) "Antoine Robidoux, Kingpin in the Colorado River Fur Trade, 1824–1844," *The Colorado Magazine*. Denver: The State Historical Society of Colorado, Vol. VII, No. 4, pp. 125–132.

CHAPTER 11
Uncle Sam Investigates

The definitive biography of John Charles Frémont is found in:

Nevins, Allan (1955) *Frémont: Pathmarker of the West*. New York: Longmans, Green.

Material which focuses exclusively on Frémont's ill-starred 1848–1849 expedition is found in:

Brandon, William (1955) *The Men and the Mountain*. New York: William Morrow and Company.

Gunnison's 1853 exploration of the central railroad route is ably described by:

Mumey, Nolie (1954) "John Williams Gunnison, Centenary of his Survey and Tragic Death (1853–1953)," *Colorado Magazine*. Denver: The State Historical Society of Colorado, Vol. XXXI, pp. 19–32.

Ruffner, E. H., *Report of a Reconnaissance in the Ute Country, Made in 1873; by Lieut. E. H. Ruffner*, [H. G. Prout, James Bassel, David Campbell, and F. Hawn,] 1874.

The Hayden, Wheeler, King, and Powell surveys are covered exhaustively in:

(The 43rd Congress, 1st Session, House Exec. Doc. 193): Serial No. 1610.

Bartlett, Richard A. (1962) *Great Surveys of the American West*. Norman: University of Oklahoma Press. [The quotation by Hayden is from Bartlett (1962) p. 76.]

CHAPTER 12
Here They Dug Gold and Silver
Three works which trace the history of mining in the American West are:

Henderson, Charles W. (1926) *Mining in Colorado: A History of Discovery, Development, and Production.* U.S. Geological Survey, Professional Paper 138. Washington, D.C.: U.S. Government Printing Office.

Rickard, T. A. (1932) *A History of American Mining.* New York: McGraw Hill Book Co.

Paul, Rodman Wilson (1963) *Mining Frontiers of the Far West, 1848–1880.* New York: Holt, Rinehart, and Winston.

Two works which describe for the layman the techniques of hard rock mining are:

Young, Otis E., Jr. (1970) *Western Mining.* Norman: University of Oklahoma Press.

———— (1976) *Black Powder and Hand Steel.* Norman: The University of Oklahoma Press.

CHAPTER 13
Storm and Strife
Contemporary accounts of the Telluride labor troubles of 1901–1904 — mostly from local newspapers — are extremely partisan. The same could be said for many accounts written after the passage of half a century. One of the most even-handed treatments is:

Lavender, David (1968) *The Rockies, Revised and Enlarged.* New York: Harper and Row.

Much background material is found in:

Holbrook, Stewart H. (1956) *The Rocky Mountain Revolution.* New York: Henry Holt and Company.

A recent study with a prolabor bias is:

Williams, Roger Neville (1977) *The Great Telluride Strike. Labor Struggles and Martial Law in San Miguel County, 1901–1904.* [The material in this pamphlet appeared in three installments in the *Telluride Times*, during September 1977.]

An account which has a more owner-oriented bias — Robert Livermore was the brother-in-law of Bulkeley Wells, one of the central figures in the struggle — is found in:

Livermore, Robert (1968) *Bostonians and Bullion; the Journal of Robert Livermore, 1892–1915.* Edited by Gene M. Gressley. Lincoln: University of Nebraska Press.

CHAPTER 14
From Here to There
Much of the material on pack mules in this chapter has been taken from:

Griffiths, Mel (1955) "Those Marvelous Mountain Mules," *Empire Magazine,* The Denver Post, March 27, pp. 8–9.

U.S. Army Engineer Field Manual, Animal Transport, 1917.

The description of the Cumbres and Toltec narrow gauge railroad is from:

Ingersoll, Ernest (1885) *The Crest of the Continent: The Record of a Summer's Ramble in the Rocky Mountains and Beyond.* Chicago: R. R. Donnelley & Sons Company.

The economics of aerial tramways is discussed in:

Rickard, T. A. (1903) *Across the San Juan Mountains.* New York and London: The Engineering and Mining Journal.

CHAPTER 15
Power
The primary sources for the history of the pioneer alternating current generating plant at Ames are:

Bailey, Stephen A. (1933) *L. L. Nunn, a Memoir.* Ithaca, New York: Telluride Association, Cayuga Press.

Nunn, P. N. (1905) "Pioneer Work in High Tension Electric Power Transmission," *Cassier's Magazine,* Vol. XXVII, No. 3, January 1905, pp. 171–200.

Britton, Charles C. (1972) "An Early Electric Power Facility in Colorado," *The Colorado Magazine.* Denver: The State Historical Society of Colorado, Summer, 1972, pp. 185–195.

Lavender, David (1964) "The Electrifying Mr. Nunn of Telluride," *Empire Magazine,* The Denver Post, Oct. 11, 1964, pp. 10–13.

CHAPTER 16
Water in the Valleys—Herds in the Hills

"Uncle Dick" Wootton's drive of 9,000 head of sheep from New Mexico to California in 1852 is narrated in:

Wentworth, Edward Norris (1948) *America's Sheep Trails.* Ames, Iowa: The Iowa State College Press, pp. 167 ff.

John Wesley Powell's blueprint for arid land utilization is contained in the first two chapters of:

Powell, J. W. (in charge) (1879) *Report on the Lands of the Arid Region of the United States, with a more detailed account of the lands of Utah (2nd Edition).* United States Geographical and Geological Survey of the Rocky Mountain Region. Washington, D.C.

The quotation from the twelfth century Arab geographer Al-Idrisi is taken from:

Gies, Frances (1977) "Al-Idrisi and 'Roger's Book'," *Aramco World Magazine,* Vol. 28, No. 4, July/August, pp. 14–19.

The brief discussion of water law in this chapter had been modified from two sources:

Moses, Raphael J. (1976) "Very Basic Colorado Water Law." A paper delivered at the *Water in Colorado Workshop* convened at Western State College, Gunnison, Colorado, July 19, 1976. [Mr. Moses is a senior member of the law firm of Moses, Wittemyer, Harrison, and Woodruff, P.C., Boulder, Colorado.]

Cummins, Densil Highfill (1951) *Social and Economic History of Southwestern Colorado, 1860-1948* (Unpublished Ph.D. dissertation), University of Texas, Austin, June 1951.

A thorough study of the Gunnison-Uncompahgre diversion and the Gunnison Tunnel is found in:

Beidleman, Richard G. (1959) "The Gunnison River Diversion Project," *The Colorado Magazine.* Denver: The Colorado State Historical Society, Vol. 36, No. 3, July 1959, pp. 187–201, and Vol. 36, No. 4, October 1959, pp. 266–285.

The problem of integrating grazing and crop agriculture in the Uncompahgre Valley Irrigation Project is explored in:

Beyer, Jacquelyn L. (1957) *Integration of Grazing and Crop Agriculture, Resources Management Problems in the Uncompahgre Valley Irrigation Project.* Chicago: Department of Geography Research Paper No. 52, University of Chicago, December 1957.

CHAPTER 17
Village, Ranch, Mine, and Open Space

Population figures in this chapter are taken from:

U.S. Bureau of the Census (1973) *Census of Population: 1970,* Vol. I Characteristics of the Population, Part 7, Colorado. Washington, D.C.: U.S. Government Printing Office, 1973.

The comments of William Rathmell about David Day are from an unpublished manuscript by Rathmell entitled: *A Brief History of Ouray County, Colorado.*

The term "Bonanza Victorian" appears in:

Stoehr, C. Eric (1975) *Bonanza Victorian.* Albuquerque: University of New Mexico Press.

Information on "Captain Jack" Stoiber and "Waldheim" comes from interviews with Sara (Maxwell) Baily, in Denver during early 1982, and from:

Wolle, Muriel Sibell (1977) *Timberline Tailings. Tales of Colorado's Ghost Towns and Mining Camps.* Chicago: Sage Books, the Swallow Press Incorporated.

Livermore, Robert (1968) *Bostonians and Bullion; the Journal of Robert Livermore, 1892-1915.* Edited by Gene M. Gressley. Lincoln: University of Nebraska Press.

Ouray Herald, May 1896 (newspaper).

The story of the Cow Creek School comes from:

Up the Hemline (Being a true account of 100 years of classroom experiences in Colorado). Published by the Omega State (Colorado) Chapters of the International Delta Kappa Gamma Society. Margaret J. Lehrer, Editor. Colorado Springs: Williams and Field, Inc.

The descriptions of school experiences at the Camp Bird and Sneffels schools have been greatly strengthened by interviews and correspondence with Verena Rucker Jacobson, Barbara McCullough Spencer, and Mary Kuchs Griffiths.

CHAPTER 18
On High Hills

Wright, Carolyn and Clarence (1964) *Tiny Hinsdale of the Silvery San Juan.* Denver: Big Mountain Press.

The Livermore description of his mountaineering activities during the course of his surveying work is found in Livermore (1968) already cited in bibliography for chapter 17.

During the last two decades, a plethora of mountaineering guides and histories have been published. Many of these have dwelt on San Juan mountaineering history, or serve as guides to its higher and more difficult peaks and routes. A sampling, in alphabetical order, might include:

Borneman, Walter R. and Lyndon J. Lampert (1978) *A Climbing Guide to Colorado's Four-teeners.* Boulder: Pruett Publishing Company.

Bueler, William M. (1974) *Roof of the Rockies, a History of Mountaineering in Colorado.* Boulder: Pruett Publishing Company.

Eberhart, Perry and Philip Schmuck (1970) *The Fourteeners, Colorado's Great Mountains.* Chicago: Sage Books, The Swallow Press, Inc.

Godfrey, Bob and Dudley Chelton (1977) *Climb!* Boulder: Published for the American Alpine Club by Alpine House Publishing, Distributed by Westview Press.

Jones, Chris (1976) *Climbing in North America.* Berkeley: Published for the American Alpine Club by the University of California Press.

Ormes, Robert M. (1952 – 7th Edition 1979) *Guide to the Colorado Mountains.* Colorado Springs: With the Colorado Mountain Club, published by Robert M. Ormes.

Most of the material on the naming of Lavender Peak is found in:

Griffiths, Mel (1981) "Destined for a Better Name," *Empire Magazine,* The Denver Post, December 20, 1981, pp. 10–28.

George Darley's ski crossing of the crest of the range between Lake City and Silverton is chronicled in:

Darley, George M. (1899) *Pioneering in the San Juan* (First copyright, 1899, by Fleming H. Revell Company). Reissue copyright (1976) Community Presbyterian Church of Lake City, Colorado.

EPILOGUE
Here and There

The quotation from John McPhee is found in:

McPhee, John (1976/1977) *Coming into the Country.* New York: Farrar, Straus and Giroux, p. 126.

The dissertation on "pasties" first saw print in:

Griffiths, Mel (1978) "Some Like 'em Hot," *Westways:* Los Angeles, January 1978, p. 12.
Denver Times, July 28, 1901 (newspaper).

246